WITHDRAWN

The
Big Enough
Company

The
Big Enough
Company

Creating a Business
That Works for You

Adelaide Lancaster
and
Amy Abrams

PORTFOLIO/PENGUIN

PORTFOLIO / PENGUIN
Published by the Penguin Group
Penguin Group (USA) Inc., 375 Hudson Street,
New York, New York 10014, U.S.A.
Penguin Group (Canada), 90 Eglinton Avenue East, Suite 700,
Toronto, Ontario, Canada M4P 2Y3
(a division of Pearson Penguin Canada Inc.)
Penguin Books Ltd, 80 Strand, London WC2R 0RL, England
Penguin Ireland, 25 St. Stephen's Green, Dublin 2, Ireland
(a division of Penguin Books Ltd)
Penguin Books Australia Ltd, 250 Camberwell Road, Camberwell,
Victoria 3124, Australia
(a division of Pearson Australia Group Pty Ltd)
Penguin Books India Pvt Ltd, 11 Community Centre, Panchsheel Park,
New Delhi – 110 017, India
Penguin Group (NZ), 67 Apollo Drive, Rosedale, Auckland 0632,
New Zealand (a division of Pearson New Zealand Ltd)
Penguin Books (South Africa) (Pty) Ltd, 24 Sturdee Avenue,
Rosebank, Johannesburg 2196, South Africa

Penguin Books Ltd, Registered Offices:
80 Strand, London WC2R 0RL, England

First published in 2011 by Portfolio / Penguin,
a member of Penguin Group (USA) Inc.

1   3   5   7   9   10   8   6   4   2

LIBRARY OF CONGRESS CATALOGING IN PUBLICATION DATA
Lancaster, Adelaide.
The big enough company : creating a business that works for you / by Adelaide Lancaster
and Amy Abrams.
p.   cm.
Includes index.
ISBN 978-1-59184-421-1
1. Small business.   2. Business enterprises.   3. Businesspeople—Case studies.
I. Abrams, Amy.   II. Title.
HD2341.L265 2011
658.1'1—dc22   2011013124

Printed in the United States of America
Set in Berling
Designed by Jaime Putorti

For Ruby, Noa, and Eloise

. . .

For KLR
This all started with an e-mail from you.
We are forever indebted.

CONTENTS

PART TWO

THE CRITICAL SKILLS:
Mastering Everyday Actions for Business Success

The
Big Enough
Company

INTRODUCTION

The Promise of Entrepreneurship

They didn't start out unhappy. They started out eager, excited, ready for a challenge, and hungering for meaning. Looking for freedom, autonomy, and a sense of accomplishment, they had decided to start their own business and were determined that their company would provide them the satisfaction no other job could. But somehow they lost their way.

Maybe they had compromised on what they wanted, or maybe what they wanted had changed. In any event, their businesses no longer met their needs and they were stuck with jobs they didn't enjoy. They came to us looking for advice.

There were those who had settled for a business that worked well enough: the consultant who had grown weary of consulting but kept doing it because that's how she made money; the counselor who had perfected her craft and was making a decent living but still found herself asking, "Is this all?"

And there were others who had pursued growth for growth's sake: the recruiter who hired staff, only to learn she hated managing people; the jewelry designer whose collection grew stagnant because she was too busy handling wholesale clients to actually design new pieces.

These entrepreneurs aren't unusual. In fact, their stories are all too familiar, their fates all too common. In nearly ten years of working with entrepreneurs through our business In Good Company, we've heard countless stories and lamentations like these. And that's what concerns us. All of these entrepreneurs started their companies because they thought it would give them freedom—freedom to work on their own terms, be their own boss, and create a company that met their needs. But in the end the opposite happened, and they ended up encumbered by businesses that bore little to no resemblance to those they had envisioned. They were working for their companies, but their companies weren't working for them.

Chances are, if you run a small business, you've felt the same way at one point or another. But that doesn't mean the game is over. The beauty of entrepreneurship is that no matter how off course you may feel, your future and fate are in your hands. Even the best of us can get stuck from time to time. We just need a little help to get going in the right direction again. And that's what this book is meant to do: help you overcome the hurdles of entrepreneurship so you can create a business that really works for you.

• • •

Get more of what you want and less of what you don't—that is the promise and potential of entrepreneurship, plain and simple.

The problem is that it doesn't stay plain and simple. It's easy to let popular advice cloud your vision and confuse your goals, losing sight of what you sought to achieve in the first place. It's tempting to relinquish the driver's seat, allowing outside opinions and trends to dictate growth. It's enticing to believe in short-term celebrity and business fads, jumping on a bandwagon heading in the wrong direction.

Deep down, we know better.

We know that the real goal isn't size (necessarily); it's success. Success doesn't come from following formulaic systems or looking for quick results. Nor does it come from measuring how big or profitable your venture is compared to others. It isn't just about having a big company; it's about having a company that is just big enough to deliver what you need and achieve what you want. Real success comes from growing your business in a way that keeps what you want at the forefront, whether that's financial security, creative autonomy, professional opportunity, personal meaning, intellectual challenge, or something else entirely.

But just because you know what you want doesn't mean it's easy to get it. All entrepreneurs face tough decisions, bouts of uncertainty, and periods of exhaustion. All have hiccups, detours, and distractions and have to work hard to keep their goals in mind. Nevertheless, the work is worth it.

We know this fact firsthand. In starting and building our company, we've faced the same entrepreneurial challenges ourselves, transforming our business several times over and rejecting obvious growth paths in favor of those that worked better for us. Even though we haven't always gotten it right and have no idea what the future will bring, we feel confident in our ability to do two things: (1) be clear about what we want, and (2) be creative about the ways to achieve it.

Understanding this makes the journey enjoyable, our unknown future exciting, and the promise of entrepreneurship real. And we want to make sure you feel the same way!

Whether you're looking to build a business that better supports your vision, grow according to your goals, or transform parts of your business that you may have already compromised on, we are going to help you.

Through the course of this book we will work with you to:

- **Think "from the inside out."** Before you examine your company, you have to examine yourself. We will help you focus on your needs, motivations, goals, and aspirations and construct a growth plan from there.
- **Change the way you think about growth.** Growth is not just about getting bigger but also about how companies transform and evolve over time to meet a variety of goals. We will help you recognize the many growth options available and stop limiting your thinking about what's possible.

- **Connect to the amazing world of entrepreneurs.** The business world is rich and interesting, filled with companies of all sizes, means, objectives, styles, and goals. We will help you use this diversity and abundance of examples to serve as inspiration and fodder for your own venture.
- **Learn common best practices and principles.** There is no need to reinvent the wheel, and there are some lessons you just don't need to learn the hard way. We will help you benefit from the collective wisdom of our peers and discover the universal principles and practices that can help strengthen any business.

Where We Stand

Before we spend two hundred-plus pages together, it only seems fair that we tell you a little about the way we see things. You may agree. You may not. But we feel it's important to put it out there. These beliefs have been shaped not only by our own experience but also by that of the thousands of entrepreneurs we have worked with over the last ten years.

Entrepreneurship of Today

Until recently, "entrepreneurship" has been tightly associated with the old dotcom-era model—that is, technology companies with a trajectory of fast growth and quick sale. The true definition is much more expansive. Now more than ever, entrepreneurs define the endgame in a variety of ways, proudly pursue multiple purposes and goals, and select a variety of paths to get there.

Old-school thinking commends businesses and founders based on size, scale, and sales. New-school thinking, which we embrace, heralds business owners who have exercised creativity and leveraged entrepreneurship as an opportunity to achieve their own unique goals and needs. Old-school thinking applauds growth for growth's sake. New-school thinking believes that growth should be determined by your goals and that the right size and direction is a matter of personal opinion.

After all, entrepreneurship is not about bingeing, blindly and automatically ingesting every opportunity that comes your way. Nor is it about executing a ready-made business plan. The art of entrepreneurship is about undertaking smart growth that is strategic, creative, and goal-driven. It is about feeling out the options, understanding what is best for you and your business, and consistently selecting the next best direction—all with your goals and needs in mind.

We are challenging you to think differently about your business and your definition of success. Instead of asking yourself how big and how fast, consider what size is big enough to get the job done. Instead of just evaluating your progress with a numerical multiplier, consider whether your company is having the impact you want. Instead of asking yourself how your company stacks up against another, consider how satisfied you are with the company you created.

A Word About "Entrepreneur"

In this day and age, it is impossible to describe what an entrepreneur or the experience of entrepreneurship looks like. We now come in all shapes and sizes.

However, many of us still shy away from the title and struggle to recognize ourselves as part of the ranks. Instead we may call ourselves small business owners, independents, freelancers, designers, or consultants, or we may simply say that we work for ourselves. All of these titles are accurate, and we encourage you to find something that feels comfortable.

But for the purposes of this book we are going to call you entrepreneurs. Why? We believe the term "entrepreneur" captures more than the other titles and hints at the risk and reward involved in striking out on your own. It conjures up a blank slate and intonates the boot-strappy-ness of it all. It reflects the opportunity to create something new, unique, and meaningful.

We think that if you saddle yourself with all the innovation, positioning, motivation, execution, and decision-making required to run your own venture, then you deserve the title and the credit it carries.

The Entrepreneurs in This Story

You can't have a good book about entrepreneurship without some really great entrepreneurs, which is why we've featured plenty of them in this book. Here are some of the characters you'll become familiar with:

You

The most important entrepreneur in this story is you.

If you're anything like our clients, you are engaged, optimistic, and motivated but also want more—more from your business and more from your experience of entrepreneurship. You see your business as an investment and a vehicle for getting what you want. Instead of running a business that works well enough, you want to create a business that delivers what you want, one that continually adapts to meet your unique needs.

Another thing we know about you is that you are busy. Our clients sometimes say, with a good deal of remorse, that they don't have the time to step back and think about what they need and want. Sure, they'd like to have clarity around their motivations and goals, but they've got a job to do! We don't think it's about time, we think it is actually about permission. Our clients often don't give themselves permission to spend time on what can feel like intangible and conceptual work. And believe us, we know it is hard when there are a million smaller concrete tasks begging to be checked off the to-do list. But trust us. It is important. In fact, it is vital. Far from fluff, the effort you put in here will pay off tenfold. Give yourself permission and let this book help you.

Us

In addition to talking about you, we will also sprinkle our own story throughout the chapters. Our experience will probably feel familiar, as we too have had to work hard to build a business in keeping with our needs and goals. Along the way we have felt stuck, tried things that didn't work, and had to reconcile conflicting desires. We don't claim to have figured it all out and we certainly aren't suggesting that our own decisions are right for your business. But we hope that sharing our efforts to make our business work for us will encourage you to make your business work for you!

Entrepreneurs We Like and Admire

We believe in the importance of community and the power of example. Learning from other entrepreneurs is a key to business success. Therefore, you will find examples of many other entrepreneurs embedded within these chapters. Their stories are meant to serve as inspiration, validation, and fodder for insight and creativity. Some of the entrepreneurs are our former clients. Some are members of our business, In Good Company (IGC), a community, business learning center, and workspace for women entrepreneurs. Others we interviewed for the purposes of this book.

We chose the (nearly one hundred) women we interviewed in large part because we admired them and found their businesses and style of entrepreneurship to be interesting. And though some are local heroes, they certainly aren't famous, and they haven't experienced overnight success. They are real people who have remarkable yet relatable stories.

As we created the pool of interviewees, we looked for a diversity of goals, industry, and entrepreneurial experience. We had only two hard-and-fast criteria for the women we interviewed. They had to be:

- **Creating their own road map.** We wanted to talk with women who had been innovative in either what they were doing or the way they were doing it.
- **Authentic.** They had to be willing to shed the glossy PR story and share the real unvarnished thinking behind their choices and experience.

Of the women that we interviewed, the following is true:

EMPLOYEES
- 20 percent have no employees
- 28 percent have between one and three employees
- 18 percent have four to ten employees
- 4 percent have eleven to fifteen employees
- 15 percent have sixteen to twenty-five employees
- 11 percent have more than twenty-six employees

NUMBER OF BUSINESSES
- 30 percent have had more than one business

LENGTH OF TIME IN BUSINESS (FOR CURRENT VENTURE)
- 23 percent have been in business two to three years
- 30 percent have been in business four to seven years
- 25 percent have been in business eight to eleven years
- 10 percent have been in business twelve to fifteen years
- 12 percent have been in business for more than sixteen years

FINANCES
- 92 percent have used personal savings to fund their business
- 60 percent have received money from their spouse, domestic partner, friends, or family, either in the form of a loan or an investment

- 30 percent used equity investment to fund their business; 15 percent have a formal angel investor; 7 percent have venture funding

RELATIONSHIP STATUS
- 75 percent are married or in a domestic partnership; 25 percent are single

CHILDREN
- 50 percent do not have children; 25 percent have one child; 25 percent have two or more children
- 80 percent did not have children when they started their business or within a year after starting their business

AGE
- 10 percent are under thirty years of age
- 42 percent are ages thirty to thirty-nine
- 36 percent are ages forty to forty-nine
- 12 percent are over fifty-five years of age

To be sure, our work has primarily focused on women, but we have collaborated with and drawn inspiration from many male entrepreneurs as well. It should be no surprise that thoughtful, deliberate, and creative entrepreneurship is not a gendered experience. We know that anybody can leverage these lessons to create a more satisfying business for themselves, and we hope you are among those that do.

How This Book Works

The Big Enough Company is broken into two parts reflecting the dual challenge that every entrepreneur faces: crafting the big picture of what your company should be, and executing it on a daily basis.

The first part asks big questions to help you identify your motivations in pursuing entrepreneurship, your ideal role, the impact you want your business to have, and a successful future for your business. These are the questions that help to create a foundation and should be revisited at critical junctures and during strategic decisions.

Each chapter includes:

- **A Look At**—the key lesson and why it's important
- **In the Company of Others**—examples from other entrepreneurs
- **Your Turn**—an opportunity to apply the lesson to your own experience
- **Troubleshooting**—examples of the issues that get in the way of success

The second part focuses on critical skills. It highlights lessons such as learning to take small steps toward progress, the importance of experimentation, learning to say no, and the impact of community and colleagues. These are lessons of the everyday variety that all entrepreneurs should know and use to keep their business on track. They will help you avoid the common challenges that can wreak havoc on even the most finely tuned businesses.

Each chapter includes:

- **The Problem**—a look at common challenges that interfere with everyday satisfaction
- **The Solution**—a detailed discussion about the key lesson
- **Troubleshooting**—examples of the issues that get in the way of success

We encourage you return to this book as your business continues to evolve. You will find that different lessons and examples will speak to you at different points in time. It is our hope that each read further helps you to build a business that works best for you.

PART ONE

THE BIG QUESTIONS:

Building Your Business from the Inside Out

In order to best direct and grow your business, you have to know what is fundamentally important to you. We believe it makes much more sense to start with yourself and create a growth plan from there rather than foist a particular strategy or mandate on your company and hope it provides the benefits and rewards you are looking for.

A business that works for you needs to:

- Deliver the benefits you want (chapter 1)
- Create the impact you desire (chapter 2)
- Give you a job you enjoy (chapter 3)
- Attain the outcome you envision (chapter 4)

Each of these elements can change or take on a different meaning over time, but each is exceedingly important in informing the best structure, path, and direction for your business. It is critical for you to keep your finger on the pulse of these factors, acknowledging and anticipating current and potential changes so that you can adjust your business accordingly.

This kind of "inside-out" approach will ensure that your decisions are deliberate and the outcomes reflect what you want. It assumes you are the expert and the best and most appropriate decision-maker. It assumes that given the right information, inspiration, and insight you will make the choices that are best for you and the business.

What's In It for *You?*

Clarify What You Want from Your Business

The biggest benefit is being able to do whatever I want to do with the business when I see an opportunity. I love the absolute freedom to explore, to play, to think, to satisfy my own needs.

—SARA HOLOUBEK, FOUNDER OF LUMINARY LABS

"So, why did you decide to become an entrepreneur?" This is the first question we ask each of our clients when they come to us with a question or concern. It may seem obvious, but the answer is critically important in helping us understand the relationship that our clients have with their business. For some people it is a romantic story filled with dreams and inspiration. For others it might have been an accidental occurrence. Others might have acted out of necessity. Sometimes you can still see traces of this story in the present-day business—perhaps the accidental entrepreneur is still a bit ambivalent or the romantic is still grappling with the reality of just how much work there is to be done.

We listen to the story carefully, noting indications of what our clients hoped to get out of their experience. What were the original benefits they sought when they started their own business? What motivated them to start it in the first place?

A Look at Motivations

The experience of entrepreneurship is different for everyone and each of us brings unique ideas, hopes, skills, and needs to the table. But what's really important to know is what specifically motivated *you*. And in order to ensure that your company works for you, you need to ask yourself this question too. Why did *you* decide to become an entrepreneur?

Were you looking for freedom, prestige, autonomy, creative control, mobility? Perhaps you wanted to make room for things in your life outside of work. Or maybe you just like to call the shots or were drawn by the allure of uncapped earnings potential.

Keep in mind, we aren't asking you what you want your business to achieve. (We'll get to that later.) Your motivations are distinct from your business goals and include:

- What you bring to the table before the business is even formed or decided upon
- What draws you to entrepreneurship over other employment options
- What makes all the work and responsibility of running your own business worthwhile

Your motivations aren't just what bring you to entrepreneurship in the first place; they have a lasting effect on your business. Ideally, your motivations influence the kind of business you choose to run and the way you choose to structure it. The greater the clarity you have about what you want, the better able you are to build a business that continues to meet your needs far into the future.

After all, an entrepreneur who needs financial stability would likely make radically different business decisions from one who needs complete creative freedom. A person who wants to make space for the extracurricular interests in her life will go about things differently than the entrepreneur who is seizing upon a time-sensitive opportunity. So before we get into the specifics of what to do with your business, you first need to understand what you want from it.

The Story of Angela and Zoe, Part 1

Consider for a moment two women, Angela and Zoe, who have a passion for gourmet food. Both want to start a business. What should they do? What kind of business should they start? Those are both big questions and can't be answered without a better understanding of who these women are and what they want from a business. Let's take a closer look at their individual motivations.

Angela has felt stifled in a corporate role. She resents the office politics and disorganized decision-making processes. It seems that as soon as people get on board and in the groove, a new direction is set and priorities named. The cycle has left her uninspired and unmotivated. What's more, she's got a bad case of the entrepreneurial itch and has long been intrigued by the start-up world. She keeps thinking of ways to make a business out of her love of good food. She knows the marketplace could use lots of improvements, but isn't sure which avenue to pursue.

Being a foodie, Angela is always on the hunt for specialty foods and spends lots of time trying to find little gourmet shops in different locations. It bothers her how hard it is to find shops that have what she wants, especially when she's traveling. She originally considered trying to make an online directory or editorial site that would collate and catalog these stores, but she knows she wants to be more involved with the actual food rather than with other store owners. Plus, she believes it will be harder to monetize this Web site than an actual food store. After thinking about it more, she realizes what she really desires is the opportunity to help change the marketplace by making high-quality gourmet food available in lots of locations. She considers developing a wholesale line but ultimately decides to start a store of her own so that she can be involved in creating a specific customer experience.

Zoe, who also loves gourmet food, considers herself a chef first and has always shied away from the business side of things. She has been an apprentice to many famous chefs in cities across the United States and has long had her heart set on becoming a well-known name in and of herself. Recently she was offered a head chef position at a yet-to-be-developed urban restaurant, which was supposed to be part of a larger development project. It would have given her significant exposure, but she turned down the offer in favor of opening something of her own. Some called her crazy, telling her she had just committed career suicide, or at the very least undermined what she had worked so hard for. Zoe thought otherwise.

Although she appreciates her training and experience, Zoe is exhausted from being in the business for nearly fifteen years and has always believed that there is another way to do things, a way that doesn't require an insanely frenetic pace. She is determined to do what she loves without sacrificing her health and family. Not one to be deterred by a challenge, she adds another complexity to the equation—moving her family to her hometown about thirty minutes outside the city. Frustrated by the notion that notable cuisine can be found only in urban centers, Zoe wants to create a place of her own where she can exercise her creativity and passion, on her terms.

So while at first glance Angela and Zoe may appear to be starting the same business—a gourmet food store—they each have very different personal motivations, want very different things from entrepreneurship, and would be satisfied by building two very different businesses. We will see how their businesses evolve in later chapters.

In the Company of Others: Working for What Is Important

Not long ago the term "entrepreneur" was synonymous with "unemployed." Now it conjures up a multitude of stereotypes: risk-happy, multitasking, difficult to work with, and sales-y, to name a few.

Despite the varying images, there seems to be a fascination with profiling the common characteristics of an entrepreneur. Magazines are awash with headlines such as "What it takes to be an entrepreneur" or "Are you cut out to be your own boss?"—as if the experience is really that predictable and generic.

The truth is, the decision to become an entrepreneur is quite nuanced. Our conversations with the women we interviewed reflected a wide range of reasons for ultimately taking the leap.

Some of the entrepreneurs we spoke with were eager to pioneer the great unknown, but others were seeking refuge from corporate life. Some suggested that their decision was a reflection of who they are as a person, while others pointed to their stage in life or professional trajectory. Some indicated that they were making a long-term choice whose benefits would be borne out over the course of their career, while others simply felt it was the "next best step." Some talked money, while others talked meaning. The diversity displayed by the women we spoke with serves as a great reminder that the entrepreneurial experience is far from stereotypical.

Despite the rich variety, however, there were certainly some prominent themes that stuck out among all the stories, namely freedom, meaning, money, and opportunity—the hallmarks of the entrepreneurial experience.

Freedom

Freedom is much more expensive than money.

—SELIMA SALAUN, FOUNDER OF SELIMA OPTIQUE

More than anything else, entrepreneurs revel in the draw, allure, value, and rewards of freedom: the freedom to own their time, express their creative vision, and call the shots. After all, it's terrible to work at someone else's pace, compromise on your vision for a shortsighted client, or support a decision you know isn't going to work. What most entrepreneurs want is the freedom to do good work and be responsible for their own future.

Not surprisingly, many entrepreneurs don't seem willing to give up these hard-fought freedoms, and many of the women we talked to said they would never like to work for someone else again. Some joked that they were simply unemployable, while others like Claire Chambers, founder of Journelle, said that "my worst day as an entrepreneur was better than my best day as a consultant," and that is from someone who had lots of very nice things to say about her former firm!

Of course, having freedom doesn't mean you get to slack off. Sometimes the word "flexibility" is used pejoratively, implying that the entrepreneur is not serious and the business is not a top priority. To the contrary, we find that most people who start businesses work more hours than they ever did before. The benefit lies in being able to *choose* those hours. As Allison Hemming, founder of The Hired Guns, says, "I still work seventy- to eighty-hour weeks, but I call the shots on my time. At least I can organize my time and efficiency around building a business that I ultimately own. I can control my destiny."

MEET:

Jessica Sutton, owner of JSGD, a graphic design studio, loves that she is able to work during the hours that are most productive and creative for her, which are often 11 a.m. to 8 p.m. instead of a traditional workday. This works well both for her and her graphic design clients, most of whom are small business owners themselves. Jessica has turned down several larger contracts that require a closer to full-time commitment, in part because they would require her to compromise on the freedom she currently enjoys and worked so hard to get!

Ellen Diamant, owner of Skip Hop, is a creative at heart. Her background was in marketing and creative design for several large product companies, and when she had her son she initially started a graphic design business that she nurtured for several years.

However, it was an idea for a product that truly allowed her to flex her creative muscles. Ellen was frustrated by the unfunctional and unstylish baby market, which at that point was a sea of pastel and Winnie-the-Pooh-themed items. She had an idea for a diaper bag that easily converted to a messenger bag and could be clipped onto any stroller. The Duo diaper bag turned out to be the perfect product to launch the now famous brand Skip Hop. After her initial success, Ellen has leveraged her creative instincts to revamp the baby product market one category at a time, from toys to feeding items to home décor. Being an entrepreneur has allowed her the freedom to pursue and implement her creative vision, forever changing the industry in the process.

"CORPORATE" IS A DIRTY WORD

Sometimes a step toward something new comes as a result of a negative experience. For many entrepreneurs that negative experience can be summed up in one word: CORPORATE. In our conversations this word was used as an adjective, a place, a state of being, a mindset, and even an insult. We can't tell you how many people spoke to us about the prospect of "going back to corporate" as just about the worst thing that could happen to them. On the positive side, many talked about how the unhappiness of their previous work environments in turn motivated them to create very positive work environments in their own companies.

Michelle Madhok, CEO of SheFinds.com, an online shopping blog, says that the SheFinds culture and policies are inspired in part by what she hated while working in corporate. She hated Mondays and she hated the pressure to be at the office exactly by 9 a.m. So at SheFinds, everyone works from home on Mondays, and on other days employees need to check in online by 8 a.m., but they don't need to be in the office until 11:30.

Meaning

For me the benefit of entrepreneurship is the sheer sense of satisfaction of working on something that you are passionate about.

— ANDREA MILLER, CEO AND FOUNDER OF TANGO MEDIA

Many entrepreneurs strike out on their own in order to do work that is meaningful to them, from those who "follow their passion" to those who want to have a particular impact on people or the world around them.

Some are drawn to the positive messages that entrepreneurship conveys to those around them and the influence it has on both their identity and relationships. This certainly rang true for Hannah Macdonald, owner of Bump Brooklyn, a hip maternity store in Park Slope, Brooklyn. She shared with us some of the many reasons for starting her own business. "I needed to rediscover myself, I wanted to bring back some equality to my marriage, and I really wanted my son to see his mother going to work. I felt responsible for my son's perception of women. I wanted him to see what I was capable of."

For other entrepreneurs it's really important to be able to work in a meaningful way that is reflective of their personal values. Rebuking the mantra "it's just business," these business owners take great pride and satisfaction in establishing work practices that are congruent with their personal philosophies. Claudia Romana, owner of Claudia Romana Enterprises, a ladies' golf apparel line, reminds us that "it's not just the goal but how you get there. If you lose your integrity then you lose everything."

MEET:

Melanie Notkin, founder of Savvy Auntie, a multiplatform media company, was tired of defining herself by what she wasn't—a wife and a mom. As a dedicated aunt of six nieces and nephews, she knew there were a lot of women like her who did so much for the children in their lives but frankly didn't get the credit they deserved. Becoming an entrepreneur gave her the ability to recognize and celebrate this part of herself and to support, acknowledge, and honor all those like her. After much brainstorming and behind-the-scenes work, she launched SavvyAuntie.com and more recently a book called *Savvy Auntie* for the niche she dubbed PANKs® (Professional Aunt No Kids). By establishing herself as both an entrepreneur and a role model, Melanie has been able to embrace her Savvy Auntie self and champion all the other aunties who contribute to the "American family village." In her mind, entrepreneurship is "the most amazing journey that you can take to find yourself."

Michelle Kedem, founding partner of On-Ramps, a full-service talent search firm, became an entrepreneur in order to be a part of something interesting. When she worked in corporate, Michelle felt as though there were a lot of important and compelling things happening in the world, but she ultimately "didn't feel like part of the conversation." She said, "I felt squired away in a corporate position observing things that I wanted to be a part of." Now her company gives her the opportunity to effect change and be in the thick of it. Her work has meaning and allows her to engage with the topics she cares about, such as talent best practices and organizational excellence.

A WORD ABOUT PASSION . . .

When it comes to entrepreneurs, there is a lot of talk about passion. The media is saturated with stories of women who "followed their passion and started their own business" and advice to "find your passion and the money will follow." We don't take issue with the concept of passion and its presence in business; we just don't like how the word is used. It feels so vague and inaccessible, an amorphous magical ingredient that will solve your business, personal, or financial problems, and it unfairly ties success to a singular thing. In our minds, this approach doesn't come close to fairly acknowledging all the hard work that actually goes into building and sustaining a business that works for you.

More important, and perhaps problematical, we have seen this word serve as a barrier. We have talked to women who feel like their idea or business is lacking because they aren't 100 percent passionate about "XYZ." And we've encountered those who would love to start a business but hesitate because they don't have an ardent "passion" to follow. Instead of looking for interesting and viable business opportunities, these women soul-search for passions that may or may not yield a satisfying business. While it may sound liberating, the call to "find your passion" can also create a lot of pressure!

Money

I wanted to set the ceiling. I wanted to feel I could earn whatever I could earn. I wanted it to be on me.

—EMILY, FOUNDER OF E. WOLPER INC.

Any conversation about what people would like to get from entrepreneurship is sure to feature the topic of money. After all, people don't start a business for their health! Some of the women we interviewed started with a specific financial objective in mind, while others became increasingly focused on and motivated by financial performance as the business grew.

MEET:

Emily Wolper, founder of E. Wolper Inc., had worked as an admissions officer at Columbia University before starting her own firm. She loved her job. However, she also knew at a very young age exactly what her earnings potential was should she choose to stay within the academic institutional structure. In such an environment, each pay level is preestablished, and while it might increase over time, it can be quite limiting to know exactly how much you will make as you ascend through the ranks. Emily wasn't thrilled with the pay ceiling of the institution and knew she could dramatically increase her earnings potential over time should she open a private admissions consulting practice of her own.

Teresa Chang, ceramist and owner of Teresa Chang Ceramics, didn't expect to get jazzed about the financial side of things, but she ultimately had a change of heart about the business's numbers. She initially regarded the accounting and invoicing tasks of her business as a necessary evil. However, she was surprised to learn that she really enjoyed keeping the books for her business. For her it helps to keep her focused and establish the rhythm of the business. It also allows her to keep in touch with the "empirical evidence" of her work. She says the accounting not only keeps a whole other part of her brain active but also keeps her honest about how much she is making and how the business is really doing.

HARD TO PUT A DOLLAR SIGN ON IT

As important as money is to some entrepreneurs, others are willing to take a financial hit in exchange for other benefits that are more important to them. They know they might make more money if they took a corporate job or even ran their business in a different manner—but that's not what drives them. Sometimes you have to trade a higher income for something more valuable to you. "Do you want to work corporate for the rest of your life, and work for the man, or do you want to work for yourself and potentially live a really nice life and still get to live your dreams?" asks Chloé Jo Davis, owner of Girlie Girl Army, a blog and 'Glamazon Guide to Green Living.' "There are so many perks to owning your own business, especially with what I do. If I can make enough money that I can work from home, support myself, live a relatively decent life, that's more than enough for me."

Opportunity

I couldn't not do it.

—JULIA ARCHER, OWNER OF @WORKDESIGN

Are you ever transfixed by an idea, so much so that you literally feel as though you're being pulled toward something, tractor-beam style, unable to resist? The thought gets stuck in your head and suddenly everything you see seems to confirm how fantastic it is.

We know the feeling, and so do many of the women we interviewed. For these ladies, their venture began as just an interesting opportunity they spotted in the marketplace, a flickering thought that started with "wouldn't it be cool if?" Once they identified it, they simply couldn't leave the idea alone. Interestingly, not all of them immediately considered starting a business. Several even tried to pitch the idea to other corporations, but turned to entrepreneurship once they realized they would have to bring it to fruition themselves.

MEET:

Cyndee Sugra, owner of Studio 7 Media, saw a job posting at Sony for her dream job at the peak of the dotcom bust. Good jobs were hard to find, but this one was a perfect match. They were looking for someone with a music background and knowledge of music software and Internet marketing. Cyndee had both. She is a classical pianist and guitarist, studied studio recording, and had a record deal during high school and college, but had also done online marketing for several large entertainment and media properties, including BMG Entertainment and DirecTV. Cyndee was jazzed about the opportunity and potential the position presented. However, for some reason or another, she was turned down. Frustrated and unwilling to watch a dream position slip away, Cyndee decided to do the same thing but on her own. At the time there was a tremendous need for Web services and development, but people didn't have the budget for big agencies or permanent staff. Cyndee's new boutique agency filled the void perfectly. Over time, the company was able to broaden its services to include original software development in addition to more mainstream online marketing, Web development, and graphic design projects. Since launching, Studio 7 Media has become a force to be reckoned with, developing lots of never-seen-before technology solutions and products. With the same fervor that encouraged her to strike out on her own in the first place, Cyndee has consistently pushed the industry by taking on the next most challenging opportunity. We wonder if Sony knows what they missed out on.

Joyce Szuflita, founder of NYC School Help, had no intention of starting her own company. She was raising her family in Brooklyn, where she had lived since 1981, and working in set design. Despite knowing the neighborhoods inside and out, when it came time for her twin girls to start school Joyce was cast into the world of the unknown. Determined to make sure her girls got the best education available, she acquainted herself with the extreme nuance and complexity of the Brooklyn public and private school systems. As Joyce tells it, she became obsessed with educational information and ended up with insider knowledge of nearly every institution around. As her kids advanced through the years, her knowledge only grew deeper and deeper. When her daughters were accepted to the high school of their choice, it dawned on Joyce that she really had a unique and highly desirable bank of information at her disposal. Sure, she had helped friends along the way, sharing the inside scoop and little-known facts, but there were thousands of families in Brooklyn who would kill for the expertise that she had amassed. So she decided to turn her years of data gathering into her own business. Now Joyce leverages her encyclopedic knowledge to help Brooklyn families navigate the school system, finding institutions that best meet their unique needs.

Jessica Jackley, cofounder of Kiva and also cofounder of Profounder, was inspired by a three-month stay in West Africa interviewing grant recipients. She approached numerous organizations to sponsor a participatory microcredit platform, but no one would bite. Ultimately only one organization out of the many asked was willing to sponsor a pilot study. Motivated by the opportunity to create something with such significant impact, Jessica ended up pursuing the idea independently, involving friends, family members, colleagues, and classmates from her Stanford MBA program. We're sure the nearly half a million loan recipients are extremely grateful she did!

• • •

Of course, sometimes opportunities arise out of necessity. Many entrepreneurs we spoke with said their initial foray into entrepreneurship was due to life circumstances that were beyond their control.

For example, Jennifer Hill was a graphic designer with the beauty brand Fresh. She loved her job, but her situation suddenly changed when her dad got sick and she took on a big caretaking role. In order to keep herself afloat she quit her job and began to do some freelance work as time permitted. These freelance clients ultimately helped her turn an unfortunate situation into an opportunity to build her own business. Not only did Jen enjoy having the flexibility she needed to care for her family, but she also loved the creative freedom entrepreneurship offered her. Today, several years later, Jen not only continues to do custom design work, but has a significant online retail operation as well, where she sells prints, calendars, stationery, and invitations. She has been offered many in-house positions over the years but is unwilling to give up her business and the benefits it brings her.

Angie Davis, owner of Byrd & Belle, also turned an unfortunate situation into an opportunity for entrepreneurship. Like too many people, Angie was laid off from an architecture firm during the lows of the recession. It turned out to be a gift. Dubious about the poor hiring market, Angie turned to making things at home to keep her busy and posted them on Etsy as a bit of an experiment. She was amazed by the response. With the launch of her amazingly cool felt laptop sleeve her popularity skyrocketed and her hobby was effectively turned into a business. As the economy improved, she began to be approached by various firms with a range of opportunities, none of which she seriously entertained. However, each offer provided her with the chance to pause and consider what it was that she really valued about and wanted to get from entrepreneurship. Aside from her newfound freedom, it was the satisfaction that came from introducing great design and functionality to everyday people. Something that always bothered Angie about the field of architecture was that often great design is reserved for the wealthy. In her new business, she loves that she creates well-made products that anyone can experience. That realization allowed her to further define the work she wanted to do under her new brand, Byrd & Belle.

Your Turn: Clarifying *Your* Motivations

Now that we've talked about the different motivations that inspire entrepreneurs, it's a good time to reevaluate your own needs. It is important to remember both what gave you the entrepreneurial kick in the pants in the first place as well as what is important to you today.

> *Question 1:* What motivated you to strike out on your own?
> *Question 2:* What must your business afford you in order to be worth it?
> *Question 3:* What happens when your needs and motivations change over time?

For some entrepreneurs the answers to these questions may seem obvious, but we think it's important to consider them nonetheless. After identifying your answer, think about how your motivations have shaped the course of your business and the decisions you have made. Have your decisions so far honored your original goals? Have your motivations changed? How might someone else with different personal motivations have shaped your business?

Question 1: What motivated you to strike out on your own?
In order to know where you are going, you have to figure out where you've been. That's why it's important to consider why you decided to launch your own venture in the first place. In order to build a successful company that works for you, these motivations must inform everything you do.

For example, Adelaide originally pursued an independent path because she couldn't find an inspiring place to do the kind of work she wanted to do—counsel women making professional choices and changes—that would also boast healthy earnings potential over time. She wanted to have the autonomy to work on things she found interesting without being constrained by organizational rules and restrictions. By the time the idea for In Good Company (a community, business learning center, and workspace for women entrepreneurs) was developed it was the sheer opportunity that drove her forward. Adelaide knew she would regret letting this possibility pass her by. She wanted the chance to create something bigger and to find even more ways to connect with the clients and content she found rewarding.

Amy's first foray into entrepreneurship (aside from grade-school lemonade stands) was a recruiting agency called Interactive Pipeline. She had already been managing someone else's recruiting firm, so she knew she had the skills to run the show. However, since she wasn't in charge, she didn't have the ability to set her own priorities or the company's direction. She also wanted the opportunity to make more money. She realized that if she was going to be working as hard as she was, it had better be for herself. That way she would get both the autonomy and financial upside of an entrepreneur. In Good Company was a little bit closer to her heart. After investing in a graduate degree in counseling and spending time working with entrepreneurs in a one-on-one capacity, she wanted to create a bigger business that was personally fulfilling and offered the flexibility and space to have a family.

Together we work to keep our motivations and needs in mind when making decisions about the business. There are many paths we could have taken that might have worked for the business but would have ultimately changed it in a way that didn't work for us. For example, others might have decided not to teach and facilitate programs as often as we do. Perhaps they would decide to spend time on other tasks, such as strategic partnerships, online offerings, or operational logistics for the space. However, we find it really meaningful to connect with our members and work with them to troubleshoot business challenges. And meaningful work is one of our primary motivations. At various points in the business we have had to temporarily scale back our programs in order to focus on something else, but overall we make sure facilitation is a significant part of what we do.

FOR YOUR CONSIDERATION

- Why were you initially motivated to do your own thing?
- What do you get by being your own boss that you wouldn't if you worked for someone else?
- How have your motivations shaped the way you run your business?

Question 2: What must your business afford you in order to be worth it?
Some days it's easy to recite a long list of the benefits of being self-employed . . . and some days not so much. Once upon a time working in PJs seemed like a dream . . . until you experienced the stir-craziness that goes along with working from home. Calling the shots is cool . . . until you really need someone's opinion. The truth is, not all the characteristics of entrepreneurship appeal to everyone, and many are a double-edged sword. So rather than accept the generic benefits extolled by others as worthy of sacrifice, we want

you to know exactly what benefits ring your bell. More important, we want you to know which benefits are, for you, nonnegotiable.

Perhaps you don't want to undermine your financial security, or maybe you want to be able to travel for three months a year. If you treated these motivations as nonnegotiables, imagine how differently you would start or shape your business. For example, Jessica Sutton, owner of JSGD, softened her leap into entrepreneurship by first taking on freelance work, then scaling back her "real job" to two days a week, before finally "kicking the crutch." This transition not only allowed her to maintain her financial security but also enabled her to start with clients she enjoyed rather than feeling pressured to take any kind of work.

Likewise, her friend and officemate Jen Hill (known for her *Places I Have Never Been* print series) loves to travel and makes sure to keep her business as virtual and portable as possible so that she's able to run it from locations across the globe. Consider how different priorities compel these entrepreneurs to make decisions about their company structure, say no to clients and opportunities, or steer their company's growth in a particular direction.

We too have needs that IGC must accommodate in order to truly work for us. Both of us believe our time is our most valuable commodity, and therefore we want to spend it in a way that is not only enjoyable but productive. But that means something different to each of us.

Adelaide relishes the ability to work from home and to attack a mile-long to-do list without interruption. There have been many periods in the business when it's been necessary to spend lots of time in New York while the mail piles up at home in Philadelphia. While she can certainly endure this for a few months at a time, she would never choose to run a business in a way that made this the norm. That is one of the reasons she has resisted the pressure to expand to other cities, which would force her to be away from home more often.

On the other hand, Amy is an off-the-charts extrovert who

sometimes calls people to keep her company on her walks to the subway. To her, a full day at home with her computer is a cruel punishment. Her need to work around others on a regular basis is very real. However, as we all know, loads of coworkers are not exactly a given when you run a small company. That's why the opportunity to create In Good Company was so appealing to her; it provides the kind of office and peer community that Amy and others like her crave.

As you can see, some of our needs are quite different from each other, yet we have managed to build a business that accommodates both of us.

FOR YOUR CONSIDERATION

- What must your business afford you in order to be worth the work it requires?
- What compromises are you willing to make in order to preserve this?

Question 3: What happens when your needs and motivations change over time?
As time chugs on you may find that your motivations change or evolve. This is by no means a bad thing and in fact makes sense. After all, your personal needs and motivations will change over time, and if you intend to keep your business for many years, it's likely that those changes will spill over. For example, what if you started your business because you wanted to make some additional income? Now you'd like to travel and have more autonomy over your time, but the whole darn company is built around you and requires your presence to run it.

Or what if you started this business because you wanted to keep your feet wet while you had young kids at home? Predictability and stability were of great importance, so you chose a few stable institutional clients who came with long-term contracts. But now your kids are in school and you want to take advantage of the time and creative energy you have available.

In both of these scenarios, you'll need to adjust your business in order to remain satisfied. Otherwise you'll be stuck in an outdated business that no longer works for you. But don't despair; this is the exciting opportunity that entrepreneurship presents! You have the freedom to make the changes necessary in order to make your business accommodate your needs.

Several of the women we interviewed were able to adjust their businesses to meet their changing needs in really interesting ways.

Sunny Bates, a consummate connector and well-known name in the start-up world, loves innovation and being on the leading edge of information and discovery. Sunny initially had a recruiting business, which she started when she had two small kids at home and stability and predictability were of great importance. After about seventeen years, she started to feel a little discontented.

She loved to go after new and interesting clients who were diverse in terms of both industry and need. This was what kept her stimulated and engaged. However, she realized that it also presented problems for her business. Recruiting firms do better when they have narrow and deep areas of expertise, not necessarily when they tout an eclectic client portfolio. With a narrow and deep focus you can leverage existing knowledge of industries and candidates, relationships, and procedures. Conversely, when you're always scouring for something new, you waste a lot of time reinventing the wheel.

Ultimately, Sunny recognized this conflict. She sold her business to her employees and, leveraging her deep Rolodex and love of connecting, hung out a shingle as a consultant of sorts who was able to jump in and participate in multiple projects. From her new position she has been able to play a critical role in the launch of several high-profile ventures and even serve as an adviser to the TED conferences.

Another entrepreneur, Judi Rosenthal, originally started as a financial adviser for Ameriprise because she was motivated to increase her earnings potential (in part so she could invest more money in the nonprofit programs she was so passionate about). After building a very successful financial planning practice, primarily with a focus on women clients, she realized that her motivations had changed. Now with a baby at home she wanted to have less face time in her business without being limited by her own ability to see a certain number of clients.

Judi saw the opportunity to create a separate business platform, Bloom, within the Ameriprise system, supporting the company's fleet of women financial advisers by teaching them the skills that had made her so successful. She sold off the majority of her planning practice to another adviser, retained her choice clients, and opened her new business. She has very deliberately created Bloom with her schedule and time in mind.

Now, just because your needs change doesn't mean you have to sell your business and start anew. Entrepreneurs make more minor adjustments all the time.

For example, since the start of the business, Adelaide has been accustomed to traveling from her home in Philadelphia to the office in New York up to four times a week if necessary. She always liked to work from home but didn't have any reason to specifically limit her travel other than expense. However, once she was expecting a baby, she knew her needs would change dramatically. No longer did she want to schlep back and forth several times a week with an infant at home, so she decided to travel no more than once a week. She knew this shift in her needs would directly impact her role, so she looked at her responsibilities and determined that several things would need to change in order to make things work for her. First, programming was consolidated and rescheduled to fit a once-a-week trip. Second, she began to shift her in-person responsibilities to other staff members and beefed up duties that could be done remotely. The shift in tasks actually worked out well, as Adelaide had been eager to dedicate more time to writing and social media. Had she not made these changes she would undoubtedly have been unsatisfied by a business that no longer worked for her. That's not to say there aren't times she misses events at the office that she would like to attend, but there are trade-offs even when you get what you want.

FOR YOUR CONSIDERATION

- Have your needs changed over time? What adjustments have you made as a result?
- How do you anticipate your needs changing in the future? What adjustments might that require?
- What can you start doing now to make that transition smoother?

RECOMMITTING TO ENTREPRENEURSHIP

Many of the businesses we have worked with have had accidental or experimental starts. But inevitably there has been a pivotal moment where the entrepreneur has paused, reevaluated, and reaffirmed her commitment to entrepreneurship.

Joy Cho, founder of Oh Joy!, had one such moment. Joy had moved to Philadelphia with her husband, who was in medical school. A graphic designer by trade with experience in home and textile design, she hoped her next design job would be to work for Anthropologie, the clothing retailer, as a textile designer. At the time, however, the position she sought wasn't available. Disappointed, she started to freelance and blog on the side while continuing the job hunt. Before long, Joy had developed quite a following and was actually surprised to realize how much she loved her new independent work/lifestyle. Interestingly, after she was on her own for a year, Anthropologie called her back up, as they were now hiring for the position she had so coveted. Of course, enamored with her new entrepreneurial life, she didn't take it, but it did provide her with a very useful and important opportunity to step back and evaluate her situation. She was forced to really consider the benefits and reality of entrepreneurship and contrast those with an ideal internal position. She found so much happiness in being her own boss and knew she'd be giving up too much if she left her business. She surmised that "the work is a lot more but the payoffs are a lot more too."

If you think about it, you renew your commitment to entrepreneurship each day. Make sure that you are renewing on the right terms.

Troubleshooting:
When You Get in Your Own Way

Now that you've reflected on your motivations and the important role they play, let's turn our attention to a few things that can get in the way of success.

We see many clients who are unsatisfied with their business for one reason or another. Sometimes the source of this discontent has to do with getting what she wants from entrepreneurship, particularly when her motivations conflict with each other or aren't clearly established to start with.

Have Competing Needs?
Know What You Want When Push Comes to Shove

As we've already explained, you have to know what you want before you can get it, but it's also important to recognize that everything comes with trade-offs. What you want may not always be possible, especially if you have conflicting motivations. I want big *and* calm. I want to ease in *and* have fast fame. It's easy to see why these kinds of conflicting motivations can cause all sorts of business problems. The solution is simple but not easy. You must remember and remind yourself which motivations are greater priorities. When push comes to shove, what do you really want most? What motivation will you protect at all costs?

The challenge in our minds with conflicting motivations and expectations is the loss of time and energy. We hate seeing our clients feel badly about what they have created, especially when it's completely in line with what they intended to create. We have often encountered entrepreneurs who just simply don't give themselves credit for achieving the goals they set out to achieve. Somehow, even with explicit goals and terrific outcomes, some people use someone else's yardstick to measure their own success.

The Case of Too-Tired Tabitha

For years Tabitha had been in marketing positions at corporate institutions. However, she had a background in product design and had continued to nurture her interest by following trends, companies, and products in the home décor market. She was good at her job, and some days she really liked it, but she felt frustrated that it monopolized her life and she didn't have enough time for all she enjoyed. There were certain times during the year when the travel required was quite extensive. And soon she grew less and less inspired about the projects she was being given. She had always dreamed about running her own shop and would fantasize about having a well-appointed small office that she could comfortably pad around in.

She started working with us and put in motion the plans to leave her job. She had gotten quite excited about going back to her product design roots and launching a line of functional kitchen products, starting with a multiuse food storage system. In discussing what she wanted the business to become, Tabitha made it clear that she wanted a well-known brand that could be found at major retailers such as the Container Store and Bed, Bath & Beyond. She was accustomed to being well paid and working with a bright team of people, and she wanted those characteristics to be present in her own business as well. After two small production orders, Tabitha gathered together some angel investors and put up a hefty sum of her own as well.

About eighteen months into the new business, she expressed dissatisfaction. She was bone-tired. Ironically, the pace she had set really didn't seem to be that much different from what she was trying to get away from. She wondered if she was doing something wrong. What happened to that serene office and a life with more balance, she wondered?

Her business really was quite different from the fantasy she had conjured up. But the reality is that the business size and impact she wanted necessitated a certain pace and intensity. She could have had the quiet office, slippers, and never-ending cup of herbal tea, but it is likely her business trajectory would have looked quite different.

We spent a lot of time that meeting talking about what she really wanted from the business. Deep down Tabitha knew that brand recognition and the opportunity to really impact the marketplace in a *big* way was her first priority. We talked about the challenges of having your cake and eating it too and concluded that her fantasy was fairly incompatible with the goals she had built the business around. We talked about the importance of prioritizing her motivations and recognizing the trade-offs that came with them. If Tabitha was going to pursue these motivations, she couldn't beat herself up for not having achieved the fantasy she wanted. The lack of a serene office wasn't a failure or a shortcoming, it was a choice. And more important, it was a choice that reflected her needs and goals.

However, since it's never all or nothing, we discussed how Tabitha could balance her existing pace a bit more. There were ways she could better enforce boundaries and carve out more quiet time for herself. We also strategized several operational and logistical changes she could make at certain future milestones. She set up a small office at home, and when the next big milestone was reached, she would try to work from there on Fridays. We all thought this would help her maintain a creative outlet and room for strategic thinking.

With time, Tabitha has been able to institute more of the balance she desires. As with many entrepreneurs, it is a battle, but at least it is one she is winning. Her experience has given her greater perspective on the value of her time, and she has been much better at determining which opportunities are really worth her attention and resources. More important, she's stopped holding herself to an impossible standard and has become comfortable with the trade-offs that come with her choices.

FOR YOUR CONSIDERATION

- Do you continually feel torn about saying no or enforcing boundaries that you established in order to make the business work for you?
- Does the experience of others make you feel badly about your own progress and choices?
- Are you plagued by a persistent case of "the grass is always greener"?

Forgot to Define What You Want?
Clarify Your Needs and Realign the Business

It's pretty easy to clearly define and recognize your personal motivations at the beginning when your start is actually a clear and concrete event. But there are many ways to "plunge" into entrepreneurship, and sometimes it happens by accident. Consequently, some ventures are launched with a complete identity and proclaimed purpose, while others linger in entrepreneurial purgatory for a bit, waiting to find out exactly what they are.

There is no right way to approach entrepreneurship, and certainly a whole constellation of factors can influence how deliberate and discreet is the formation of your business. However, sometimes a less deliberate start can cause the entrepreneur to miss out on the opportunity to be crystal clear about what her motivations are. This can cause a lot of ambivalence or ambiguity, which can be quite harmful to the business.

Don't get us wrong, there is absolutely nothing wrong with start-ing slow. We often suggest that people look for ways to experiment and test out elements of the business they want to launch before going whole hog (see chapter 6, "Perfection Is a Trap").

However, we get concerned when folks are never deliberate or premeditated in their plans. We pause when we hear people say they simply fell into their business and followed it to where it was today. In these cases we often have to do a little more work to help our clients define their motivations and intentions. Always taking the path of least resistance is a sure way to end up with a business that you don't like. Falling into a business is totally fine, but you don't want to hand over the reins for the rest of the journey.

The Case of Hijacked Helen

Helen calls herself an "accidental entrepreneur." With a background as a buyer and merchandiser, she has always helped friends with their wardrobes. Once, while in between jobs, she agreed to help some of her friends' friends and let them pay her for her services. Before she knew it she was spending more time with these "sort-of clients" than she was looking for a new gig. She decided that, actu-ally, she loved setting her own schedule and was dreading going back to a "real" job. So she kept on seeking clients, staving off a possible return to corporate. Fast-forward two years, and Helen had become disenchanted. She came to us wondering what she should do.

It turned out that Helen had more client demand than she could currently service. She was keeping long hours and was exhausted from seeing multiple clients a day. She had been told she should hire someone to see clients under her name, but she wasn't sure she wanted the responsibility and commitment that requires. We asked Helen how she liked to spend her time, and she said she enjoyed the client work, depending on who the client was. She also mentioned that she had recently done some media work, which she loved. She told us that she was disappointed to have missed out on the chance to a spokesperson. Not long prior, a fashion Web site had approached her to represent them, but she had taken so long getting back to them that she missed out.

It was clear from our conversation that Helen's "accidental" start had encouraged a bad habit—saying yes to any kind of work without having a clear understanding of whether it met her needs. As a result, Helen's services were very hodgepodge and she ended up accepting a lot of work she didn't like doing. Plus, because she wasn't clear about what she wanted from her business, she had no good way of evaluating or making time for future opportunities. Helen had been hijacked by her business.

We asked Helen to talk to us about what benefits she wanted her business to provide her. She replied that what she really wanted was to make a good living, doing work she liked, and to have a better balance of work hours. She also wanted to start sharing her advice and knowledge with a larger audience. We were confident that Helen could adjust her business to give her what she wanted.

First, we had Helen prioritize the services she offered. We told her that the work she loved should come first. We also talked with her about the importance of adopting business practices that really set her up to be successful. No more squeezing in three clients on a day when she should see only two. It compromised the results and made her less satisfied. Also, there was no need to see all new clients within two weeks of the initial call. She was at a point where she could set the terms in her favor. From now on, bigger projects could be scheduled farther out and a deposit could be collected to reserve the time on her calendar.

As for the services that she didn't enjoy, we encouraged Helen to either contract with an apprentice to do some of that work or partner with someone whom she could refer the work to, who would be likely to refer work back to her.

Second, we had Helen think about the future and the kind of work she'd like to be doing two years from now. She told us she was really disappointed about the spokesperson opportunity and that she would really like to do more of that. She also wanted to be featured more regularly in local media for her expertise. Helen carved out two blocks of time each week for business development, where she would focus explicitly on cultivating the kinds of opportunities that she wanted more of.

Lastly, we had Helen think about the course of her week. When in her mind were ideal times to be working? Since many of her clients were available only on the weekends, what time could she allot for herself so that she too would get a break? For now she decided to take only one client on Sundays and to take all Mondays off. Also, by limiting herself to no more than two clients a day, she would be able to maintain better balance on the days when she was seeing clients. Helen now has a business that works for her and provides her with what she wants. She is satisfied and secure in her experience of entrepreneurship.

FOR YOUR CONSIDERATION

- When did your business feel "real"? What have you done differently since then?
- Are you set up in a way that allows you to do your best work?
- How do you handle business that you don't want?

Cheat Sheet: What's In It for *You?*

POINTS TO REMEMBER:

1. Your motivations reflect your unique goals for becoming an entrepreneur. They sum up what you want from your business and are different from the goals you have for your business.

2. Your motivations should play an important role in influencing the kind of business you choose to run and the way you choose to structure it.

3. Sometimes what you really want can conflict with other goals and expectations you have. It's important to prioritize.

4. We should all take the time to revisit and reclarify our motivations, especially those entrepreneurs who had more of an accidental or experimental launch.

5. It is likely that what you want from your business will change over time. It's important to realign your business with your motivations in these instances. This may result in a small tweak or a total transformation.

QUESTIONS TO CONSIDER:

1. What motivated you to go out on your own?
2. What must your business afford you in order to be worth it?
3. How have you structured your business to meet your needs?
4. Are there any needs you have that are currently unmet?
5. What changes can be made to better deliver the benefits you are looking for?

BUSINESS SPOTLIGHT

"I thought I would jump out of my art studio for a few months and hire some people and put some systems in place. That was about fourteen years ago. I never finished the portrait on the easel."

An unintended (and wildly successful) detour to entrepreneurship
Trish Karter, cofounder of Dancing Deer Baking Company

Trish didn't intend to be an entrepreneur. She wanted to be an artist but landed in business when the family company was in trouble and from there went on to get an MBA. After graduation she worked in new ventures and business development. When that didn't add up to professional happiness, she left the business world in order to reclaim her life as a painter and spent more than five years in the studio, selling her work through galleries and patrons. Never did Trish suspect that she would soon become a cofounder and CEO of Dancing Deer Baking Company, one of the most admired brands in the natural gourmet food market. In some ways, it happened by accident.

When she was a painter, Trish and her ex-husband, Ayis Antoniou, became acquainted with Suzanne Lombardi, who was a very talented baker in need of business advice. Suzanne was carrying her pots and pans to rented kitchen facilities at night and delivering fresh all-natural cakes, cookies, and pastries to coffee shops in the morning. This was in the days before the natural food market had exploded. People loved her products and there was the potential to create something much bigger.

Trish saw an opportunity. She and Ayis became Suzanne's angel investors and helped her set up a former pizza parlor with a couple of ovens. With the couple's assistance, the business was launched. Getting orders was not the problem, but keeping up with demand was tough. Trish knew that without better infrastructure Dancing Deer would crumble under its own success. She thought it would take just a few months to hire some people and put systems in place and then she'd be back at her easel. After all, she loved her life as an artist.

So Trish rolled up her sleeves and dove in. The day-to-day challenges of running a small growing business were rewarding and the creative opportunities were endless. The partnership with Suzanne was a joy, as they were both workhorses with similar values, aesthetics, and ideas about food and fun. Before long she was hooked.

The good times took a pause, however, in 2000, when a divorce resulted in Trish's carrying on without her two founding partners, Ayis and Suzanne. Over the next ten years she grew Dancing Deer into one of the most respected and innovative brands in the specialty goods business, with nationwide distribution, multiple channels including a highly successful Internet gift business, and piles of awards and honors.

While Dancing Deer's prominence is a success story, what's notable about the business is how clearly its growth over the last sixteen years has reflected Trish's personal motivations and values.

From the beginning, the business was "about more than just great-quality food." In addition to making delicious, all-natural, and high-quality products, Trish aspired to exemplify a meritocratic, worker-empowered, environmentally progressive, double-bottom-line business, one that measures success not only by economic performance but also in terms of positive social impact. Presented with opportunities to grow into a variety of different businesses, Dancing Deer is what it is because of what is important to the woman behind the scenes.

This has meant different things at different points in the company's development. In the early days it meant, among other things, a commitment to progressive, low-impact packaging and scaling back a broader product line in order to focus on what Dancing Deer did best. It also meant saying no to a huge opportunity to sell its famous Molasses Clove cookies in Williams-Sonoma stores nationwide. Because the all-natural product would not survive the time required in distribution and Trish and Suzanne had no interest in putting preservatives in the product, they took a pass. (On the upside, Williams-Sonoma came back a few days later and requested a custom gingerbread dry mix instead, which launched a very successful long-term relationship.)

In 2001 Trish started the Sweet Home Project, which gives 35 percent of the retail price of cake and cookie gifts to help Boston families sustainably transition out of homelessness—a challenging issue in their inner-city neighborhood and for some of their employees. When the economy went south the team never even discussed cutting back on its commitment to Sweet Home.

The search for new production facilities as the company grew was also an exercise in staying true to the mission. The company expanded many times with adjunct facilities, but moved its main manufacturing twice, in 1998 and 2008. Both times the priority was to find excellent production space but stay in the urban center on public transportation lines and retain the inner city workforce. Trish didn't want the Dancing Deer staff to be burdened with a long commute. More recently, this requirement meant waiting an extra three years to find a location that was the right size and price. However, with both moves, the company eventually landed on solutions that were better for business, operations, and morale than she could have imagined. Trish's consideration of and loyalty to her staff has certainly been repaid. Many of the employees who work in her factory have been with Dancing Deer for upwards of ten years.

Trish believed that success would come from perfecting their core business and sticking to their core values. It was often challenging, but the value system always trumped other pressures. She believes this is what made the brand and the product quality not only hold strong but grow even in tough times. There were many opportunities to dumb down and accelerate volume but this was never on the table for Trish. There were temptations to chase the shiny objects such as establishing a retail division or doing line extensions in unknown territory, "but, it was something we'd have to learn, how to do those new businesses, and we were still learning how to do the business we were in. We had to get that right first."

The goal was not to pursue growth at all costs, and the focus was not purely on economic gain. The business goal was to build a national brand of exceptional quality, creating value for investors, employees, and the community. Clearly Trish didn't believe that Dancing Deer was "just business."

Over the years, Trish chose strategic business extensions that did complement the core wholesale offering and didn't divert precious resources from the primary goals. Dancing Deer developed a large consumer and corporate e-commerce presence, as well as gift lines for resellers, which gave the brand national visibility with marquis accounts. Recently, Trish stepped down as Dancing Deer's CEO, handing over the reins to the COO. She remains on the board of directors, but she felt it was time for something new. "After sixteen years I squeezed as much good karma out of cookies as anyone possibly could. It was painful to separate but now that I'm on the other side I've swamped myself with cool new possibilities." She reports that she is incubating a variety of new ventures that bring together (not surprisingly) her interests and personal values, including sustainability, social justice, and dematerialization.

What Will Your Business Be Known For?

Provide Your Business with a Purpose

The process of building a brand is the most fascinating. You start with nothing and it just grows.
—SELIMA SALAUN, FOUNDER OF SELIMA OPTIQUE

"Can I give you a piece of advice?" It seems like a harmless enough offer, yet anyone with even the slightest amount of experience gets uneasy when they hear this question. They reflexively tense, bracing themselves for an unwelcome barrage of opinions. As entrepreneurs, we know feedback is critical to our success, yet we are wary of others telling us what to do . . . that's why we're entrepreneurs! The problem with most advice is not that it's bad or ill-intentioned, but that it is devoid of context. The giver assumes to know what you need and to understand what you want. They forget that one size doesn't fit all and that the right course of action is completely dependent on the goal. Good advice needs a deep understanding of the issues and a clear picture of the goal. In order to give an appropriate and helpful business suggestion, you need to know not only someone's motivations and skills or the services and products their business provides; you need to know what their business, at its core, is about. You need to know the business purpose.

A Look at Business Purpose

Now that we've spent some time focusing on you, let's turn our attention to the business itself. It is not enough for your business to be a means of fulfilling your personal motivations. Your business needs a purpose of its own in order to last in the marketplace.

We often work with clients who are grappling with a significant decision or have reached a business crossroads and want to know if they are making the right choice. It depends, we say, on what they want their business to accomplish, stand for, and represent.

Some entrepreneurs use a mission and vision statement to help answer this question. Now, before you roll your eyes, bear with us. Contrary to popular belief, your company's mission and vision are not simply an esoteric exercise fated to die amid the glossy pages of a business plan. Nor are they simply a mirror reflection of your own personal goals. Rather, they create real business value. They fortify your business, allowing it to stand on its own two feet, and also act as a decision-making litmus test as you consider opportunities in the marketplace. In contrast to independent strategies or goals, your business purpose is the overall impact you want your business to have in the marketplace and the world. It helps to distinguish your business from seemingly similar others within your category or industry. It serves as a reflection of what you think is important and enables you to declare what matters.

Business purposes are visible and compelling. It is what makes Hanky Panky, which revolutionized the thong in the name of comfort and quality for all, more than just underwear, and Malia and Carol Mills, who create a personalized and empowering customer experience, more than just swimwear. It is Sweetriot's dedication to positively impact each piece of its supply chain and in turn champion enlightened trade and change the chocolate and cacao markets. It is eyewear designer Selima Salaun's ability to rebrand the entire product category as fashionable and sleek. It is Cyndee Sugra of Studio 7 Media's insistence on allowing her business to be a platform for development, experimentation, and innovation.

To clarify, business purpose is not the same thing as social or charitable purpose. To be sure, some business purposes are tightly interlaced with elements of social good, but most, at least in the way we are defining it, do not indicate whether or not a business gives back or "does good."

Knowing what you stand for and how you measure success not only helps to distinguish and add meaning to your business, it also provides much-needed direction and guidance, sifting out directions that *could be* pursued from those that really make sense and bring satisfaction. As entrepreneurs we are intrigued by opportunity but often spend a lot of time wondering whether a particular direction is a good one to pursue. A strong business purpose helps us to navigate and evaluate these decisions and crossroads.

The Story of Angela and Zoe, Part 2

You may remember from the last chapter that Angela is driven by what she sees as a gaping hole in the marketplace, while Zoe wants to cook on her own terms, in a way that allows her to experience sanity, balance, creative control, and ownership. After much thought and research, both women opened gourmet markets.

Angela is eager to change the marketplace by providing a new upscale and consistent option for specialty and prepared foods, while Zoe is compelled to create a business that will be able to cement itself as an institution within her community and bring acclaim to the town itself, challenging the assumptions of where fine cuisine is found.

Angela knows it is important for her to develop a recognizable and highly regarded brand that will transfer well to many domestic and international markets. She also sets up a strong online retail presence and wholesaling program. On the other hand, Zoe creates a business that in her mind offers the best of both worlds: it serves specialty and prepared foods by day and turns into a four-table gourmet restaurant by night. She can have the pleasure of cooking without the stress of a huge restaurant. Her retail store allows her to develop a strong presence within her community.

So in the end, both are gourmet grocers, but since they have dramatically different purposes and motivations, they will develop dramatically different businesses. Their business purpose serves not only to distinguish their ventures from one another, but also to inform every decision each of them will make about the direction the company will go.

In the Company of Others: Creating a Business Legacy

When you ask entrepreneurs about the purpose of their business, they will most likely start with the specific needs it fills or the problem it solves. This is good. We should hope that all businesses fill a need or solve a problem of some sort. If you push a little further, however, you will most likely hear the entrepreneur express a deeper hope or a loftier goal for the business, and it is this deeper purpose that lends the business not only its unique DNA but also its markers for success.

Obviously, each of the women that we spoke to in the making of this book had a distinct and unique business purpose, but a second look revealed several interesting themes. These themes may help you identify your business purpose or provide you with other like businesses that may offer lessons to learn.

Raising the Bar

The way that I can change the world is by teaching everyone to communicate better. To me, that's something worth fighting for.

—JODI GLICKMAN, PRESIDENT OF GREAT ON THE JOB

There are many markets that are stagnant, places where we as consumers have become content with the status quo and fail to ask the question, "How can this be done better?" Sometimes we notice our discontent, but often we don't. Instead we are complicit in our continued endorsement of subpar products, methods, and services. It is not until change rolls around and our experience is radically improved that we all collectively smirk and say, "Of course!" This change is often brought about by innovators who aren't content with the way things are done and want to do something about it.

We spoke with several women whose business purpose reflected this sentiment. They wanted to raise the bar and push the envelope. They wanted to move markets and industries, forcing them to evolve and improve. These women leverage their businesses as vehicles to create this change.

MEET:
Shazi Visram, founder and CEO of HappyBaby, is determined to raise the bar in a major way. In 2003, one of her close friends became a mom of twins, and Shazi witnessed several common new-mom challenges firsthand. She was particularly dismayed when she saw how difficult it was for her friend to find good healthy food to feed her infants. The only alternative to processed jarred baby food was to make your own, which many busy moms don't have the time to do. This gap in the marketplace really troubled Shazi. She couldn't figure out why there weren't healthy and organic alternatives. After all, our nation was experiencing a health crisis, particularly among children. In Shazi's mind, instilling good eating habits at a young age was the best way to promote a lifelong relationship

with health and nutrition. So Shazi launched HappyBaby, which offers a complete line of premium organic infant and toddler food and is sold in more than five thousand stores nationwide. Shazi's goal has been not only to provide moms with peace of mind, knowing their babies are getting optimal nutrition, but also to establish great business practices that are both environmentally and socially responsible. In addition, HappyBaby works hard to support the organic farms where the food is sourced, the retailers who carry the products, and the families who purchase them.

Jodi Glickman, founder of Great on the Job, was dismayed by how ill-prepared well-educated students were for successfully navigating the workplace. She believes that effective and professional communication is one of the most critical skills for workplace success, yet it is largely overlooked by traditional corporate and business school training programs. So Jodi, a skilled communicator herself, single-handedly rewrote the script in order to teach and empower young professionals to be "great on the job." But ultimately she is not just satisfied with reaching those she can teach herself. She won't be happy until the curricula of business schools nationwide are fundamentally changed to include these important skills. That's why Jodi has worked hard to create broad visibility for her brand and ideas. Her weekly blog on Harvard Business School's Web site consistently puts her on the "most read" list, and her first book, eponymously titled *Great on the Job*, came out in May 2011.

Blazing a Trail

> I always like to be focused on the next innovations that we are going to be doing.
>
> —SARA HOROWITZ, FOUNDER OF FREELANCERS UNION

Pioneering is about being one of the first. It's about breaking barriers and exploring new territory. Several of the entrepreneurs we spoke with considered their businesses to be a way to explore the unknown and create change. Once a particular feat was achieved, the founders and their businesses moved on to the next frontier, always ready and eager to push into the unknown. The pursuit is intriguing for them and they rise to the challenge. Their businesses are engineered to be trailblazing vehicles.

MEET:

Sarah Horowitz, cofounder of Freelancers Union (formerly Working Today), grew up under the influence of the labor movements of the 1960s and 1970s. This gave her an eye toward social justice, and as a young labor lawyer she determined that independent workers would be the new face of the labor movement as they are excluded from traditional employer supports and benefits. She founded a nonprofit to meet the needs of this market by grouping them together to build their power in both politics and in the market. Over the years, Sara kept advancing the agenda, eventually taking up the role of political advocate and lobbyist and outlining the areas of critical concern for today's freelancers. Ultimately she created a first-of-its-kind social enterprise that would offer group-rate health, dental, life and disability insurance, as well as retirement plans, to members, who might not be able to afford them otherwise. Sara has continually pushed the organization into new waters, always looking for the next best way to support those who are independently employed. As soon as a particular goal is adequately addressed, Sara is already defining the next destination. Most recently, she helped introduce legislation in New York State that would protect freelancers from clients who don't pay.

Ellen Galinsky, cofounder and president of the Families and Work Institute, a research think tank that studies the changing workforce, family, and community and then translates that research into action projects, has had a tremendous impact on educational and workplace policies and practices. Ellen is constantly advancing the field of study and shaping the national conversation about work and family. The Families and Work Institute conducts the most comprehensive representative studies of the U.S. workforce and employers. Its research keeps a finger on the pulse of our changing work and family lives and helps us map the present as well as plan for the future.

Championing an Idea

We catalyzed a movement. We cleared the way for other similar companies to exist.

—JEN BOULDEN, COFOUNDER OF IDEAL BITE

Ideas are powerful. They can change the world and they can certainly change a marketplace. Several of the women we interviewed created their businesses in order to champion an idea. As the idea spread, their businesses became both magnet and megaphone, sharing information and drawing people in.

MEET:

Jen Boulden, co-founder of Ideal Bite, cared a lot about green issues. After graduating with a "green" MBA, one that focused on environmental policy and management, Jen was looking for a great job to flex her new muscles. But she was disappointed to find that most of her corporate options seemed to be about helping companies meet regulations and achieve the bare minimum. So she decided to start her own green consulting company, Anavo. During this time she also met her to-be business partner, Heather Stephenson. They shared a passion for sustainable living and soon became go-to people for their friends and colleagues who had questions about improving gas mileage, finding eco-friendly fashion, and composting. These one-off questions quickly led to a business idea when they recognized the huge void that existed for advertisers to reach these same folks, whom Jen dubbed "light green" consumers. Light green consumers were neither tree huggers nor litterbugs. They were average folks who drove an SUV to Whole Foods. They wanted to do their part but didn't want to sacrifice everything. So Ideal Bite was formed. Jen and Heather set up a subscriber-based e-mail blast that specifically targeted this market. As predicted, Ideal Bite was attractive to both subscribers and advertisers. Once launched, it made a significant contribution to the green movement by demonstrating that it was "not just okay but fun for the masses to go green." Before it was sold to Disney, Ideal Bite was sharing light green love with more than half a million readers each day.

Janet Hanson, CEO of 85 Broads, thought big investment banks like Goldman Sachs, the one she worked at, were losing out by not staying connected to the women who were so frequently leaving their ranks. These institutions saw little value in investing in a network for former employees. But Janet saw these Goldman refugees differently. They weren't just former employees; they were alumnae who had powerful shared experiences, not to mention a heck of a lot of brains, expertise, and valuable contacts. Who knew where they would land next and what they would be working on? Although it took a few years for the big financial institutions to come around, the women whom Janet was recruiting to be a part of the network immediately got the idea and recognized the value. Today 85 Broads is a global network with twenty-five thousand members who are graduates of the world's leading educational institutions. The 85 Broads members provide professional support and have been a source of advice, jobs, business, and even investment for each other.

Redefining an Industry

I would love to have created a brand that still exists when I'm no longer here.

—SELIMA SALAUN, SELIMA OPTIQUE

Sometimes business is about fame—not necessarily for you, the entrepreneur, who toils to move the venture along, but for the business itself. Our cultural history and business landscape is punctuated by larger-than-life brands that have come to mean much more than the literal translation of their simple names: Coke, Apple, Ugg . . .

Several of the women we spoke with were motivated to achieve this kind of renown. They want their brand to have a dramatic impact on the market and the mind of the consumer. They are ultimately building institutions that stand out in their industries and have long-lasting reputations. Talk about legacy!

MEET:

Selima Salaun, founder of Selima Optique, is a Paris-trained optician and optometrist who came to New York in 1990 to manage the Alain Mikli boutique, a 5,000-square-foot optical store on Fifth Avenue. She was always encouraging the owner to add different brands of eyewear and adorn the store with complementary accessories such as hats and scarves. He would politely listen, but never took up her suggestions. Eager not only to enjoy the freedom that goes with being your own boss but also to express her creative vision, Selima decided to open a small optical boutique of her own. Before long a client came in and asked if she could help him find a pair of glasses that had a standard shape but were a little funkier. So Selima created a pair especially for him. She took a standard design, the Le Corbusier style, and produced it in bright red. The client loved the result (and still wears them to this day), and Selima loved the design process. So she created a few other frames in fun colors to offset the typical black and tortoiseshell frames found elsewhere. She was the first person to design bright two-tone colored frames, and these early designs caught the attention of a buyer at Barneys, who immediately asked to carry Selima's small line in their store. Hesitant but excited, Selima expanded her collection and began wholesaling. Early on she was given advice on how the typical eyeglass designers work: two collections per year that quickly get phased out to make room for more designs. This approach didn't sit right with Selima, who wanted to create high-quality, luxurious, timeless accessories that were fashionable but not trendy. It's not surprising then that most of her designs can still be purchased today. Over the last two decades, Selima's business has grown to include private-label and wholesale accounts as well as eight dedicated boutiques: five in Manhattan, two in Paris, and one in Los Angeles. Her designs can be found all over the globe, and in addition to eyeglass frames and sunglasses she designs other accessories, lending her creative eye and signature style to umbrellas and one-of-a-kind hats. For Selima it's all about her brand. She loves that she has created something from nothing and wants her brand to remain vibrant and well-known long after she is gone.

Claire Chambers, CEO of Journelle, believes the lingerie industry is due for an overhaul. Disappointed that lingerie is often marketed as something you wear for someone else, and only on special occasions, Claire wants to reposition it as a treat you give yourself, every day. She originally set out to be a lingerie designer. She started taking weekend sewing classes while she worked at a consulting firm, and then managed to take a three-month sabbatical to further pursue her entrepreneurial ambitions. During that sabbatical she had a serendipitous conversation with a friend about the impact of Sephora on the cosmetics industry. Claire told her friend she was a Sephora addict and would never shop at a department store for makeup again! As she was saying it, she realized that the same problem existed in the industry she was pursuing. A quick look at her own lingerie-buying habits confirmed that even for lingerie connoisseurs like her, department stores were the most reliable source for designer lingerie. Inspired by Sephora's example, she immediately changed course and morphed her business into a retail concept. With three physical store locations and an online store, Claire is on her way to shaking up the Victoria's Secret status quo.

Solving a Problem You Understand

I come at it from a position of authenticity. It's really easy to talk about because I'm living it too.

—ROBIN WILSON, CEO OF ROBIN WILSON HOME

Lots of businesses are created by entrepreneurs who have walked many a mile in their customers' shoes. This was the case with several of the women we interviewed. Keenly aware of what it felt like to be without something they needed, these women were determined to make sure others didn't experience the same lack.

MEET:

Malia and Carol Mills, owners of Malia Mills, were bothered by the common swimsuit-buying experience. Despite their slender builds, they always left this insecurity-ridden ritual feeling depressed. They knew that other women felt the same way and resolved to do something about it. Not only did they decide to design fabulous-fitting and fashionable swimsuits, but they also dedicated themselves to creating a friendly and comfortable customer experience. From their "love thy differences" campaign to using real women as models on their site to sizing their suits to reflect a more specific bra-sizing scale, their brand inspires confidence in everyday women. Sold primarily through nine dedicated Malia Mills retail locations, suits are recommended and adjusted by carefully trained fit experts who work hard to put you at ease and accentuate your assets. In the company's early days, Malia Mills tried wholesaling to department stores, but they found they couldn't impact the customer experience in the same way as in their own stores and with their own staff. So they canceled their accounts and wholesaled only to small boutiques with a congruent and complementary ambiance.

Amanda Hofman, founder of Urban Girl Squad, spent her junior year at Barnard, an all-female college, as a resident adviser on a freshman dorm. As a result, she came to understand the importance of female friendships. Upon graduation, Amanda missed the instantly accessible camaraderie and watched other women struggle to meet new friends in Manhattan. She wondered why there weren't more fun and friendly ways to meet gal pals as an adult. From what she could tell, most offerings focused on either dating or professional networking. Eager not only to keep her vibrant group of friends intact but to grow her social circle, Amanda launched Urban Girl Squad, a social group for women in their twenties and thirties who want to try new things and meet new people. UGS sponsors a range of events each month, from rifle shooting to hairstyling, from wine tasting to snowshoeing. Knowing how expensive, and therefore inaccessible, Manhattan can be for women of this age, Amanda was determined to keep her events relatively inexpensive. As a result, almost all of Urban Girl Squad events are cheaper than if you did the same activity on your own. More than three thousand women have participated in UGS events, and most of them become repeat customers.

Robin Wilson, CEO of Robin Wilson Home, has suffered her whole life from allergies and asthma. She was interested in real estate development and interior design but noticed how unfriendly the process and products were to those who suffered from health problems similar to hers. So after establishing an industry reputation for her creative use of green products and clean construction practices, Robin started her own project management and design firm, which has diligently worked to transform "sick homes" into "eco-healthy" ones. She gets tremendous satisfaction from helping families create spaces that provide refuge from harmful allergens and toxins. Robin knows her services are a premium, but being available to the everyday family is important to her. She has given lots of thought about how best to position her brand for the market she wants to serve. Different from most designers who clamor for the luxury market, Robin tries to keep her prices in check. Her goal is to create aspirational but affordable products that the majority of the market can afford. She finds herself calibrating her prices by asking herself, "Would my mom pay for that?"

Your Turn:
Determining the Impact *You* Want Your Business to Have

Here's the chance for you to dig deep and consider your own business purpose. For some of you, it may be a matter of just reacquainting yourself with what you already know. For others, it may be a long-overdue opportunity to solidify what your business stands for. To start, answer the following questions.

> *Question 1:* What do you want your business to be known for?
> *Question 2:* How does your business purpose help define your
> business growth?

Question 1: What do you want your business to be known for?

Too frequently the women we work with don't really understand just how unique and special their businesses are! They lump their business (or get lumped by others) within a broader industry or field, only to be lost in a sea of generalities. Now, of course, we need to be able to categorize our own and others' businesses and see how they fit into the larger marketplace, but what a shame it is to have your business swallowed by a vague, broad banner such as coach, Web site, or clothing company. Or to be blurred by industry headings such as marketing or design.

Of course, your business should be known for what it does or provides customers. However, given the amount of time and energy you give your business, shouldn't you take the time to be a little more specific? We aren't necessarily talking about business strategies, e.g., sell the most T-shirts, customize the T-shirts, get T-shirts to the consumers the fastest, have the best-quality T-shirts, etc. We are talking about legacy. We are talking about what you want your business to be known for.

We don't believe that the bare minimum is rewarding for most people, and you probably don't either, considering you're reading this book. We do believe, however, that your business purpose is an exciting opportunity to customize and tailor your business, making it all the more satisfying, meaningful, and rewarding for you *and* exceptional within the marketplace.

Please don't misunderstand us, though. We are not encouraging you to set up the business equivalent of superwoman. It is unlikely that you will create a business that strives to be an exceptional place to work, align itself with a strong cause, engage customers in the business decision-making process, revolutionize the industry, challenge notions of the status quo, and bring a leading innovation to the marketplace. Well, at least not all at once! Seriously, it is prudent to remember the conventional wisdom here. You can try to do all of these things, but you likely won't do them well. Your business purpose is a great place to exercise your discerning eye.

We revisit our own business purpose frequently in order to make decisions about growth. In our business, we have always sought to make entrepreneurship a more accessible and successful endeavor for women. For those who are considering going out on their own, we want to help pull back the curtains of entrepreneurship and show them it is very doable when you have the right tools at hand. For those who have already gotten started, we want to make sure they are building a business that works for them and that is set up to help them achieve what they want. These two focuses have helped to define the relevant field of options for our business. We could have pursued these ends by establishing an IGC in every major U.S. city or by building a national online platform. Both of these directions could have supported and fulfilled our business purpose, but they weren't congruent with our personal motivations or roles. So far, we have chosen to continue fortifying our New York footprint while reaching women across the country through writing, publishing, and speaking, because this option yielded all the benefits we wanted.

We have also entertained many ideas that, no matter how interesting, ultimately didn't support our larger business purpose. For example, a particularly creative member suggested that we aggregate our members and approach retailers for discounts on their behalf. This was in the days before Gilt Groupe and Groupon had achieved the ubiquity they now enjoy. We also considered allowing members with products to sell them at our location, providing common store infrastructure and taking a percentage of sales. This approach is similar to Art Star, a business we interviewed, which offers a brilliantly juried boutique that supports and provides helpful business infrastructure to artists. We determined both of these to be "off mission" and were glad to see other businesses so adeptly fill the voids. It was easy to get excited about these opportunities, but it took only a brief revisiting of our business purpose for us to say, "That's not the business we are in."

FOR YOUR CONSIDERATION

• What do you want your business to be known for?

• What would be the best compliment your business could receive?

• What would make you proud?

Question 2: How does your business purpose help define your business growth? It is easy to underestimate just how much seemingly similar businesses can differ. To demonstrate this we intentionally interviewed companies that inhabit the same general business category but have each carved out their own unique and remarkable toehold in the larger market.

Take for scrumptious example these three bakeries: Fat Witch, Dancing Deer, and BabyCakes. All make delicious treats, but each goes about it in a totally different way. Sure, there are obviously differences in their business models: Fat Witch is primarily a retailer, which after twenty years still has one location, a very robust phone order service, and lots of licensing programs; Dancing Deer, which started as a wholesaler, selling in many markets but most notably Whole Foods, has more recently enhanced its online retail presence; BabyCakes is also a retailer that has at least three well-appointed locations and a bestselling cookbook to please the gluten- and allergen-free fans in the rest of the nation.

However, more than these structural distinctions, these businesses are driven by three specific and distinct business purposes.

Trish Karter of Dancing Deer has not only established her brand as a beacon of all-natural, high-quality treats, but as a double-bottom-line company and an exceptional place to work for her employees.

Patricia Helding has leveraged Fat Witch Baking Company as an incubator for her creativity. She is always finding new ways to take the witch theme to new levels and new ancillary products to offer. Patricia's humor and whimsy are part of the reason that customers fall in love with Fat Witch.

Erin McKenna of BabyCakes is determined to change the way we think of allergen-free desserts, which thanks in part to her are no longer relegated to the dusty shelves of obscure health food stores but instead are regarded as delicious, stylish, and, dare we say, sexy.

These business purposes enhance each of the ventures, providing personality and a particular focus. They separate the businesses from generic would-be competitors and serve to define the field of what is not only possible but worthy of pursuit. They allow the respective entrepreneurs to go above and beyond the narrow quantitative scope of the dollar to create a business that has significant meaning.

Given what she wants to achieve, it makes sense that Erin McKenna has become a media darling and foodie celeb. It makes sense that she partners with trendy clothing designers to produce her shops' uniforms. It also makes sense that Trish has stayed focused on doing what she does well and reinvests her creative energy into her business practices and culture in addition to developing new products and partnerships that are congruent with Dancing Deer's existing offerings.

As far as Fat Witch is concerned, it makes sense that in order to better indulge Patricia's creative side the company has served as a platform for her various ideas, from a book on entrepreneurship for preteens, to a licensing program in Japan, to a cookbook. These kinds of initiatives have been a more appealing road to growth for her than opening additional locations, which undeniably requires a much more operational focus. In addition to their in-store sales, Patricia has developed robust phone order and e-commerce programs. Alongside their signature brownies they also sell a whole slew of branded products, such as witch make-at-home mixes, witch T-shirts, and tote bags. Patricia has also come up with a creative extension of the Fat Witch "green" initiative—"Witch Ends."

In the process of making perfectly square brownies, the brownie cutter leaves behind the edges and corners for disposal. Now, instead of being thrown away, these leftovers are bagged and sold.

FOR YOUR CONSIDERATION

• How does your business embody your business purpose? Where can you see its fingerprints in your policies or offerings?

• How can your business purpose help to define your growth moving forward?

• How might someone else with different business goals have shaped your business?

Troubleshooting:
When You Get in Your Own Way

Many entrepreneurs fear that someday they will regret the road not taken and are therefore hesitant to turn down business opportunities that seem even remotely promising. Many get preoccupied thinking about things they *could* do, things they feel like they *should* do, and seemingly proven formulas that appear to be a shortcut to business success. The reality is that these opportunities often become distractions from your main goal.

Below we introduce three examples of entrepreneurs who let their fear of missing out on an opportunity interfere with the direction they wanted the company to take.

Distracted by All the Shiny Things You Could Do?
Stay Focused on What's Important

In this fast-moving, information-saturated world it's easy to be overwhelmed by options. You could try on ten ideas a day, every day for a month, and still be in new conceptual territory. You probably know a particularly itchy entrepreneur, who is constantly in pursuit of the next hottest trend, or perhaps you are that person.

While it's a good habit to look at business trends and see how they might be adapted for your own purpose, there is a cost associated with always being on the chase. The truth is that for those of us who are easily excitable it doesn't take much to become enamored with an enticing but ultimately off-track opportunity. Consider it the curse that plagues optimistic and curious people.

When it comes to these "wouldn't it be cool if?" moments, there are two things we always remind ourselves and clients:

1. **They are expensive.** We're not talking about cash. As an entrepreneur, the most valuable thing you have is your time and energy, and you need to be extremely judicious in how you spend these precious resources. There is a real loss that occurs from consistently following dead-end directions. Remember that the time spent here is time taken from your ultimate goal.

2. **They are distracting.** And not just for you! Business identities need to be harvested. A business that tries to tackle everything becomes unwieldy and loses itself in the marketplace. It is confusing for consumers and difficult for you to synergize your existing efforts.

We certainly aren't the first to say that your business actions should be tied to an overall strategy, and we won't be the last, but it seems that we all need a good reminder every once in a while. Now, that doesn't mean there isn't room for experimentation (we have a whole chapter on this), but we are saying you should choose wisely what activities to spend your time on and use your business purpose as a guide.

The Case of Could-I Katie

A few years ago, we worked with a client named Katie who owned an interior decorating company. She worked with clients to redesign their living space to better reflect their family and stage of life. Katie was quite passionate about environmental sustainability and felt it was important to incorporate her philosophy into her work. She focused on repurposing her clients' existing pieces and finding ways to donate items that were no longer needed. By establishing lots of strategic donation partners, Katie created win-win-win scenarios and was able to ensure that instead of being discarded, unneeded items were put to good use.

She also wanted to be able to provide her clients with more eco-friendly suggestions for the items that did need to be purchased. However, compiling these green sourcing resources required a lot of up-front research and relationship-making, and Katie was having difficulty finding the time to invest in this infrastructure.

Katie came to us wanting feedback on an idea. She had found over the years that because of her relationships and passion for people doing good work, she had made lots of very successful "marriages" between entrepreneurs who wanted to help and causes that needed help. She was a natural connector, and seemed to be a magnet for people pursuing social justice. Recently someone had suggested that she find a way to monetize this great skill of hers! She wondered what we thought. Could she be a consultant of sorts who helped to facilitate this matching process? Well, certainly she could. But what we didn't yet know was whether it made sense given what she was trying to accomplish.

We asked Katie some questions that helped illuminate her personal motivations and business purpose. Katie told us she loved being visually engaged and using her creativity to physically change the way a space looked. More than anything, she really loved how her work actually transformed her clients' lives. She wanted her work to help serve as a metaphor for her clients, teaching them that improvement is about clarifying your vision, editing what you already have, and incorporating a few select high-impact new items. She wanted to demonstrate that it is not about purging everything you have and replacing it wholesale with an entire new getup.

Ultimately she wanted to be known for her unique approach to design and for getting big results in a meaningful and responsible way. Most important, she told us she wasn't willing to give up the opportunity to use her visioning and design skills in order to pursue her social cause matchmaking. This proved she knew the consulting idea wasn't the real deal. Like Katie, we have had many clients position an enticing "could be" option as something they could do "too," in addition to their existing business. Yes, they could. "But at what cost?" we ask.

This is the very question we asked Katie, and through our discussion we determined that pursuing this consulting option was not a prudent use of her time and energy. She acknowledged that she would likely continue to do it informally but would rather invest her time into creating the green sourcing infrastructure she had been wanting for years. She was concerned that the addition of her social good matchmaking would undermine her ability to really build up her reputation in the design field.

Had Katie talked about her desire to create change in many arenas by integrating good practices into existing ways of living, we would have encouraged her to consider the consulting option more closely. Her own business could have served as a first client or an example to follow.

FOR YOUR CONSIDERATION

- Have the recent opportunities you've considered furthered your business purpose or detracted from it?
- Have there been any costs?
- Do you currently invest time and energy in any projects that take away from what you're ultimately trying to achieve?

Pressured to Follow a Specific Course of Action? Remember What You Want to Be Known For

Nothing frustrates us more than when entrepreneurs curtail their own business savvy and creativity to follow a growth path they believe they "should" follow. In most cases the "should" direction is one they have been told will quickly lead to a high degree of scale and increased potential revenues. There is nothing wrong with scale and high potential revenues—so long as it allows for the things you want to get out of your business. Sometimes this "should" direction works out, but more often than not we find that these entrepreneurs have effectively pigeonholed themselves into running a business that doesn't work for them.

The Case of Should-I Shannon

When Shannon came to us, she was running a Web design company and was in a period of transition with her business. She had previously worked with a team of other independently employed folks on several large client projects and told us she liked this arrangement because it allowed her to stay close to the design work rather than focus on client management or "business" tasks. Mostly the team worked with larger creative companies, which Shannon really enjoyed. When we asked what it was about the work that she liked, she told us that, ultimately, she loved helping beautiful products get noticed.

Unfortunately, several of the team members had recently moved and one had taken a full-time position. So she adjusted by taking on one large client who kept her busy thirty hours a week. The problem was that she didn't really find this work very interesting, and the client, being a nonprofit, paid a little less than she liked.

She was, however, fielding tons of requests for short-term work. She did enjoy the income consistency that her current client provided her, so she really didn't want to leave them in order to take on shorter-term, higher-paying projects. She also hated the sales cycles of project work and being in between clients. However, someone had suggested that she accept those jobs and staff them out to someone who charged less than she did, keeping the difference. In fact, they told her, she could have a whole cadre of people working for her and there would be no limit to what she could make, plus she wouldn't have to do the work!

Shannon wanted to know what we thought. She had been sitting on this idea for months but hadn't taken any steps toward making it happen. She was hesitant. She told us she kept coming back to the idea because it seemed like a "smart business" thing to do. She thought she probably "should" just do it.

Maybe, we said, but after some discussion, we learned a few things about Shannon we hadn't realized.

For one, she loved photography and was learning on the side how to take great landscape shots. She has shown some of her pieces in small shows and sold a few prints through online retailers. Likewise, many of her smaller clients had been photographers, and she had a lot of great ideas about compelling ways to display their work on their own sites. In fact, she had a great idea for a larger site where lots of photographers could display their work so that prospective buyers could find it easily. The site presented a lot of revenue potential (by taking a percentage of sales or by levying a fee to post); she just hadn't had the time to develop it.

We also learned that more than her dislike of sales, Shannon really hated client management; she just wanted to be left alone to do her work. She also told us, "If it was up to me, I would spend two or three months out of the year traveling to places where I could take great landscape pictures," which she could then sell online.

We told Shannon that, actually, it *was* up to her! We told her that accepting work, which she would then farm out to other designers, would most definitely entail a lot of client management and most likely sales too. Once you start to feed projects to people, you have to keep supplying work if you want them to be available. It was a perfect business direction if that was the role she wanted and if she felt it was the best way for her to achieve her business purpose.

Shannon was certain that that wasn't the role she wanted long-term, and she also didn't want to have to take on any old client. She really wanted to stay true to helping people's beautiful things be seen and recognized. If the photography site worked out, she said she'd love to expand the same design and algorithm to other goods.

Instead of accepting and farming out these smaller jobs, she decided to wean her one large low-paying nonprofit client while cultivating her reputation for working with photographers who would be able to pay a higher rate and would help her develop her network. Once she had started making this transition, she would also be able to free up enough hours to dedicate a little time each week to creating the photography site she was excited about. This strategy actually enabled Shannon to achieve her goals much more quickly than she had anticipated. Within a few months, she had increased her earnings and was working with clients that she enjoyed much more. Her more specific target client strengthened her reputation and made it easier for the right clients to find her. Also, her new arrangement has allowed her to free up enough time to move her site forward.

Building a Strategy, Not a Business?
Connect with Your Customers and Get Soul

Business is about creating value—whether it's providing a useful service, offering a much-needed product, or changing someone's experience. Sometimes in the process we also collect or create something that is valuable to someone else—user data, information, access to a specific market. These by-products can be enormously helpful and important. They can help diversify the revenue stream, open new doors of opportunity, or create intriguing partnerships. However, it becomes problematic when entrepreneurs are so overly focused on the by-product that they neglect their actual business, leaving it hollow and soulless. The business strategies get tangled and confused, and their secondary market starts to define what their business does while the real offering suffers.

The Case of Strategy-Only Stephanie

Since graduating college, Stephanie had worked in the public relations industry at both large and small firms. While she loved being in the know, she dreamed about working for herself and for years eagerly plotted her escape to independent employment. Her firm represented a lot of small business owners and entrepreneurs, so Stephanie solicited some advice about what kind of business to start and how to go about it. Many of them were happy to help and encouraged her entrepreneurial ambitions. She consistently told people that she wanted to start a business but she didn't know what kind. She loved the idea of having a retail store but was hesitant about the overhead and the prospect of having employees. Several people advised her to stick to what she knew well—cool insider information—and leverage her enormous contact database. More than one person suggested she consider building a business model "like Daily Candy"—a Web site that recommends events, restaurants, and attractions for people in different cities. People said it was a straightforward and lucrative business model and one that could be started with relatively little money.

Stephanie loved Daily Candy and was intrigued by the idea of having a low-cost but high-profit business. She spent several months researching the e-mail subscription business model before submitting notice to her firm. Due to her research diligence, she had a clear sense of what subscriber milestones she had to hit in order to attract advertisers. She called on some of her graphic designer friends, who came up with an adorable site and a catchy name. She wrote the first several months of content and began sending out her e-mails to her contacts. Her subscriber count steadily increased at first, but then seemed to plateau. She knew it could take some time to build a large and loyal following, but she was having a hard time hanging on to her subscribers. People seemed to sign up and then randomly unsubscribe a few weeks later. Plus, she wasn't getting great feedback from her first tier of advertisers. Stephanie wondered what was going wrong and decided to seek our advice.

As we listened to Stephanie's story we realized we didn't really understand the essence of what her business was about. We knew she sent weekly e-mails with city-specific shopping and event information, but we weren't sure why. We asked Stephanie to talk with us about the impact that she wanted her business to have. What did readers get from subscribing to her e-mails? How did her product impact or change their lives? What was she hoping to accomplish? Stephanie admitted she hadn't given much thought to our questions. She thought she offered an easy way to get information about city happenings. We asked her how that need fit into the marketplace and, more important, whether that reflected something that was important to her.

It was clear to us that Stephanie needed to work on developing her business proposition and especially her business purpose. We told her it was great that she had all the information about how to grow this kind of business model. Many people flounder without that, and we were impressed by her clear road map. However, we were concerned that she was not entirely clear about what her business really meant to her customers or even to herself! We gave her some homework and scheduled a follow-up visit.

We told Stephanie to research the marketplace to see what she thought was missing. It wasn't enough to be an alternative to an existing offering. What was she going to do that was different and better? Most important, we challenged her to identify what problem she solved and why it mattered.

Stephanie came back to us a month later invigorated with a totally new take on her business. She realized the market was missing something that helped young professionals get the most out of the city despite their limited salaries. She wanted to give them a taste of the good life. Instead of just telling people about a new restaurant or store, her e-mail would show people how to dine well at well-known places for under forty dollars. Instead of just highlighting new designers and stores, Stephanie would scour the city for high-style and low-cost items. This "more with less" message was something she felt really strongly about. Too many of her friends racked up big credit card bills in their twenties on meaningless events that they didn't remember or clothes they didn't own a season later. She realized her insider knowledge had always enabled her to dress and live well without spending a fortune and that this was the contribution she could make to the marketplace.

We were glad to see Stephanie so excited about this new direction. This was the kind of soul her business needed! In addition to the need for a clearer editorial focus, we talked with Stephanie about the value this positioning offered in terms of marketing and sponsor relationships. After our meeting she immediately began making changes to her offering, tweaking the business name and putting a new marketing plan in place. She found it much easier to write the editorial content and get people excited about the concept. It took only two months to really see an impact in terms of numbers too. She was experiencing less reader drop-off and her subscriber count began to grow. What was most important, of course, was how much more satisfied Stephanie was with her business. She was able to focus on something important to her and bring value to others in the process.

FOR YOUR CONSIDERATION

- Why does your business matter to you and your customers?
- How well is the underlying purpose and meaning of your business conveyed?
- How well do you balance your focus on creating value and making money?

Cheat Sheet:
What Will Your Business Be Known For?

POINTS TO REMEMBER:
1. Your business purpose is the overall impact that you want your business to have in the marketplace and world. It defines what you want your business to accomplish and is a reflection of what you think is important.
2. Knowing what you stand for allows you to measure success, distinguishes your business from others, and adds meaning to your work.
3. A clear business purpose also provides critical guidance, separating growth options you "could" pursue from those that really deliver satisfaction.
4. Not every opportunity that comes along is right for your business. Pursuing lots of tangential options is distracting and expensive.
5. Sometimes a seemingly obvious growth option, such as duplicating what you already have in place, is not the best way to achieve your business purpose. Avoid getting sucked in by strategies you are told you "should" do just because they have the potential for size.

QUESTIONS TO CONSIDER:
1. What do you want your business to accomplish?
2. What do you want your business to be known for?
3. How does your business purpose help to define your direction and growth?
4. Do all of your current offerings further your business purpose or do they detract from it? How about initiatives that you are considering?
5. What directions "could" you have pursued but chose not to? Why?

"I was scared out of my pants. I remember the first year and a half I would have to get up and go running every morning just to get the butterflies out of my stomach. It was something that I felt I had to overcome."

Utilizing business purpose to determine business growth
Shobha Tummala of Shobha

After working at some larger corporations, Shobha Tummala took a position working for a tech start-up. It was here that she had her "glass slipper moment." Like Cinderella understanding that she would be a princess, Shobha realized that not only did she love the small business world but that she too wanted to be an entrepreneur.

Far from her background in electrical engineering, Shobha decided to launch a company in the beauty industry. She decided to create a salon that specialized in hair removal. Drawing on her Indian heritage as well as her own experience, she established her business as a place that promoted not only natural products but effective and professional services.

Shobha knew from her Harvard MBA classmates that running a business was no piece of cake. She was well acquainted with her strengths and weaknesses and prepared for the beginning to be especially tough.

While she found support and solace in other entrepreneurs, Shobha did have her own share of skeptics and some of her own fears as well— "fear of not knowing how to lead a company, fear of being the one person who was supposed to have all the answers, fear of not choosing the right direction, fear of having the responsibility to do these things." Every morning for the first year and a half, Shobha would have to go for a run in order to get the butterflies out of her stomach. But for her, fear was simply not a good enough reason to refrain from pursuing her dream.

So in 2001 she took her first step by renting space from a local hair salon and hiring a few practitioners to see clients while she managed the business side. Slowly the business gained traction, building a strong reputation and word-of-mouth referrals. A few months later she was able to open her first dedicated salon, Shobha Soho. Ten years later, Shobha boasts three Manhattan locations, fifty employees, numerous industry awards for excellence, a comprehensive list of hair-removal services for women and men, and a professional training program for other estheticians.

About a year and a half into the venture, Shobha had a turning point that helped her solidify her business purpose. She had grown accustomed to hearing her employees complain about the working conditions in the industry. They would share stories about mistreatment by other employers and poor hygienic practices from the other salons. Determined to do something about it, Shobha decided to raise the standard in the beauty industry. But in order to meet her goal and have the impact she wanted, her business needed to be bigger.

These realizations made Shobha commit to creating not just a profitable company but also a great work environment. She became passionate about cultivating and maintaining the right company culture in addition to providing high-quality, professional, and friendly service for her clients. Shobha didn't want to create something that was great on the outside and rotten on the inside. She wanted to feel like she had done something really great in this world. She wanted her business to have an impact.

Over the years, this business purpose—to raise the standard in the beauty industry—has helped to shape the growth of the business. The primacy placed on maintaining a great culture and work environment has influenced which strategies have been employed and has helped to define success.

For example, Shobha had a brief foray into other salon services, such as facials, before steering back to its core area of expertise. It turned out that the additional services made everyone's job harder. They complicated operations and put strain on the staff. Even though clients enjoyed them, Shobha decided these extra offerings were not in accordance with the broader business goals and didn't help the company achieve the success it was looking for. This was a great reminder for her that her business was really about achieving excellence in a few areas rather than trying to do many things half as well.

Perhaps the most significant way the business purpose impacted strategy was Shobha's decision not to open a location in another city—Washington, D.C. For months she prospected the city, sought out the right spot, ran the numbers, and put the expansion wheels in motion. But something didn't feel right. Despite having the capital to expand, Shobha worried about the additional stress this location would put on the company. The economic downturn had already been challenging and she worried that this move would further undermine her efforts to preserve and maintain her signature culture. Some things needed fixing before moving on, and this move wasn't going to help, nor would it bring the company closer as a team. Shobha ended up not signing on the dotted line and, as she puts it, left her broker at the altar.

This experience caused her to shift her growth strategy and focus. She realized she wouldn't be able to manage and maintain ten, fifty, or a hundred salons with the type of culture she desired. So she began to consider growth options that wouldn't put her business purpose at risk. Ultimately she decided on a two-pronged growth strategy. First, she would create and sell high-quality proprietary professional and retail products that are natural and effective. These would allow her to gain further customer reach without jeopardizing the company culture. Second, she has established comprehensive training programs for other professionals who don't work at the Shobha salons. The Shobha certification helps estheticians to improve their technique, efficiency, and professionalism. Participants are able to advertise their certification status with signage at their location as well as in an online directory on myShobha.com. This will not only allow Shobha to increase her company's brand recognition but also, in keeping with her goal, dramatically influence the industry as a whole.

What Do You Do Best?

Give Yourself a Job You Enjoy

> People put entrepreneurship in business terms, but it is a
> creative profession and a creative drive that makes us entre-
> preneurs.
>
> —TARA HUNT, COFOUNDER OF BUYOSPHERE

You are not just a doer of things that need to get done. As an entrepreneur, you have the freedom to create the job you want. You also
have a mandate to make sure that the tasks you enjoy don't get lost
in the rest of the business stuff. After working so hard to finally be
in the driver's seat, it only makes sense for you to drive the way you
want to.

Sure, being an entrepreneur means you will have your fair share
of unglamorous tasks: taking out the trash, unclogging a toilet,
sending invoices, standing in line at the post office. But these are
the exceptions. The beauty of having your own business is being
able to create your ideal job, one that reflects your individuality.
Despite people's best efforts to catalog the common traits and skills
of entrepreneurs, not every entrepreneur does the same thing, nor
should they.

Sometimes our clients treat the parts of the job they like the
most as dessert, savoring these tasks as a well-deserved reward for

slogging through all the other junk. Instead we encourage them to imagine a business where they get to do the things they like most, most of the time. Instantly their faces brighten. That would be cool, they say. So do it! we reply.

A Look at Role

In order to have a business that works for you, one that is worth all the work it requires, you need to enjoy your job. This is possible when you are in a role that engages your strengths and interests.

The right role will:

- Make for work that is rewarding and satisfying
- Ensure that your business is leveraging the best you have to offer
- Prevent you from squandering your time on the wrong types of tasks
- Help your company develop its unique shape and place in the market

Casting yourself in the right role is all about understanding the optimal way for you to contribute to the business. This requires knowing both the value of your time and your greatest strengths. It's important to recognize that your role is more than the summary of the tasks you perform. While it should serve as a good indicator of the kinds of duties that make up your job, the whole concept is much broader. Role is an expression of who you are in the business and how you relate to it.

Before we go further, it is important to cover five universal truths:

1. It is hard for almost everyone to transition out of the "I wear every hat" phase that often accompanies the starting years. And it is easy to fall into a pattern whereby you saddle

yourself with "easy but unappealing tasks" and ultimately pigeonhole yourself into a role that you don't like.

2. Delegation is a thorny issue that gets tangled up in feelings of control and perfection and trust. However, learning to delegate effectively and comfortably is one of the most important lessons that an entrepreneur can learn—but that doesn't mean it's easy.

3. There are many prevailing philosophies about what a founder, partner, CEO, or entrepreneur *should* do or be good at. The truth is there are infinite possibilities for how you interact with your business.

4. As an entrepreneur, your most valuable asset is not capital, previous professional experience, a clever business name, or a plum client. With a whole company to run and a limited amount of hours in the day, your time is your most precious commodity.

5. It's a real shame when you don't enjoy what you actually do, especially when you are the one in charge of your own employment. If you wanted a job you didn't like, there are tons available that require less work, stress, and time.

An entrepreneur can often underestimate the strategic influence of her own role. It's important to recognize that your role doesn't just relate to your own personal satisfaction but also determines the direction of the whole company. Take for example two women's clothing design companies, Built by Wendy and Lilla P, run by two very different women with very different roles. Built by Wendy is run by Wendy Mullin, an independent fashion designer and seamstress extraordinaire. Wendy is the creative force behind the entire collection. She does 100 percent of the designing and has a team that manages nearly every other piece of the business, including the operations of her two stores. Having a retail component allows her collection to literally live together in one physical place, creating a complete manifestation of Wendy's vision. It also allows the company to maintain personal relationships with many of its customers.

Wendy also publishes a line of sewing books and patterns, teaching fans and crafters alike how to make their own styles.

Lilla P, on the other hand, is a women's wear company, which boasts an impressive wholesale business in addition to a successful e-commerce site. The founder, Pauline Nakios, is not a designer by training and instead serves as the creative director and liaison of the brand. Pauline's vision drives the company, which was started with a quest to create the perfect T-shirt, and she represents the brand both to the designers and in the marketplace, carefully maintaining each of her wholesale vendor relationships. Key to Lilla P's success are these relationships, stores who "get" the brand and Pauline's way of doing business.

Both of these businesses have been influenced by and developed for the founder's role. The distinctions between them are meaningful and allow the founder to focus on her greatest strengths.

The Story of Angela and Zoe, Part 3

Let's revisit our example of Angela and Zoe to see an example of how two people with similar businesses take up different roles and thereby influence the direction of their respective companies. If we look at how both Angela and Zoe spent their first couple of years in business, we can see how their roles began influencing the direction of their gourmet shops right from the start.

Angela, in addition to being a foodie, loves the big picture, spotting new opportunities and making strategic relationships. She likes forming strong partnerships with her clients and finding new ways to introduce more and more people to the brand. A year after she set up shop, Angela began looking for ways to expand her footprint and bring her vision to other markets. She hired very talented chefs and together they collaborated on the prepared-foods menu. She spent much of her time testing and investigating various growth options. She established a couple of local wholesale accounts and began talks with some real estate developers on an additional location in a nearby town.

Zoe is the type of person who loves working with food, getting her hands dirty, and tinkering with recipes. She also wants to be intimately involved in the customer experience. For her, direct customer interaction is how she gets both feedback and inspiration. She spent the better of her first year cooking and perfecting recipes and menus. The shop established a carry-out dinner program and offered a limited four-table dinner seating. She knew she wanted to create something unique, and dedicated time to researching and visiting other chefs with small restaurants but big reputations.

Over the course of the next several years both Angela's and Zoe's businesses grew. Angela opened several new locations, while Zoe's intimate restaurant consistently enjoyed a yearlong wait list. Angela developed a well-known brand that people in multiple markets have come to rely on. Zoe, on the other hand, brought culinary acclaim to her small town and feels completely fulfilled creatively.

It is easy to see that these two entrepreneurs would be quite happy within their own businesses, but imagine for a minute if they were transplanted into each other's ventures. Not necessarily a perfect fit. However, there are ways that each business could adapt to accommodate the preferred role of the new leader.

If Zoe were magically transplanted into Angela's business, she could invest much of her time and energy into creating the recipes, products, and cookbooks for the multistore chain that Angela had created. She could select a specific café to call home and satisfy her desire for customer interaction. Or perhaps she could creatively leverage various social media tools to put her in touch with customers around the world. Also, since Zoe might not like the operational responsibilities of multiple locations, she could explore having local partners or perhaps even a franchise.

If Angela were magically transplanted into Zoe's business she could start a wholesaling program that would allow her to expand the footprint of Zoe's small shop. She could explore doing pop-up stores or opening seasonal locations in small communities similar to the one where they are currently located. She could also look for ways to feature the market in multimedia outlets and sell the "story" of the business. Over time and with Angela at the helm, Zoe's business might go the route of the Silver Palate, a local shop with a national presence and multiple brand extensions.

What wouldn't work, however, would be pushing either woman into the preferred role of the other. Both would be miserable and come to dislike their business.

In the Company of Others: Crafting the Right Role

When you talk to a hundred women about their experience of entrepreneurship, you are going to hear about a hundred distinct roles. Our interviews certainly demonstrated that no two entrepreneurs have the same job. However, from the sea of distinctions some familiar archetypes emerged. We think they will be helpful in the consideration of your own role.

This list is not exhaustive, nor are the options mutually exclusive. And to be sure, none of the women's roles were limited to these archetypes either. Each of the women we spoke with had a multifaceted role and was also responsible for the fiscal health and growth of her company. However, they all invested a certain amount of creative energy and focus on cultivating a particular relationship with their businesses. These relationships, or roles, not only strengthened the company but also complemented the woman's natural skills.

The Evangelist

I love talking to people about this. I love evangelizing. I love performing. That's what I love the most.

—GENEVIEVE THIERS, FOUNDER OF SITTERCITY

Some messages are worth evangelizing. They are meaningful, wide-appealing, and poised to make an impact. Some of us are natural preachers, itching to tell the world all about what fires us up.

We have met, known, and interviewed many entrepreneurs who love to champion the larger cause connected to their businesses. These Evangelists leverage their businesses as a vehicle to participate in a larger movement. Most of them are the public face of their companies and spend a good portion of their time speaking to people and the press about issues that they believe in.

MEET:

Chloé Jo Davis, owner of Girlie Girl Army, has established a business that champions the concept of a cruelty-free lifestyle that doesn't require sacrificing indulgence. She teaches so-called Glamazons how to have their (vegan) cake and eat it too. Chloé's Evangelist roots go back to her late teens when she made money as a party promoter. She regularly turned out thousands of people at parties and sample sales and was known for her ability to spread the word. As Chloé matured she become more politically and socially aware, particularly about animal treatment.

As a promoter she had thousands of people on e-mail lists, and it didn't take long before she started sending her contacts messages that had a dual focus. Alongside the latest sample sale or party, Chloé began featuring animals that needed to be rescued. Eager to make a difference, she donned the name Girlie Girl Army and set out to share what she knew with the masses. Soon, Chloé's own commitment to a "cruelty free" lifestyle deepened as she became a vegan and began working with Farm Sanctuary, an organization that works to protect farm animals from cruelty. As her priorities changed she was faced with an evergreen set of dilemmas, such as how to find a good vegan mascara, leather-like boots, fashionable clothes made from sustainable materials, or a recipe for an organic margarita. Girlie Girl became the microphone that allowed her to share what she found as well as the virtues of being cruelty-free. As Girlie Girl has evolved, the power of that message has grown. With more than 30,000 weekly newsletter subscribers and even more daily readers, Chloé has really been able to orchestrate an interesting and compelling conversation with her subscribers and companies. What's really meaningful for Chloé is hearing how her efforts have paid off. She gets hundreds of e-mails from girls who say how instrumental Girlie Girl has been in changing their lives.

Genevieve Thiers, founder of Sittercity, began her business in college, while studying to be an opera singer. Genevieve, the oldest of seven children, had been babysitting her whole life and was well acquainted with the word-of-mouth network that most moms used to find sitters for their kids. She didn't witness the challenges of this system until she was a senior in college and saw a nine-months-pregnant woman climbing two hundred stairs to post flyers at her school in an effort to find a babysitter. This was the first time that Genevieve was privy to the desperation that often accompanies the hunt for a childcare provider. Realizing that most moms were at the mercy of random chance or the quality of their friends and family networks, Genevieve began to think about the problem and, of course, the opportunity to solve it. She thought it would be great if someone put all the babysitters in one place online and created a matchmaking service for moms and babysitters.

Within a year Genevieve launched Sittercity.com. Her first order of business was personally spreading twenty thousand flyers over the city of Boston, which helped her to sign up six hundred sitters. And to say she's undergone some changes in role over the last ten years would be a radical understatement. In the beginning the business consisted of her, her cell phone, her laptop, and her bold idea to solve a very big problem. But in time the business grew and led to more employees. At first it was hard to trust others with her creation, but as the staff matured and a c-level team was groomed (including a new CEO), Genevieve was able to transition into a role that allowed her to do what she does best—perform, which is not surprising given her musical roots! During her tenure as CEO, Genevieve was able to spend a good deal of her time working with the press and educating people on the issues and topics surrounding care: what it means today, what is the etiquette, how it is changing. Investing her energies evangelizing the messages that are important to her enabled Sittercity to solidify itself as a thought leader in the industry and, of course, helps Sittercity garner attention from both sitters and clients!

The Expert

I didn't think that I would become such a personality. But it turns out if you Google "online shopping expert" I come up near number one.

—MICHELLE MADHOK, CEO OF SHEFINDS.COM

Instead of spreading the word to all who will listen, some entrepreneurs like being the go-to person. These folks brand themselves as "all things ____." To them, success is being the first person who comes to mind when you think about their areas of expertise. These entrepreneurs accumulate deep knowledge and pepper the media with their words of wisdom.

We interviewed several women who have successfully positioned themselves as the Expert. They are the public faces for the companies and are tapped frequently to speak on their carefully honed perspectives.

MEET:

Michelle Madhok, CEO of SheFinds.com, has been a pioneer in women's online content for over a decade. She cut her teeth at CBS and AOL before launching her own Web site dedicated to online shopping, particularly to solving what Michelle calls the paradox of choice. Like all online experiences, shopping is a bit of a double-edged sword. It offers convenience and accessibility, but it also brings with it disorganization and clutter. A Google search for black pants will return thousands of hits. So SheFinds.com, which is a blog, offers three things: shopping guides that help you find the best of what you are looking for, overall online shopping advice and deals, and finally updates on the latest styles and fashion gossip. SheFinds.com provides an added benefit by including links to featured products to make the online shopping experience easier. It is a fashion lover's dream. Over time, Michelle has expanded her online empire to include other shopping properties aimed at women, MomFinds.com and BrideFinds.com.

In addition to steering the direction of the company, Michelle has leveraged what she's learned from SheFinds.com in order to establish herself as an online shopping expert. As an early eBay addict with a natural penchant for frugality, she is quite suited to the role. Her Expert status and persona has ended up netting her some very lucrative spokesperson deals with companies such as PayPal and Bank of America in addition, of course, to shining a spotlight on SheFinds.com.

Marie Scalogna Watkinson, owner of Spa Chicks on the Go, originally had the idea to create a mobile spa in 2002. Prior to that, she had been in high demand as a medical massage therapist, with her own private practice for more than five years. But she knew her business needed to change. The physical nature of massage was too taxing, as was being at the mercy of hourly billing and schedule fluxuations. Marie was well acquainted with bringing her massage table to her client's location for an appointment, but she wondered if there was a bigger business opportunity to make other spa services mobile as well. Within months of getting the idea, Marie launched Spa Chicks on the Go. At first she targeted private events, such as birthdays and bat mitzvahs. However, Marie quickly realized there was an even greater opportunity to deploy her talent, expertise, and team to promotional private label events for clients such as Molton Brown, Nivea, and Aquafina. During these events, the Spa Chicks on the Go brand took a backseat to that of the corporate client.

Initially Marie was involved with every event both as massage therapist and as event director. She loved being "hands-on" and was excited about the event management tasks. It was a refreshing shift from the physically draining massage therapy work. But as the business evolved and added private-label corporate events, Marie knew she couldn't continue wearing two hats. She gave up the massage, focused on the event production and began positioning herself as a spa expert. This role shift has paid off big time. It has allowed her to focus on building her expertise, knowledge bank, and proprietary best practices and tips. It has also secured her spokeswoman positions and contributing writer gigs. Additionally, Marie believes her Expert role has added security and stability to her business because her reputation is something that she owns no matter how crowded or competitive the market may get.

The Visionary

> I like thinking beyond the four walls we tend to box ourselves in.
>
> —SARA HOLOUBEK, FOUNDER OF LUMINARY LABS

Some entrepreneurs always have their eyes set on the horizon, fixed on where they want to go next. The Visionary focuses on leading the company to its next destination and charges herself with deciding what that is.

We spoke to many women who considered this perspective and focus to be integral to their work. They are always trying to free themselves up for the next thing and are interested in pushing the bar upward, defining new space, and often "disrupting" the status quo. They spend a large portion of time with their feelers out, investigating new options and directions.

MEET:

Sara Holoubek, founder of Luminary Labs, a boutique consultancy focused on strategy and innovation, helps companies solve problems and catapult themselves forward. With innate acuity and an all-star multidisciplinary team, Sara has always been well poised to help her clients achieve the growth, change, and transformation they are seeking, mostly because she doesn't settle for an easy answer, quick fix, or the lowest common denominator. Dead set on excellence and eager to employ unconventional wisdom, Sara plans to succeed by doing things differently and helping her clients to do the same. Within her company, she takes on the role of Visionary and sets the stage for great work to be done. She spends a good deal of her time thinking about how to inspire her team to go above and beyond, and the rest of the time with clients talking about how to change the way they think and act. With one eye on traditional consulting firms like McKinsey or BCG, and the other on the start-up world, Sara is leveraging the best of both mindsets to forge her own path and create her own legacy.

Tara Hunt, cofounder of Buyosphere, a company that puts consumers in charge of their shopping history, calls herself a visionary strategist. It is a role that she loves and one that she has assumed in each business venture she has had. It is in her nature to ask big questions that require innovative answers. Tara loves the agility that entrepreneurship provides and challenges herself to always be on top of where the world is going. For her, bringing humanity back to business and advancing the conversation around social issues provides meaning. As the steward of this process, Tara has to appeal to both customers and investors, convincing both of the huge potential for change and innovation.

Tara instinctively aligns herself with the customers and works hard to advocate for equity and empowerment. Her role becomes about finding the best ways to solve critical social problems. She was one of the founders of the coworking movement and worked to empower the "little guy" by fostering collaboration among entrepreneurs. She is currently directing her attention to the everyday shopper by helping put them in control of their own purchasing data. It concerns her that as consumers we have so much less information about our own shopping history and patterns than large companies do. Given Tara's preferred role, it is no wonder that one of the things that appeals to her about entrepreneurship is the evolving nature of the work. Ten years ago she could never have imagined where she'd be today, and it excites her to think that the same is true about where she will be ten years from now.

The Caretaker

> It's all about the team. I wouldn't want people to think that I'm the one that is responsible for everything because it's really our team that does it.
>
> —JENNIFER WALZER, CEO OF BACKUP MY INFO!

Many great leaders are not defined simply by their own role but instead by their team. The Caretaker is no exception. Several of our interviewees focused on nurturing their teams by creating exceptional organizational ecosystems that encourage high performance, loyalty, and success. They were dedicated to creating great places to work, cohesive and functional teams, sensitive and innovative policies, and the like.

MEET:

Amy Voloshin, cofounder of Printfresh Studio, is a textile designer by trade. When she started her own print design firm, she knew she wanted it to be bigger than just herself, so she began to hire other people soon after launching. The addition of these early employees made Amy shift away from designing, instead taking on the roles of art director and manager. It became her job to cultivate the conditions that breed creativity and manage the overall creative direction. One of her primary tasks is to create a positive work environment, one with a noncompetitive and open culture where designers are supportive and supported. By her tending to the company and culture in this way, her employees are empowered to produce their best results. Amy's skill at creating a positive work-place is evidenced by the very high retention rate of her staff. Many have been with the company since close to the beginning, and several even began as interns.

Jen Walzer, CEO of Backup My Info!, plays the role of team mom for her online data backup company. Over the years she has played every role in the business at some point, but now, with a capable staff of eight, she focuses a lot of her time on cheering her employees along. In addition to keeping her finger on the pulse of the company's overall status and metrics, she makes sure to cultivate a productive, fun, and supportive work environment. Jen focused on her staff in establishing the company's seven core values, which in addition to things like "obsessive customer service" includes "celebrate," "all about the team," and "enjoy yourself." She says it's really important to celebrate even the personal events and milestones in her employees' lives and that all business decisions take into account each team member's interests. Jen will decline an opportunity or direction that would potentially hurt or disservice an employee. She also says it is important for them to live by their own rules. In fact, each week the team nominates one member based on their demonstration of the core values. And at the end of each quarter those nominations are tallied and winners for each of the seven core values, as well as one overall winner, are declared.

The Creator

When you buy from me you're buying from a person and I give you a little peek into how it gets done.

—ANGIE DAVIS, OWNER OF BYRD & BELLE

Some entrepreneurs relish doing the actual work the business is known for. Instead of heaping on the organizational responsibilities, these women keep unnecessary work and infrastructure at bay in order to preserve space for the business's central task. These companies are engineered to allow the Creator to really focus on what she loves best.

MEET:

Wendy Mullin, owner of Built by Wendy, is a designer at heart. She loves the whole process, from the inspiration to the sketching to the pattern-making to the sewing and production. However, as her clothing line has grown over the last twenty years to include two retail stores, a strong e-commerce site, a warehouse, and six full-time employees, she has had to learn the business side of things as well. She credits her success and staying power in part to the fact that she always considered her business a business and allocated the time necessary to manage it well. Ideally Wendy spends 50 percent of her time designing and 50 percent running the business. In order to make this balance possible, she had to give up a lot of other tasks and responsibilities. There have been times in the past, though, when Wendy's role moved too far toward the business side of things, leaving 20 percent or less of her time for designing. These shifts left her feeling frustrated and creatively constrained. It was clear she needed to design to be satisfied. In order to get back to doing more of what she loved, Wendy had to bring on some more help and also scale back some of the company's initiatives. Since that time, she has been careful to monitor her role and ensure that she spends a good portion of her time doing what she does best and what Built by Wendy is known for—her classic minimalist designs.

Angie Davis, owner of Byrd & Belle, loves designing products, and she struck gold with her sleek felt iPod cases shortly after she launched her business. Once the initial product took off, Angie expanded her collection to include laptop, iPhone, and iPad cases as well. In her first two years she has sold more than thirty-five hundred of her felt cases, and her popularity has resulted in a consistent two-week wait time for any product. Although she has received offers to move the production overseas, she won't do it. It is hugely important to her that her work stays handmade and fairly paid. However, in order to maximize her time creating her products, Angie has brought on an assistant to manage other parts of the business. This seemingly small change has turned out to have an incredible impact on Angie and Byrd & Belle. She is able to sell a lot more and no longer feels overwhelmed or lonely. And most important, it has allowed her business to do more while keeping her in the role she loves.

The Chief

I became an entrepreneur because I love running things. I wanted to call the shots.

—PATRICIA HELDING, PRESIDENT OF

FAT WITCH BAKING COMPANY

Perhaps the biggest surprise for many entrepreneurs is how much they actually enjoy "running a business." Predisposed to think of tedium and details, many are pleased to learn how creative being the Chief can be. After all, anything you say goes, and a company is really just one big blank canvas. The Chief gets to decide how things will be done and where to go next. Even when business responsibilities eclipse the other work she previously did, the Chief stays happy.

MEET:

Megan Brewster and Erin Waxman, owners of Art Star, met each other in art school. After graduation they joined forces and got a space where they both could practice their craft. They also included a small retail component, showcasing the work of other local independent artists. Despite the large artist community in Philadelphia, they were frustrated by the lack of retail outlets where they could sell their goods. Their small boutique would help solve the shortage of stores and offset some of their rent as well. So Megan and Erin took turns minding the shop, figuring they could work on their own projects during downtime. The gals quickly discovered that after managing the boutique there was little time left over for their own projects. But to their surprise they were all right with that. It turned out they really enjoyed running the business. It was not only meaningful but creatively fulfilling as well. Within the first year, they phased out their creative work altogether in order to focus solely on the Art Star boutique as well as the Art Star Craft Bazaar, an annual Philadelphia event boasting more than 160 vendors.

Linda Lightman, owner of Linda's Stuff, had always been a consummate shopper. She loved fashion, she loved deals, and she loved the hunt, but this former attorney never thought they would turn out to be critical business skills. In 2000 she helped her kids sell some of their video games on eBay, which was still in its relative infancy. With only cursory computer knowledge, Linda got the games photographed and posted and sold within hours. Thrilled by both the ease and the financial return, she tried a few of her own belongings. When they too easily sold, she knew she was hooked. Word got around about Linda's new skill, and friends started coming out of the woodwork asking her to help them offload stuff as well. Linda soon needed help photographing and listing the merchandise. Eleven years later, she has more than sixty-two thousand items posted on eBay and employs more than fifty full-time people. In the early days, the interaction with buyers and sellers was one of the most rewarding parts of the job for Linda. However, as the company has grown she has enthusiastically settled into the role of Chief. Linda loves focusing on running the business and establishing the company's brand and culture, so much so that she has rarely missed a day of work. She takes tremendous pride in the way the company operates, and engages with both their buyers and sellers. And like many entrepreneurs, she has found that turning over responsibility to others has often resulted in a better product overall. Linda enjoys spending her time overseeing all of the company's operations as well as improving its processes and business infrastructure.

The Brand Ambassador

As an entrepreneur I fully own my brand and manage that promise. I will never compromise that.

—MELANIE NOTKIN, FOUNDER OF SAVVY AUNTIE

Some entrepreneurs choose not to focus on the company's inner workings but on the brand itself. They naturally scout the marketplace for new opportunities to grow brand awareness and additional ways the brand can carry itself forward. The Brand Ambassador is focused on the next extension, product, or collaboration. All these efforts serve to further fortify the brand and to reinforce it as an institution. Not surprisingly, Brand Ambassadors are often people who personally reflect and emulate their own brands, or perhaps it is their brands that reflect and emulate them.

MEET:

Melanie Notkin, founder of Savvy Auntie, considers her primary responsibility to be upholding her brand promise to her fellow savvy aunties. When Melanie started and was in the process of designing her Web site she knew she wanted the brand to reflect her personality while still highlighting every auntie's experience, not just hers. The Savvy Auntie movement wasn't just about her story, it was about the nearly 46 percent of women through the age of forty-four who do not have children of their own.

Melanie wanted to make sure the brand reflected the uniqueness of this audience. She designed her site and brand with "playful luxury" in mind. As Melanie says, it is "playful because this is about a woman's experience with children, and luxury because she has discretionary income and time that she spends on the children in her life, and on herself." The brand lets these women know they are understood and respected. No matter what Melanie is doing, she always has the Savvy Auntie brand at the forefront of her mind. With every decision she carefully weighs whether she is upholding or compromising the brand promise that she has made to her community. Melanie makes sure that each sponsor fits into the vision, that each online feature authentically reflects the intention of the company, and that each new brand extension further reinforces the company's mission.

Lotta Anderson, founder of Lotta Jansdotter, began her business with a screenprinting experiment. She was living in Santa Cruz, California, and had been taking classes trying to identify what she wanted to do with her life. After trying her hand at jewelry making and ceramics, she fell in love with screenprinting and textile design, which wasn't surprising given her Scandinavian roots. Soon one pillow collection turned into an assortment of textile products and fabrics, all with beautiful colors and contemporary designs. Lotta developed a loyal and broad following at a time when the DIY and craft markets were peaking in both Japan and the United States. Over time her fans started expressing interest in not just her products but Lotta herself. They were intrigued by her skills, style, and process. They were inspired by her example and wanted to follow suit. So Lotta expanded her role beyond designing products and began looking for various ways to carry her brand forward. Her role shifted from designer and producer to that of Brand Ambassador. She has since published five books on fabric printing, simple sewing, and handmade living and has begun licensing designs to other companies. These other endeavors have proved to be a wonderful and complementary creative outlet to the design and production of her fabrics.

Your Turn: Giving Yourself a Job *You* Enjoy

Now we're asking you to spend some time considering how you employ yourself. We want you to think about whether you like what you do and whether you are leveraging the best of what you have to offer.

Question 1: What are you known for?

Question 2: What do you want to do more of in the future?

Question 3: How can your role help to define and transform your company?

As you consider the questions and scenarios below, please don't despair if you discover you're in the wrong role. This happens more frequently than you'd probably think, and there are lots of remedies.

Question 1: What are you known for?

Despite common training, beliefs, and goals, we, Adelaide and Amy, are really quite different from each other. In our business, our roles are where that difference shows the most.

In a nutshell, Amy is an ideas and people person, while Adelaide is an ideas and details person. This influences not only the way we work together but also the different roles we assume within the company.

Amy is known for her infectious energy and optimism. She loves meeting and connecting with people and can remember the darnedest details about conversations and personal stories years after a first-time meeting. People love to be around her and feed off her enthusiasm. Queen of metaphors, she enlists her creativity to relate any situation to any person. Amy plays the role of evangelist, willing to tell anyone about the things we believe in and wanting to help everyone find the right solutions for them.

What does that mean in terms of tasks? Quite simply, it means that she talks to people as much as possible. Amy meets with all potential members, works with clients, fields press inquiries, and maintains a presence at the workspace. There is rarely a person outside of our community who ends a conversation with her without knowing about IGC and our beliefs about women and entrepreneurship.

To say that Adelaide is not quite as outgoing is an understatement. As an introvert and homebody, her in-person time is dedicated to cofacilitation of programs at IGC and collaborative work with Amy. Too much interpersonal interaction is draining for her. While she loves connecting with members, she is energized by thinking, implementing, moving things forward, and making them happen.

She shines in her ability to dig deep into an issue and take a stand on what she finds important. She loves information and is constantly reading and hunting down resources and data. Business trends and stories are of great interest and get mentally cataloged for future reference and example. She also has an eye for detail and an unparalleled sense of urgency, which are decidedly both a blessing and a curse. Adelaide plays the role of thought leader and expert. Not only is she eager to push the status quo, but her research and writing help to credential her in the field.

What does that mean in terms of tasks? Aside from cofacilitating the IGC programs, which she loves, Adelaide sticks to information, namely gathering, processing, collating, and sharing it. She writes, manages the social media platforms, reads, researches, and implements. She also manages the financial and operational aspects of the business.

You can probably see how we complement each other well. All of our products and offerings are a complete mind meld, but, aside from idea generation, we interact with the business and our offerings very differently.

Now, before you run out and look for your corresponding Amy or Adelaide, remember that while a partner can certainly be advantageous, in our case it also means that our business has to be structured in a way that is interesting and meaningful to both of us. Writing this book with the hundred interviews—scheduling, brainstorming, writing, and the promotional plan it required—was the perfect task for us to collaborate on. Other directions most certainly would have yielded a more ill-fitting combination of roles. A straight consulting practice is too draining for Adelaide and an exclusively online platform is not engaging enough for Amy.

Now, does our current business and division of labor mean that we get to do everything we love and nothing we don't all of the time? Certainly not. But our goal, and what contributes the most value to the business, is to spend the majority of our time in a position where our contributions are both unique and significant.

FOR YOUR CONSIDERATION

- What are you known for? What aspects of your business reflect your unique handprints?
- What percentage of your work time do you spend in your preferred role?
- If you were to write your ideal job description, what would it say?

Question 2: What do you want to do more of in the future?
This is an important question to consider at every stage of your business. What you do in the future might look quite different from what you do today, or it may just be more of the same. We don't believe your role has to change for you to have a successful and satisfying business, but many of us want it to. Reflective of our overall philosophy, when it comes to role, it is not so much what you want but more that you *know* what it is that you want.

Sometimes it does make sense for entrepreneurs to preserve the role they already love and stay close to their initial area of skill and expertise rather than be weighed down by unwelcome organizational tasks. On the other hand, we all change. We learn new skills, acquire different competencies, and tire of old tasks. Things you like to do now may seem dull in the future. And yet uncharted territory may be quite intriguing. In addition to our own adjustments, markets, industries, and businesses evolve as well, putting surprising and seemingly impossible opportunities in front of us.

Several of our interviewees founded their companies with their future roles in mind.

Jodi Glickman, founder of Great on the Job, is building a

company that will fundamentally change the way business school students are taught to perform and speak up in corporate roles. She is quite clear that she desires to run a substantially sized company. But in order to give her business the boost and traction it needs to get going, she serves primarily as a trainer and marketer and has established herself as an expert. But as Great on the Job matures she will continue to make choices that ultimately create the role she wants. Consider how her orientation would be different from someone who ultimately wanted to be in the client-facing role for the majority of her career.

Marissa Lippert, founder of Nourish, also built her company with her future role in mind. Marissa is a trained, registered dietician and loves writing and the media industry. She wanted a way to combine all of her interests into a financially sustainable and stable career. Given the flux in the publishing industry, she turned to creating her own business instead of looking for a staff position. She built up a significant client practice in part to support her desire to write books and become a media regular. For her, media and communications work serves as both a creative outlet and a destination. Taking on more clients than she herself could handle or employing other dieticians under her brand were never goals, although she certainly had the demand to do so if she had wanted. After writing two books and appearing regularly in popular women's magazines, she has the flexibility to pursue several other directions going forward.

Jodi and Marissa serve as great reminders that you are in charge of your own business destiny, and as such it is important to think about the work you'd like to be doing as your company matures. We realize that some people are good about forecasting what they may want in the future, while others need to feel stuck or a bit lackluster about their current responsibilities in order to ask, "What's next?" Knowing in advance the kind of work you want to be doing can be extremely informative and useful as you make decisions about how your company should grow.

FOR YOUR CONSIDERATION

- Would you be satisfied if you had the same role in two years? Five years? Ten years?
- What do you want to do more of? What parts of your job are you less interested in?
- How does this influence the future of your business?

Question 3: How can your role help to define and transform your company?
As we've mentioned, the proper role not only brings satisfaction but also helps to characterize and direct your company over time. Alice Cheng, owner of A.Cheng, is a great example of an entrepreneur whose role changed over time, and in doing so shifted what her company does. Alice began as a clothing designer who worked under several other people's labels. After she gathered enough experience, she went out on her own. She opted to open a small retail store instead of diving right into the wholesale market, because it required less overhead to start and would allow her to test her vision and designs in smaller batches. After three years, that retail venture provided enough capital for her to establish wholesale accounts as well. Although the two sides of the business operate on two completely different business cycles, Alice spent several years designing and managing both her retail shop and wholesale lines. She originally planned to continue to grow her wholesale line and build her reputation as a designer.

In the beginning Alice's shop primarily featured her own collection. And although she loved to design, it was difficult to produce a collection that was broad enough to support the retail shop by itself. Creating a complete collection required her to design items that were both really expensive to make as well as those that weren't very interesting to her. It was also challenging to keep up with customers' desires for "new" items. Alice quickly decided that rather than spend her time on things that lost money or didn't sell well, she would begin sourcing items from other lines to fill in the gaps. At first she wasn't sure how it would go over, but as it turned out her customers loved the blended collection. These other collections not only added variety, but also lessened the pressure on her to produce new styles. Most important, it freed Alice up to design only the items that she really enjoyed and that really sold well. What surprised her was how much she liked the buying and merchandising side of the business. In fact, she found herself preferring this new role over strictly designing. Over time, she decided to close down her wholesale accounts in order to split her time between designing a smaller curated line for her store and buying and merchandising items from other collections.

FOR YOUR CONSIDERATION

- How does your current role fit into the longer-term picture of where you want to go?
- What would your company look like if you did more of what you like to do?
- What options for growth contain a role that is interesting and suitable for you?

Troubleshooting:
When You Get in Your Own Way

A good portion of our clients come to us because of challenges they are having with their role, particularly when they are in the wrong role, too far from their original creative outlet, or having difficulty giving up control.

We are going to introduce you to two clients who encountered these challenges and discuss how a variety of entrepreneurs have chosen to handle delegation.

Still a Square Peg? Put Yourself in the Right Role

A frequent but troubling challenge for entrepreneurs is finding themselves in the wrong role. They like their business but hate their job. There are lots of reasons why this happens. Some entrepreneurs struggle to delegate; others get too used to wearing all the hats. Some become wedded to a particular notion of what an entrepreneur "should" do.

In any case, we have worked with many clients who are no longer satisfied with the content of their work. Some come to us with a nagging discomfort, saying they aren't really as into their business as they used to be. Others are so miserable that they've all but hit the panic button and have begun to fantasize about closing up shop. It is a shame to tire, bore, or "outgrow" your company just because aspects of your role no longer work for you. There are plenty of ways to transform an unsuitable role into one that's more engaging.

The Case of In-the-Weeds Whitney

We have worked with many clients who have tasked themselves the wrong role within their companies. One of them, Whitney, stands out. Whitney ran a talent agency that helped to place freelance workers in jobs within small and medium-sized companies. She started the business because she was in touch with the freelance community and saw great potential for creating a better marketplace for their projects and also to cultivate a larger community of professionals who could support each other and benefit from common resources. Whitney was really excited about the potential for this business to change the way these freelancers were working and believed there were lots of intriguing options for growth.

In the beginning Whitney, like many entrepreneurs, wore a lot of hats. She cultivated the client relationships, marketed to free-lancers, and handled the more operational aspects of the business too. In time, she partnered with someone who loved handling the relationships on both the client and talent sides, so she relinquished those parts to her partner. She maintained the operational pieces and in particular the administration related to billing, finances, and jobs filled. This was a terrible use of Whitney's skills and talents. Despite being an optimist and a big thinker by nature, she had stuck herself in the weeds. Details weren't Whitney's strong suit and she found herself constantly making mistakes. Worse still, she was really unenthusiastic about the business. She felt constrained and bored.

Despite being dissatisfied, Whitney was reluctant to hire some-one to take over these parts of the business. Her industry was quite competitive and several newer similar businesses had recently opened. The data that Whitney was managing was very valuable, in particular the contact details, job rates, and revenue. She was uncomfortable giving someone else access to this information. Fur-ther, because operations wasn't a strength of hers, Whitney had cre-ated a very convoluted and confusing data management and billing system. She told herself, and us, that it would be way too compli-cated to explain it to someone else. We wondered if these were legitimate rationales or just excuses.

We talked with Whitney about what role she would like to play in the business if she weren't bogged down with operations. She explained that she would prefer to play a more strategic role, think-ing of new initiatives and setting the course for where the business could go. We then asked what other challenges, aside from her being frustrated with her role, was the business facing? Whitney told us that she felt the business was stagnating. Several new com-petitors were making headway in the market and gaining a lot of notoriety. She was concerned that the business as a whole was behaving in a reactive rather than proactive manner. She wished they had some more concrete goals to work toward.

It was clear to us that Whitney's role was not only making her unhappy but also hindering the growth of the company. What the company needed was exactly what Whitney could provide if she wasn't preoccupied with operations. More than that, she was excellent at setting strategic direction and mobilizing forward motion. We asked her to consider the opportunity costs associated with staying in operations.

Through a series of conversations, Whitney was able to divorce herself from the belief that it was necessary for her to be doing the operations. She wanted a change, not only for her own satisfaction but for the success of her business as well. She gave herself three months to transition a new person into the operations role. Within a month she was feeling not only relieved but energized. Allowing herself to take a role more suited to her strengths had a significant impact on the company as well. Within the next year, her business had made several important decisions and Whitney felt as if they were making progress once again.

FOR YOUR CONSIDERATION

- Is any of your dissatisfaction linked to your current role in the business? If so, what percentage of your time is allocated to things you don't enjoy?
- What would you prefer to spend your time doing? What is the cost to your company of your *not* doing these tasks?
- Do you have the ability to change your role now? If not now, when? And what can you do to facilitate that process?

Missing Your First Love? Reclaim What You've Lost

It's true that most entrepreneurs' roles will change quite a bit over the life of their businesses. To some this is exciting, for others anxiety-provoking and disheartening. There are many who went into business in order to do more of the thing they loved. And by taking on the business they may have already sacrificed a good percentage of these cherished tasks. We have worked with more than a few clients who, by taking on too much of the business side, have regrettably outsourced their preferred role.

The Case of Too-Boss-y Beth

Beth, an independent clothing designer, came to us because she was unhappy with her business and couldn't figure out why. From the outside, things seemed to be going great. She had recently scored herself a slew of new wholesale accounts, orders and production were increasing, and she had finally secured a wonderful showroom. Yet she told us about these accomplishments with a ho-hum attitude. The spark was gone. After a long discussion about what was missing and what she wanted from the business, it became apparent that Beth had moved too far away from the work she loved best—designing. Before she went out on her own, she had designed under several other labels. She started her own business in part to be able to realize her full creative potential and vision. She worked really hard during the first several years to achieve financial stability and was thrilled when her collection and business were able to sustain the life she wanted. However, her designs were in hot demand, and in order to keep up with it she had grown much faster than anticipated. Beth felt that each time she reached a certain milestone, a new one would instantly crop up in the distance. She didn't mind the rate of growth per se, but she missed a lot of what she enjoyed in the early days. We dug deeper to identify exactly what that was.

It turns out that in order to keep the business moving forward Beth had hired several designers to work for her while she focused on growing the business. This was the model she was most familiar with from her previous jobs. It hadn't really occurred to her to question whether it worked for her. If you asked Beth at any stage of the game what she loved most about her job, she would have told you it was designing. However, when we looked at how she was currently spending her time, designing occupied only about 10 percent of it. In the first couple of years she had had a lot of task variety, but she still spent at least 50 percent of her time designing. After hearing this, we knew that in order for Beth to enjoy her business, she'd have to go back to her roots and prioritize design as a significant part of her role.

As we talked about this, Beth said she thought she had to give up designing in order to grow her business. She also confessed that she had fantasized about closing or selling the company to someone else in order to start another that would be smaller, higher-end, and would allow her to be the sole designer. This was certainly an option, but we feared that in Beth's case it would be a huge waste. Her current company enjoyed great brand recognition and had a wonderful reputation within the industry.

Instead, we encouraged her to think about ways that she could either reallocate tasks under her current business model, launch another brand within the same corporate structure that focused on higher-end custom work, or both. Either choice would allow her to design more, and neither required a sacrifice in revenue, depending on how it was structured. Beth ended up taking both suggestions. Over time she limited her wholesale line to the best and highest-selling client and opened an e-commerce site to service anyone she wasn't currently reaching through the retail outlets. She also focused on cultivating her custom work, which was a huge revenue booster since she sold these items at retail prices. So that she could focus her energy on designing, strategy, and sales, Beth brought on new employees to focus on Web site and client management and operations. Overall, these changes resulted in her making more money, not less, and more important, Beth was able to spend more of her time doing what she loved.

KEEPING A TOE IN THE WATER

The desire to "go back to your roots" is a common one. After realizing that a bigger company also comes with more responsibility, expense, and work, some entrepreneurs, like our client Beth, find ways to scale back or adjust their roles to include more of their original love. Other entrepreneurs find ways to keep a "toe in the water" as their roles change and while their businesses grow. For them this is the trick to feeling completely fulfilled. We spoke to several entrepreneurs who had been creative about carving out time to practice their original craft.

Jude Sterns, owner of Judy Jetson Salon, spends most of her work time managing the business but saves Saturdays as a day to cut her clients' hair. Maribel Lieberman, CEO of MarieBelle Chocolate, leaves summers open to cooking, testing new products, and reconnecting with her recipes. Eileen Loeb, owner of BodySmart Personal Training, conducts a session with her trainers and their clients once a quarter. For all of these entrepreneurs, keeping a toe in their original craft helps to keep them creative and fresh. It makes sure they don't get too far away from their roots and from the essence of the business. It's worth your while to consider whether you've preserved a taste of your original craft, and if so, what strategic benefits that offers you.

Hoarding Bad Work? Learn to Let Go

The flip side of knowing what you do best is understanding what you don't do as well and, consequently, where you should get some backup and support. At the outset, this may seem like an easy principle to follow, but in our experience it is actually quite tricky to convince some entrepreneurs to relinquish control. There always seems to be a myriad of excuses about why a particular task should remain on a business owner's to-do list. "It's just easier to do it myself." "No one does it the way I like it." "It's too hard to find someone good." "It costs too much to use someone else."

We, of course, say just the opposite: there are lots of other people who excel in this particular area who are looking for good opportunities to contribute value, and most important, it costs too much not to use someone else. If time is your most valuable asset and you are wasting it on inappropriate tasks, your business will suffer. Besides, hiring and managing other people (employees or not) provides an opportunity to learn and grow.

Erin McKenna owner of BabyCakes, confessed to a group of women at In Good Company just how bad she was at delegating and trusting others when she first opened. She had perfected her cupcake frosting technique and literally frosted every cake that left the shelves for the first several months. She would ferociously guard her frosting spatula, giving anyone who got too close the evil eye. It wasn't until she was beyond the point of exhaustion that she finally relinquished the spatula to someone else. And guess what? Baby-Cakes continued to thrive. In fact, it didn't skip a beat. Once freed up from her frosting and other baking obligations, Erin has been able to focus her energy on media, writing two cookbooks, and opening another store in L.A. as well as one in Downtown Disney.

Now, of course that is one small, funny example, and you may be thinking that you don't have a frosting spatula equivalent, but believe us, you probably do. Most of us have a tendency to hoard unnecessary tasks, and the challenge is to identify what they are. You may be surprised to learn that they are different than you think.

It's wrong to assume that the only tasks worth delegating are those that are either too menial or too difficult. Sometimes you also need to give up tasks at which you are quite skilled, and sometimes it is smart to hang on to those that seem easily outsourceable. It is also wrong to assume that delegation is a lesson for early-stage entrepreneurship. It's actually an important rule of thumb to keep in mind as your business grows and goals change. It could be that your greatest contributions in the first couple of years are no longer necessary later in the life of your business.

Trisha Anderson, CEO of Frontier Soups, shared a great example of this. Historically she had been the salesperson in addition to the chef behind the company's dry-mix recipes. It made sense; she knew the product extremely well and could talk about it with gusto. However, as the company progressed and grew bigger, Trisha's role encompassed more and more. There came a time when doing the sales, creating new products, and managing the company's strategic growth was too much. (Imagine that!) Trisha's plate was too full. In order to accommodate all that needed to be done, she was making a lot of personal sacrifices and undermining some of the very benefits she had sought to achieve in the first place—namely, freedom over her time and a creative outlet.

About seven years ago, it came to a boiling point. She realized she had become overburdened and dissatisfied. And it wasn't just her that was suffering; having so many things competing for her attention meant sales weren't being attended to as they should. An intentional step back let her see that she didn't need to be doing sales anymore. Ideally all of her energy would be focused on product development and overseeing the company's strategic direction. With encouragement from a very helpful coach, Trisha hired a sales manager to take over the sales process. Since that hire four years ago, sales have dramatically improved. The new sales manager has been able to focus on establishing new relationships with larger distributors who sell to larger chain stores in addition to maintaining the smaller specialty store accounts. This change in strategy has resulted in an increase in sales each year, with 2010 sales up 43 percent from 2007. Most important, Trisha is much more satisfied. Her role is more focused and she is able to take advantage of the benefits that she enjoys. The business is once again working for her.

On the flip side, you may have good reason to hang on to some seemingly unnecessary tasks. We've spoken to several entrepreneurs who keep doing things that they "don't need to" because of the strategic value they gain. Selia Yang is a couture bridal designer whose business has both retail and wholesale components. Selia first got her start in 1997, and until very recently she, in addition to designing all the dresses and managing the business, personally fitted each dress purchased from her store. Adelaide actually purchased her wedding dress from Selia and nearly fell off the stool when the designer (whom she had not yet met) trotted out to make the proper dress adjustments. On the one hand Adelaide thought, "How cool! I feel special! She's going to make it just right!" On the other, "Now surely a designer of her caliber doesn't need to be doing this!" In fact, Selia saw the fittings as a strategically important task for the brand. She wanted to make sure each dress was as perfect as possible. In recent years she has taken great care to train someone to handle this sensitive duty appropriately in order to allow her to focus more on the future growth of the business.

The point is to know why you do what you do. And to do only those things that you believe are really worth your time and attention.

FOR YOUR CONSIDERATION

- What work do you avoid?
- What is the opportunity cost of doing tasks that are on your plate unnecessarily?
- What tasks allow you to make the greatest impact and contribution to your business? How do you stay focused on those?

Cheat Sheet: What Do You Do Best?

POINTS TO REMEMBER:

1. As an entrepreneur you are more than just the doer of things that need to get done.
2. Your role is more than a summary of the tasks you perform. It's an expression of who you are in the business and how you relate to it.
3. If you're going to invest the time and energy it requires to run your own business, you had better enjoy what it is you do!
4. Learning to delegate is a must, but pay attention to what you give away. Hang on to tasks that you enjoy and that contribute real business value.
5. Make sure your desired role is compatible with the opportunity for growth.

QUESTIONS TO CONSIDER:

1. What are you known for?
2. If you were to write your ideal job description, what would it say?
3. What is the cost of your not doing the things you are best at doing?
4. What do you want to do more of in the future?
5. How can your role help to define and transform your company?

BUSINESS SPOTLIGHT

"If I am going to grow, it's going to be beneficial to not only me but for everybody around us. How can we make a living for everyone? How can everybody get up to that point where they can live and grow too? That's the next step."

A woman who loves to create things builds an empire
Barbara Lynch, owner of Barbara Lynch Gruppo

Barbara Lynch decided she wanted to be a chef when she was twelve. A few years later, while working as a waiter at a private club on Commonwealth Avenue in Boston, she decided she'd like to own a restaurant as well. In keeping with her "Southie" Boston roots, she figured it would probably be a sub shop or a bar. Today there is hardly a person in all of Boston who doesn't know who Barbara Lynch is. Her seven restaurants are institutions. Tourists and locals alike brag about having completed a "Barbara Lynch weekend," where people devote themselves to eating exclusively at Barbara's joints. When you add in her catering company, it is fair to say that Barbara has created an empire.

It was a particularly nurturing and invested home economics teacher who helped Barbara recognize her intuition and cooking skill. And once introduced she couldn't get enough. Through middle and high school she cleverly found ways to work in various fancy restaurants, serving things she had never heard of and watching the chefs in awe. It amazed her that they could so skillfully nourish and please hundreds of people with not just great food but hospitality as well.

Barbara continued up the ladder from waiter to sous-chef to chef. After a while her reputation earned her an interview and subsequently a job with Todd English when he was still a chef in someone else's restaurant. When Todd went out on his own to create his now famous restaurants, Olives and Figs, Barbara followed. She worked for him for several years. As Barbara tells it, she got her ass kicked every day but she enjoyed every minute of it. Having no formal training, she felt she had a lot to catch up on in order to become familiar with ingredients and techniques. After work she would read *The Food of Italy* three times over, trying to memorize and acquaint herself with things like radicchio.

From Todd's establishments she moved on to head chef positions at other restaurants, turning bad kitchens around and starting some from scratch. She won awards and garnered acclaim. She was an established and well-respected chef. But Barbara didn't yet have a restaurant of her own. She was ready.

At the time she decided to launch her own restaurant, she was $75,000 in debt to the IRS and still living in the projects with her mom. Nevertheless, she refined her vision and put the wheels in motion. Her first angel investor chipped in $50,000, and within a year she had raised the necessary $3 million. Shortly thereafter her first and most famous restaurant, No. 9 Park, opened.

After about five years, Barbara got restless. And she realized that if she wanted to hang on to her staff, she needed to grow. She had several options, of course, one being to open an additional location of No. 9 Park, but she wanted something different. She had one winning recipe and wanted to create more.

Up until this point, Barbara saw herself as a skilled chef and food lover. It was true—her talent was without question and she had many awards to prove it. However, it was only after she had mastered her own restaurant that her real talent came into focus. Put simply, Barbara loves to create things—not just food, not just experiences, but concepts and opportunities too. Like other visionaries, she was driven to explore new territory, hone her craft, and share what she knew with others.

It was her desire to create something new, to bring her vision to reality, that would define her role in the business going forward and would continue to define the direction of her company.

Including No. 9 Park, Barbara has created seven distinct culinary establishments: one bar, one demonstration kitchen, and five restaurants. Each of these concepts satiated a specific need, desire, or curiosity. Barbara found that she was always craving oysters in the spring and didn't have a great place to get them, so she created one in B&G Oyster Bar. She was nostalgic for the general stores in Italy where you could buy meat, a snack, and something to drink, so she created the Butcher Shop.

Later, Barbara discovered that despite having several restaurants, she really didn't have a kitchen of her own to play, experiment, and test in. So she created Stir, which also doubled as a cooking school and cookbook store. Aside from being her "dream dive bar," Drink was a way to retain and promote the bar manager at No. 9 Park by giving him his own establishment.

Many have urged her to replicate one of her successes or to open a satellite in the suburbs. Or perhaps open a much larger restaurant that seats more people. But for Barbara that's not the point. She explains that she doesn't make money like other restaurants, which are more of the "turn and burn" variety. Instead she aims to create interesting and well-executed restaurants. Growth that required replication wouldn't be satisfying for her. It wouldn't be new. It wouldn't be creative. She loves the challenge of first making an idea real and then making that idea work expertly. For Barbara success is about creating establishments that are not only inspired but manageable and lifelong.

Thirteen years later, she's satisfied with the number of restaurants she has, but she's not done growing. The next step for Barbara is education. She would love to work with the city to do things like create rooftop gardens and greenhouses for its schools. She would also love to have an educational cooking show. To date Barbara has turned down every reality-based show offer. That kind of fame is not her thing, nor is that kind of drama. What she's after is much bigger. It is already a crowning achievement to have made a difference in the culinary world. But Barbara's real legacy is about more than recognition from her peers. It's about nourishing, and pleasing, and teaching. It's about honoring ingredients, experiences, and ultimately people.

4

Where Do You Go from Here?

Define a Successful Future for Your Business

There is no need to build a mansion when all you need is a house.

– JEN HILL, OWNER OF JHILL DESIGN

"It's called a Franchise!!!!" the e-mail rudely retorted. Yeah, thanks, as if we hadn't heard of that before. The sender was a woman in California who had written to ask if we had any In Good Company locations in her area. Although a simple glance at our Web site would have confirmed that we did not, we replied saying no, but that we did consult to other people interested in setting up a similar kind of business. Apparently she thought we had missed the point.

In reality, she had missed ours. We had been down the franchise research path before. In fact, in 2008 we had completed the majority of the paperwork and scoped out potential cities. But guess what? It was a business model that didn't work for us. Staggering expenses aside, it would require us to focus more on the operational and landlord-esque side of our business and less on education of entrepreneurs, which is not what we wanted.

But whether or not it was a good direction for us was not really the issue. What bothered us about the e-mail was the flippant nature in which this woman shouted her opinion about what we *should* do. We had no relationship with her and she obviously knew very little about our business. It was annoying. But we know from our work with clients that this kind of blunt proclamation isn't unusual. It isn't helpful either. It is this kind of obstinacy that leads entrepreneurs to think there is a "right" and obvious way to grow their businesses and that growth plans are divorced from your specific needs and goals.

We know better. Just as we all want our businesses to provide us with unique benefits, we are also each driven to achieve diverse ends. We each conjure up very different scenarios when we think into the future and envision a successful outcome. Yes, some scenarios will focus on size, but others will emphasize different factors such as longevity, continued opportunity, a specific change in the market, or even expert status.

A Look at the Future Goal for Your Business

In addition to knowing what you want entrepreneurship to provide you with, what you want your business to be known for, and what you want to spend your time doing, it's important to understand your overall goal for your business. We are not talking about what happens at the end of your business per se. We are talking about what your business will look like when you've achieved success. In short, what is the successful future outcome that you are working toward?

Are you:

- Creating a commodity that others value and are willing to buy?
- Building a platform that can support the projects and work that you continue to find interesting?
- Perfecting your craft and infrastructure in order to reap maximum rewards for manageable effort?

- Pushing the envelope as much as you can and positioning yourself to hand off your creation to someone who can take your dream farther?
- Engineering a business that you can scale up and scale back in order to meet your professional and personal needs over time?

There are an infinite number of "ends" that you could pursue. And from an objective standpoint, all the ends are good. One outcome is not necessarily better than the other, and only you can decide which is best for you and which will best accomplish the goals you have in mind.

Your goal will also help you define success and inform the growth and cultivation of your business. It tells you where you want to go and allows you to create a road map. With a map in hand, you will find it easier to evaluate options and know when to say yes and when to say no. Without at least a cursory understanding of what you want in the long run, you will find it very easy to build a business that doesn't work for you.

The Story of Angela and Zoe, Part 4

Let's revisit Angela and Zoe, who have created very different businesses that suit their individual needs. While of course their personal motivations, business purposes, and roles will play a big part, the growth of their respective companies will also be determined by their desired outcomes. Neither Angela nor Zoe is interested in selling her company in the near future and both want their business to grow with them over time. However, that means something different to each of them.

Angela needs her business to support her creative ideas and new interests. With a national brand, retail outlets in dozens of cities, and several high-profile wholesale accounts, she knows she has many options she could exercise. Many have suggested opening more locations (in either new markets or existing markets), but instead of doing more of the same, she ultimately wants to try her hand at new things and leverage what she has created in order to do so. She'd love to produce a branded cooking show, open a cooking school within her retail locations, and create branded cookware and cutlery. So Angela begins to think about her company as a platform from which she can experiment with several related directions and ideas.

On the other hand, Zoe wants to build something that is manageable and allows her to maximize the time she spends doing what she loves. For her that means staying focused on perfecting her craft and connecting with the customer. She's not interested in adding more staff or overhead than necessary. Zoe would like to save most of her creative energy for the kitchen, her recipes, and small-batch cooking. Growth for her would come in the form of reputation, customer interest, and cookbook sales. In her mind, a line of cookbooks is the perfect way to leverage her work for additional gain.

In these scenarios the outcomes provide an infrastructure that is big enough to accomplish the goal while also honoring their personal motivations, business purposes, and preferred roles. What would happen if either was encouraged to pursue different ends? The business might not meet their needs, which defeats the purpose of the whole endeavor.

Someone else in Angela's shoes might have chosen instead to have perfected the market experience and opened many more locations or possibly sought a franchise. This would have been a great outcome for someone who wanted to run a larger organization or penetrate more markets. It might also have appealed to an entrepreneur who loves training and cultivating staff or someone who loves the operational and numbers side of the business. However, that particular outcome would likely have been constraining for Angela, prioritizing location growth over the development of new or creative extensions.

Similarly, someone else might have chosen to grow Zoe's business into a lifestyle-focused retail outlet that features cooking lessons, serving ware, and home décor or even opened a catering branch. However, for Zoe these extensions might be unsatisfactory because they would divert her too much from the small-batch cooking and hands-on role she loves.

In the Company of Others: What We Are Aiming For

Not surprisingly, the entrepreneurs we spoke with are all working toward a variety of outcomes that reflect their own personal and business goals. Several themes emerged, which we believe will be helpful examples as you consider your own desired outcome.

Good Things Come in Small Packages

I just want a great small company. A well-paced, well-oiled machine.

—JEN HILL, OWNER OF JHILL DESIGN

Many entrepreneurs want to stay nimble and unencumbered. They seek a business structure that delivers the most bang for their buck. Success for them is maximizing their rewards and minimizing distracting or costly business infrastructure.

MEET:

Justine Lackey, owner of Good Cents Bookkeeping, for years wanted to be the H&R Block of bookkeeping. Yet she kept resisting her own plan for streamlining her process and procedures, focusing instead on client relationships and personalized service. After a little soul-searching, it dawned on her—she really didn't like corporations, so why was she trying to start one? She understood in theory the benefits of automating things in order to scale larger. But this made sense when she thought about things like hamburgers, not her client relationships. Justine realized that "hamburger-ization" was inconsistent with who she actually was. So she changed her desired outcome. Now Justine's goal is to be able to choose her clients and strengthen her niche by working with the 150 best artists and creative professionals in the United States.

Emily Wolper, CEO of E. Wolper Inc., has been quite deliberate in her efforts to remain an army of one. She has had a successful admissions consulting practice for over twelve years, and despite her always full client load, she has shaken her head at suggestions to bring on other consultants or even hire more administrative or support help. Emily doesn't want to parcel out any aspects of her job. In her mind, training others to work with clients independently not only pulls her away from her ideal role, but also puts her at risk for an employee leaving with proprietary information. Although Emily has felt confident in her assessment of her needs and in her decisions, her choices had previously made her second-guess her business instincts.

"I used to feel that not expanding was some kind of failure; that it meant I wasn't growing," she said. "Over the last few years, I have developed a different definition of 'growth.' Growth does not have to involve hiring new people or expanding the size of a business. I have been growing instead in my reach, knowledge, number of speaking engagements, professional association memberships, Web site development, and understanding of my role in the world of small business owners. I am interested in being a leading voice not only in my field, but also in the world of entrepreneurs. I am expanding myself, and I consider this significant growth."

Ellen Galinsky, president of the Families and Work Institute, demonstrates that a decision to stay small doesn't mean you have to be a party of one or two. Ellen founded the organization with a partner who ultimately left in order to honor her own work life needs. With her departure, Ellen made an important decision. She determined that the organization wouldn't grow too large. Ellen knew that in order for her to be fully satisfied she needed to spend a significant part of her time focused on research and writing. She also knew that if the organization became too large, she would be required to spend even more time on management, taking her away from her preferred role. Rather than growing larger, Families and Work Institute collaborates with other organizations when they take on big projects. By creating this boundary, Ellen has successfully set herself up to do the work she loves.

A Platform

It is not just a business for me. It is a platform to do the things I love.

—PAIGE ARNOF-FENN, FOUNDER AND CEO
OF MAVENS & MOGULS

Many entrepreneurs seek to create a business that acts as a long-term launching pad for new ideas and directions. Instead of replication, these entrepreneurs love to expand their business footprint through new creative services, products, and extensions. Often the overall brand is the glue that holds it all together. Their success is determined in part by the longevity and flexibility of their venture. Success is a business that can continue to transform with them and support their interests.

Paige Arnof-Fenn, founder and CEO of Mavens & Moguls, has engineered her business so that it can do both of these things. She loves that her business affords her the opportunities to speak at conferences, sit on boards, and write for several publications, including *Entrepreneur* magazine. These extracurricular business activities make all the difference for Paige. For her, Mavens & Moguls is more than just a company; it is a vehicle that allows her to do all sorts of things she enjoys. For her success is about both "staying small successfully" and continuing to enjoy her work and all the opportunities it brings.

Lotta Anderson, founder of Lotta Jansdotter, has grown her business in a way that allows her to pursue different creative brand extensions under one business. Her business started with screenprinting and textile design but has grown to include book publishing and licensing as well. Instead of pursuing these other avenues of growth, Lotta could have produced more of her home design products and made them available in more outlets. However, she was concerned that mass production would not just undermine the quality of the products but counter her handmade values as well. She chose instead to license her designs to companies such as West Elm and cultivate her larger brand to create DIY manuals, books, and classes. This platform has enabled her to incorporate several creative directions, diversify her role, and ultimately reach a larger audience in a way that is congruent with her values.

Perfecting the Art Of

I don't desire to be the biggest, but I do want the best reputation.

—JODI MORGEN KATZ, OWNER OF JMK CREATIVE

While some entrepreneurs use their businesses as a way to try many things, others opt to do one thing and do it very well. That one thing may be a small or large undertaking, but in either case it is focused on delivering perfection first and foremost.

MEET:

Jessica Dunne has always loved perfume and even as a child spent time concocting her own potions. As an adult, Jessica was inspired to make a scent reminiscent of her elegant and beloved grandmother, Eleanor. Despite no previous experience in the notoriously insider industry, Jessica secured a partnership with a renowned French perfumer, and together they worked to create the perfect recipe for Ellie perfume. Their creation won accolades and Jessica was hailed as a rising star. It was Jessica's vision that Ellie be special and unique, unpedestrian. It is no mistake then that the scent is a bit hard to find. It's not plastered all over billboards, nor is it in the hands of roving department store perfume gals poised to attack innocent shoppers. Keeping her goal in mind, Jessica has worked to cultivate the Ellie brand but has so far turned down suggestions and offers to develop new scents. Considering that she created Ellie to be timeless, it seems counterintuitive to follow the common perfume industry path, which typically involves churning out several new scents a year simply for the sake of announcing something new. For Jessica success is being able to attain perfection and craft the product of her dreams.

Maribel Lieberman, CEO of MarieBelle Chocolate, has always believed in everyday luxuries and works hard to create a beautiful and special experience for her customers. Every detail of Marie-Belle Chocolate is lovingly attended to, and her products are of the highest quality. Maribel has spent thousands of hours playing with ingredients and adjusting her recipes, looking for perfection. "If I was going to make chocolate it was going to be the best chocolate." And she extends the same level of attention to her entire store and product experience. Not only is her chocolate delicious, but she incorporates her early training as a graphic designer to create beautiful and luxuriant packaging. Her signature ganache chocolates even don beautiful images, making each piece a work of art.

Jodi Morgen Katz, owner of JMK Creative, knew she didn't like working for someone else, but was unsure if she'd enjoy working on her own. All it took was doing one freelance project on the side to show her that she had what it took to be independent. After working as a freelancer for a while, Jodi formalized her business, creating a full-service creative agency dedicated to the beauty industry. Since the beginning, she has been very clear about the future goal for her business. "I don't desire to be the biggest, but I do want the best reputation." This goal has not only provided direction but informs Jodi's current strategy. Instead of pursuing clients in multiple industries, she stays focused on beauty brands, cultivating her agency's expertise in particular areas that these companies need, such as packaging, advertising, Web design, and visual displays. If a given client or project doesn't help her achieve this goal—to be *the* creative agency for beauty brands—then Jodi isn't as interested.

FEELING THEIR WAY THROUGH THE PROCESS

Some entrepreneurs guide their businesses as directly as possible to a predefined target. They wouldn't dream of starting a business without a clear plan for the future. Others trust that opportunities will continue to unfold as they go along. For them, having too specific of a target feels limiting. Many of these entrepreneurs use words like "organic" or "intuitive" to describe their growth process.

For example, Amanda Hofman, founder of Urban Girl Squad, said she desired to "grow naturally." Since she never expected to be where she is today, she finds it hard to project too far into the future and so opts to take small, focused steps. Similarly, Sara Horowitz talked about the early days of Freelancers Union and how by not having a steadfast plan for the future she was able to "just keep building the organization in a way that felt right."

Building a Fleet

There was way more work than I could handle alone.

—ERICA ECKER, OWNER OF THE SPACIALIST

For some entrepreneurs success depends on building and managing a small army of skilled but independent professionals. These additional hands on deck allow for more work to be done, more change to be made, and more clients to be serviced. Managing this fleet ultimately shifts the entrepreneur's role, but many welcome that change and appreciate what having this small army allows them to accomplish.

MEET:

Erica Ecker, owner of The Spacialist, was running a wholesale cake company when she first heard about the profession of organizing. It was 1998—the days before the Container Store and reality TV shows like *Clean House*—and she was at lunch with a friend from college who had just become an organizer herself. Once Erica heard what it entailed, she knew that it was a perfect match for her. Within two months she had sold off her cake company and hung out her shingle as a professional organizer. Originally she thought she would run her business like a therapy practice. She would have low overhead and a small business footprint with more emphasis on the organizing than the business itself. She figured she'd spend her time seeing a certain number of clients per week and be free from the traditional marketing, operational, and branding concerns that most businesses have.

But soon she was presented with a (good) problem. She had more business than she could handle. Because her organizing appointments are scheduled in four-hour chunks, Erica found that limited availability meant she didn't have many appointment alternatives to offer her clients. Although she had never imagined she'd want to have others work under her name, she decided that in order to grow she'd have to get help. So she created a team of "Spacial Agents" whom she could dispatch to work with various clients. At first it seemed scary to relinquish control, but the benefits of having a team were quickly realized.

First, it has enabled Erica not only to accept more business but also to be more flexible and accommodating to a variety of client schedules and locations. Second, it has allowed the business to offer clients a choice of price points, as Erica gets billed at a higher rate than her agents. Third, by leveraging the different skills and personalities of her Spacial Agents, Erica has found that she is better able to match client needs and preferences. What's more, it has given Erica the opportunity to focus on other aspects of her business, such as marketing and branding, which she has enjoyed tremendously.

Over the last several years Erica has managed up to seven Spacial Agents and had excellent business results, winning "best of" awards from *New York* magazine in both 2008 and 2010.

Eileen Loeb, owner of BodySmart Personal Training, has always enjoyed exercise. As a former professional dancer and personal fitness trainer, being active and fit has been a way of life for her. But ironically it's the skills she learned in social work school that Eileen relies on each and every day in the management of her personal training company. She had always been bothered by how varied the experience and approach of most trainers were. There was no way to know who had years of experience and who had a certificate from a weekend class. As a client you were equally likely to get a dose of the latest fleeting craze as to get a good solid exercise plan.

So Eileen, who had already been seeing clients privately, decided to formalize her efforts and create a company that focused on delivering proven programs rooted in exercise science and not the latest fad. She wanted to help as many people as possible to cultivate a healthy relationship with exercise. Since her schedule was already pretty packed, she knew she would need to bring on other trainers quickly. At first she grappled with issues of trust as she handed over her precious clients, but she soon learned the benefits of leveraging others. Over the course of the last nine years, Eileen has employed between three and twelve trainers and worked with several hundred clients. Building a fleet of trainers has freed her up to focus on a role that she really enjoys, that of case manager and business problem-solver. Out of all the things Eileen spends time on, there are two she enjoys most: creating the systems, programs, and procedures that best care for both her clients' and her trainers' needs; and appropriately managing clients by developing a strong understanding of their unique personal and physical needs, matching them with the right trainer, and supervising their care. It is these responsibilities that ultimately require Eileen to regularly flex her social work skills and allow her to deliver on her company's promise.

The Bigger the Better

If we stayed small, we wouldn't be having impact around the world on millions of people. For me, scale equals social change.

—SARAH ENDLINE, CEO OF SWEETRIOT

While some businesses are better off staying small, others are built with BIG goals in mind and they need a BIGGER reach to accomplish the task. These are entrepreneurs who ask of each option, "How big is the opportunity?" For them success is determined by how many people they can reach and how far they can effect change.

MEET:

Sarah Endline, CEO of Sweetriot, knew for some time that she wanted to start a mission-based business. In college she studied businesses like the Body Shop and Ben & Jerry's, all the while keeping her eyes open for an opportunity of her own. In 2005 she found it, and decided to start Sweetriot, a fun, delicious, and socially responsible candy company. Her first products, which feature cacao nibs sourced directly from Latin America through equitrade standards, can be found in hundreds of retail locations nationwide. In addition to a commitment to directly sourced, all-natural, high-quality ingredients, Sweetriot uses recyclable, reusable packaging that features work from emerging artists. From a business practice perspective, Sarah places a tremendous amount of emphasis on the business's partnerships, from the farmers, to the manufacturers, to the warehousers, and even to the consumers. It is part of Sweetriot's mission to have a positive impact on the millions of people who make up the supply chain, which is why Sarah is determined to grow Sweetriot as big as possible. To her, a bigger company means a bigger opportunity to effect change. While Sarah is eager to expand the size and impact of Sweetriot, she also wants to do so in a way that maintains its high standards and allows it to operate with integrity and authenticity.

Shazi Visram, founder and CEO of HappyBaby, founded her company with the mission of improving the health of our nation by setting up children for a lifetime of healthy eating. It's a big goal and one that requires having far-reaching impact. So as Shazi looks toward the future and various growth opportunities, she is mindful of the options that help the company achieve the necessary reach. Her vision is predicated on introducing her brand to the greatest number of people possible, while honoring the founding principles of the business. She says that growing her business is not a function of increasing revenues, it's about delivering on a promise and significantly influencing the lifelong health of many people. "Running this business is not about monetary reward. It is certainly appreciated and expected, but that is not the basis. So straying from our mission in order to make decisions based on monetary reward would be a huge mistake on our part and we wouldn't do it."

Andrea Miller, CEO of Tango Media, started her career in the world of finance and entered business school with the hope of doing something both entrepreneurial and media-related once she graduated. After reflecting on an interesting conversation with her then boyfriend, Andrea began to wonder why there weren't any media outlets that focused on modern, relatable relationship content. A quick survey of the women's media landscape demonstrated that most of the messages were superficial and often aimed at trying to convince women to change themselves in order to "get the guy." What Andrea realized was missing was real, interesting, substantive but media-friendly content on love and relationships. She saw the opportunity for a multimedia organization that would really focus and own the relationship space, the same way that ESPN owns the sports market.

So Andrea formed Tango Media and made it her mission to help women live their best love life. The business originally launched by publishing a print magazine. However, as time progressed and the print industry gave way to more Web 2.0 sites, Tango Media recast itself as a digital property that lived exclusively online. Although this was indicative of where the industry was going at the time,

Andrea was excited about the opportunities that the digital realm presented for connecting with even more women. Because relationships are inevitably about dialogue and the topics easily generate conversation, a more interactive digital platform seemed like an obvious fit. Since making the switch, YourTango.com has worked to cultivate a community and leverage interactive features. Andrea is excited by the sheer opportunity she has to engage millions of women on a topic near and dear to their hearts. Harnessing that potential takes big plans, which the company is eager to put in place, not just online but through other media as well.

A Commodity

What if you don't want to do it for forty years? It's important to have the ability to create a business that can be handed over to somebody else, even if you don't ever do that.

—AMY VOLOSHIN, OWNER OF PRINTFRESH

Companies of all sizes and kinds are bought and sold all the time. Some people see a sale as a way to secure a big payday. Others know that they can take the company only so far and that ultimately a different set of skills and resources are needed to realize the business's full potential. Some entrepreneurs want the opportunity to start a new chapter. In any case, selling your company is a great way to capitalize on the value you have created when you're ready to move on. However, even if you're not ready to sell, there is value in thinking about your business as a commodity. It forces you to see your business differently. Thinking about the parts of your business that could be valuable to others has inspired many entrepreneurs to solidify systems, register intellectual property, collect valuable data, shed unprofitable services, and even create new business products.

MEET:

Amy Voloshin, owner of Printfresh, was encouraged early on to think about what made her company valuable. At the start of her business, she sought out many sources of advice and participated in an evening class for entrepreneurs at Wharton. One thing that was stressed in the class was the importance of thinking about her business as a commodity. However, being in the service industry, Amy knew that perpetually low barriers to entry can make service businesses tough to commoditize. There was one direction, though, that would allow Printfresh to create a tangible and unreplicable product: an archive of vintage fabrics. Over the next several years, Amy worked to acquire and catalog thousands of vintage garments and fabric swatches. Not only did this provide another component to her current service offerings, but this department could be separately positioned for sale if need be. Amy's not sure that it is necessarily an interesting option, but nevertheless it does help to diversify and solidify her company's value.

Your Turn:
Identifying a Future That Works for *You*

Now we'd like you to think about your own future. Taking into account all the answers you've already identified—your personal motivations, business purpose, and role—think about what it is that you're ultimately trying to create.

The following questions will help you identify what it is that you want and don't want:

Question 1: What is your definition of success?
Question 2: What options have come off the table and why?

Before we begin, do yourself a favor and shake off any preconceptions you have about what success means. Forget what your professors have told you, what your parents have said, what your competitors are doing, and certainly what magazines routinely praise.

Most important, remember the following:

- Most business outcomes are good *if* they are in line with your needs and goals.

- Growth is not all about size. It is about how a venture evolves and transforms over time to meet the needs and goals of the entrepreneur.
- Bigger is not always better. The right size depends on your personal motivations, business purpose, and role, among other things. Besides, size is relative—one person's big is another's small.
- The right growth path can be determined only by you and will most likely be one of several options that you *could* pursue.

Question 1: What is your definition of success?
People define success quite differently. Some can literally pin a dollar sign or a specific number on theirs, while others are seeking a more intangible gain. We understand that your definition may still be evolving; we know ours are. Nevertheless, it is important to think about what you want from the future and what that means for your business.

For Barbara Lynch, chef and CEO of Barbara Lynch Gruppo, success is creating a business and brands that are lifelong and manageable. For Shazi Visram, founder and CEO of HappyBaby, success is having a significant impact on the health and well-being of children by helping them establish healthy eating habits at an early age. For Chloé Jo Davis, CEO of Girlie Girl Army, success is bringing in additional income for her family, working from home, having a decent life, and staying true to the message of her business.

For Sara Holoubek of Luminary Labs, success is doing well in spite of the fact that she does things differently than most other businesses in her industry. Instead of being pressured to make something fast and cheap, Sara wants to build something that focuses on contributing real value over time. She does not want her primary concern to be the dollar amount someone else would put on her business. That doesn't take the prospect of selling her business off the table, but it means that her short-term primary focus isn't about making her business a commodity; it's about using it to create value for her clients and for herself.

FOR YOUR CONSIDERATION

- What do you ultimately want to achieve for your business and yourself?
- How have you engineered your business with this picture of success in mind?
- What are you willing to sacrifice in order to attain your goal?

THE MYTH OF AN OVERNIGHT SUCCESS

We've all heard the tall tales about an entrepreneurial Cinderella whose creative idea catches the mass market's attention and installs her as a household name in the blink of an eye. These instant success fantasies are long on celebration and short on sweat. The truth is that entrepreneurship is a marathon and everything takes time. Even situations that appear to have happened effortlessly have in actuality been a long time in the making.

Take, for example, Gail Epstein and Lida Orzeck of Hanky Panky, whose "4811 Thong" was catapulted to unprecedented lingerie fame after being featured in a front-page *Wall Street Journal* article. The article talked of a little-known company that had a few celebrity followers, and Hanky Panky's path was forever altered. They were instantly branded an overnight success even though they had already been in business for over 27years!

Question 2: What options have come off the table and why?
We've always found that we could learn a lot about what people want from the options they have taken off the table. With so many choices for each business and every entrepreneur, it is important to remember what you have decided against. These "roads not taken" are likely to far outnumber those you may still be contemplating.

So let's go back to the franchise situation we discussed at the beginning of this chapter. For us, franchise is an option that has come off the table, at least for now, but our reasons and rationale have actually been quite helpful in determining what it is that we do want.

First, the numbers don't add up. Having a franchise adds a significant amount of expense to an organization, and in order to profit you have to have a good number of franchises up and running. We weren't sure how many franchise locations were truly viable or how long they would take to make a healthy profit. We could make it work, but the risk involved was too high given how early along we were in our own venture.

Second, we believe the dynamics of many other urban centers are different enough from New York to make the replication of our exact model challenging. We believe there can be lots of great community workspaces around the country, and in fact there are, but franchise is predicated on sharing transferable systems and procedures. And at least in the beginning, we thought that our model raised too many question marks in other locations. We have too much integrity to sell a "solution" that we aren't sure will work.

Third, we were in the midst of a recession during the time when we were researching a franchise option. The availability of business loans had decreased substantially and the actual rate of new small businesses was declining for the first time in a long time. We didn't think it was the best economic climate to be testing out our franchise hypotheses.

Aside from all these reasons, a franchise didn't match up with our definition of success. We wanted to focus more on women and their businesses and less on operational matters. In fact, the appealing thing about the franchise option was the opportunity to create really meaningful relationships with franchisees and to help them grow their businesses. But conversations and research revealed that this would be the lesser part of our responsibilities as franchisors. As franchisors, success would depend on an increased focus on operational efficiency. We would need to flex our landlord muscle and really excel at standardizing the physical IGC experience. Now, Adelaide loved designing the IGC offices, but working with suppliers to negotiate good rates on a hundred of the same desk doesn't satisfy the same creative itch. She was even less excited about dedicating more time to things such as supplies and tech solutions.

We also realized that franchising would really cut down on our freedom to adapt our own business. No longer would adding a program or service, or even changing our prices, be an easy and uncomplicated matter. Each change would have wide-reaching impact and would become a process with a capital P. Ugh.

Going through this research process made it really clear. For us, success was about sustainability, not just scalability. We needed to create work we loved and to build something that we would enjoy for years to come. We wanted to reach even more women to help them build businesses that worked for them. We wanted to spend our time thinking about entrepreneurship and working directly with our clients and members. It was clear that this wasn't going to be achieved through a franchise.

FOR YOUR CONSIDERATION

- What options for the future have you taken off the table or put on the back burner? Why?
- What possible outcomes are incompatible with your goals or beliefs?
- What has been helpful in making good decisions about what directions to pursue?

Troubleshooting:
When You Get in Your Own Way

The right size is obviously a matter of opinion. Sometimes, however, our preconceived notions of what it means to grow or stay small can unnecessarily limit the direction we choose to take our business. We often work with clients who are surprised to learn that their experience of growth is different from what they thought it would be.

Letting the Unknown Keep You from Moving Forward? Experiment and Get the Scoop

Sometimes we let our fear of the unknown hold us back. Just because we don't yet know how to do something, we assume we won't like it. It happens a lot when it comes to managing people. Early on, entrepreneurs will often talk about not wanting to hire employees. They imagine the worst: micromanaging people they don't like, feeling overburdened, and having less freedom to make dramatic changes to the business if they want. Sure, employees will make it more challenging to close up shop or radically change course should you want to. Sure, employees require time, attention, and care. But the right employees can also help some entrepreneurs build a business that is even more satisfying and rewarding. What's more, many entrepreneurs are surprised to learn just how meaningful they find it to cultivate their staff and create a company culture.

The Case of Cottage-Fever Courtney

After a long career in the hospitality industry, Courtney decided she wanted to reinvent herself as a floral designer. The part of the job she loved the most was helping to manage the special events. She had always been a creative person and had recently been experimenting with creating some of her own floral arrangements. Once she had saved enough money, Courtney left her job to work under a renowned floral designer, the best in the industry. She thought this would be the ideal way to quickly get a lot of experience. But aside from confirming her love of flowers, the experience was a disaster. The woman she worked for was brutal and extremely particular about the way things needed to be done. Courtney was eager to learn from her, but her boss made things much harder on her staff than they needed to be. When Courtney made suggestions for improving the internal operations, she was quickly shot down. Still, she stayed, because she was learning valuable design skills. After three rather painful years, she decided to go out on her own. Her decision also coincided with her family's plan to move upstate to the country.

Once Courtney got settled into her new town, she began to casually market herself in local retailers and through other event-oriented services. Fortunately, her country town was a destination for a lot of weddings, and brides were eager to have a local designer who was not only well acquainted with the different venues but was also close at hand for meetings and planning. Courtney's business grew over the year, and by her second wedding season she was at her capacity. She hated turning down business, especially since there weren't very many good local alternatives for people to go to. She spent three seasons booked solid. Soon Courtney had a reputation for being hard to get, which only served to lengthen her list of reservations. All the while people encouraged her to grow her business and hire more people to help. Courtney was hesitant. She wanted to stay focused on what she loved and was reluctant to burden herself with other people. She feared they wouldn't be able to deliver the same way that she could, *and* she was worried that her perfectionism would make her as miserable as her old boss!

However, Courtney also started to experience the costs of not having staff. She hadn't taken a summer vacation in four years. She felt like her own life was on hold because any time a job came in she would change her plans to accommodate it. In addition, she was really spread too thin. Because she had been so busy she had recently made some mistakes that were upsetting. Three times she hadn't gotten an order in on time. Twice she was able to rush the flowers, but she ended up losing money because of the expense. Once she had to come up with alternate arrangements, which disappointed the bride. At the end of the busy season, Courtney decided to consider hiring people and growing the business. Before committing, she reached out to several colleagues who had employees to learn about their experience. The conversations she had were invaluable. Each person she spoke with told her they appreciated her hesitation and admitted to feeling similarly before they brought people on. But they were quick to add that they regretted not doing so sooner.

Curious, Courtney pushed the conversations further, asking about how they handled certain issues and what management strategies they found to be successful. She was surprised to learn that several of her peers found cultivating their staff to be rewarding. They were happy to train them and, once there was a certain amount of trust, relinquish the reins. Having employees had freed them up to try new things, focus on the direction of the business, and have some downtime as well. When Courtney mentioned that employees might mean she couldn't close or leave the business if she wanted, her colleagues pointed out that she was already booked two years in advance and that it was unlikely she would cancel these contracts anyhow. One of her colleagues challenged her by telling her that she already knew she was going to be running her business for another couple of years (and likely much longer than that), and it was up to her to decide how enjoyable that time was going to be. By the end of her conversations, Courtney was ready to give it a try. Persuaded by her peers' experience, she realized that while bringing on employees would mean she was responsible for other people, it would also enable her to take better care of herself, her clients, and her business.

Courtney made her first hire shortly thereafter and spent the slower months training her. By the time the next season came along, her new employee was confident in her skills and able to attend events on her own. Courtney loved the freedom this gave her, and for once she didn't end the busy season ragged and completely depleted. The following winter she brought on two additional employees and was excited to focus much of her time on marketing the business and creating some exciting strategic partnerships. Three years later she was amazed at the difference in her business. She genuinely enjoyed managing her employees and focusing her energies on the business and not just on doing flowers for her clients. Her business had developed quite a reputation and she was even in the process of opening up a larger retail presence within a gourmet food store. By bringing on employees she was able to realize the full potential of the business and experiment with other roles that were satisfying and fun.

Thought Bigger Was Better?
Revisit What Is Important to You

As a society we have a tendency to believe that bigger is better. We are consumers. We want more. This attitude certainly rears its head in business too. Sometimes bigger *is* better, but the problem comes when we think numbers tell the whole story.

It is easy as an entrepreneur to fall prey to number envy. We assume that ten locations are better than five, that revenues with an extra zero yield higher profits and are more impressive, that having a ton of employees is always an achievement. But in fact there are many businesses that have found that increased size has just brought increased expenses and decreased benefits. Bigger can be better when the goal calls for it, but growing for the sake of it is often a recipe for disaster.

The Case of Bigger-Is-Better Betty

Betty worked in public relations for ten years before starting her own firm. While she had worked with many well-known brands over the years, her favorite clients were always the smaller, lesser-known ones. She loved the challenge of helping a small company get noticed. When she decided to open her own business, Betty thought she could combine her love of public relations with her ability to teach individuals to improve their public speaking skills. She created a small coaching and consulting firm that specialized in working with small business owners.

Betty's business got off to a great start, as she was well connected to many organizations for entrepreneurs. She had a great roster of clients and felt that the work she was doing was meaningful and well respected. She loved that she got to choose who she worked with and enjoyed meeting her clients face-to-face. She helped several of her clients generate brand-name recognition and proudly watched many of the business owners turn from shaky public speakers to confident communicators.

Over time, many of Betty's colleagues encouraged her to grow her company and widen her reach. The feedback she continually received was that in order to grow she had to find ways to drive revenue that didn't rely on her time. People suggested creating products, like an e-book and Webinars, and selling them through a more robust Web site.

Betty certainly understood the value of utilizing technology in marketing and promotions, but she was apprehensive about how her client work would translate online. So much of what she did was spontaneous, and her most creative promotional ideas came during brainstorming sessions with the client. But she did a lot of investigating and learned that many people were building their businesses this way. She decided to give it a try. To start she would package the more tactical components of her work into Webinars and e-books. The products could either be purchased separately or as part of a virtual coaching package.

Betty spent six months building out course materials, a Web site, and technology to support the online presence. Her cash flow from clients was very good, but she became concerned with how much of a financial investment the new business would ultimately take. She launched the online platform in April and spent much of the next few months marketing the new service offerings. By September, she was frustrated by the small number of sales. And despite the meager results, marketing the online platform was taking a considerable amount of her time. In fact, Betty noticed that she was spending more time on marketing her new online business than on her existing traditional clients, who were still paying the bills! What's more, her pipeline of new business was also weak, as she had dropped the ball in cultivating new clients. Betty started to panic about her business's stability and future revenue stream. This is when she reached out to us.

Betty told us she was tremendously disappointed in herself. She had just spent a lot of time and money building this new part of the business, and after six months it still wasn't taking off. She felt embarrassed and worried that clients would lose confidence in her if the online business was unsuccessful. She was very concerned about the potential failure of this online platform on her existing business. What if she was jeopardizing everything she had worked so hard for over the last ten years? Betty was at a standstill. She didn't know whether to keep moving forward or go back to square one.

As with all of our clients, we asked Betty to talk about why she started her business and what aspects of it she enjoyed the most. "Well, that's easy—the clients," she said. One of the reasons she started the business was the freedom to choose her clients and work only with those whose businesses she believed in and whose owners she liked. She loved developing close and long-term relationships with her clients. She expressed how she enjoyed becoming a client's "secret weapon." Then we asked her about her goals with the new business extension. "People said that I should grow my business and reach more people and that technology was the way to do so." That's great, we replied, but we wanted to know what she wanted from that business. She said she hadn't really thought about it from that perspective. She was just worried about what it would mean if she didn't grow. Honestly, she was perfectly happy with her business before she launched her online platform. She commanded high fees from her clients on account of the in-depth and personalized services she provided. Betty also worried about the sheer marketing force necessary to drive the online business, which was clearly dependent on a higher number of smaller transactions.

We then asked Betty what was encouraging her to keep the online platform. She said she was worried about the ramifications of abandoning the project early. We asked her to think about it differently. Instead of focusing on the costs of taking it offline, we encouraged her to think about the costs of keeping it online. Betty thought she not only ran the risk of jeopardizing the whole venture, but more important, she was worried about no longer being excited about what she did. She was upset that after working so hard building her business and reputation she no longer liked her job. In our minds, her satisfaction was the more important risk. If Betty was happy and excited to run the online component, we told her we were sure she could work out the kinks and make it sustainable. But honestly we didn't see the point if it wasn't something she enjoyed doing.

Betty agreed and was incredibly relieved. She closed down the online portion of the business and shifted her marketing efforts to promote her original client work. She quickly felt like she was back on a level footing financially and back to running a business she enjoyed. She felt that while the whole experience was costly and emotionally exhausting, she did learn a valuable lesson, which was to trust her gut and make decisions based on what worked for her rather than suggestions that might work for another business owner.

Cheat Sheet:
Where Do You Go from Here?

POINTS TO REMEMBER:
1. Most business outcomes are good if they are in line with your needs and goals.
2. Growth is not all about size. It is about how a venture evolves and transforms over time to meet the needs and goals of the entrepreneur.
3. Bigger is not always better. The right size depends on your personal motivations, business purpose, and role, among other things. Besides, size is relative—one person's big is another's small.
4. The right growth path can be determined only by you and will most likely be one of several options that you could pursue.
5. Your goals should influence everything, from business offerings to policies to growth options.

QUESTIONS TO CONSIDER:
1. What is your definition of success?
2. How have you engineered your business with this picture of success in mind?
3. What are you willing to sacrifice in order to attain your goal?
4. What options have come off the table and why?
5. What has been helpful in making good decisions about what directions to pursue?

BUSINESS SPOTLIGHT

"I tried outsourcing because I had been told multiple times that if I wanted the business to grow the only way to do that was to get bigger. And so I experimented. I put a lot of time and money and energy into two different outsourcing experiments. And both of them were real failures. What I learned at the end was that outsourcing was ridiculous for me, because the part I love the most is actually making the stuff."

A ceramist who scaled back and got more
Teresa Chang, owner of Teresa Chang Ceramics

Teresa didn't plan on having a ceramics business. She had trained to be an architect throughout both college and graduate school. Ceramics had been only an on-and-off hobby, but no matter how many times she dropped it she kept getting pulled back to working with clay. That is until a fellow loftmate showed her it was possible to make a living as a so-called craftsperson. It felt risky to push aside her formal education to pursue the unknown, but Teresa had an inkling it would make her happy. She decided to try it, allowing herself to return to her traditional path if a career in ceramics didn't work out.

It took a couple of years to get traction, but Teresa was able to build up her name and secure several wholesale accounts for her high-end dinnerware. Once momentum kicked in, she garnered a following and terrific press coverage. Soon she was running a "real" business and with four full-time assistants working in her Brooklyn studio. It wasn't until she had an established company that she realized she'd really gone into business for herself. And despite the very long hours, she didn't want to do anything else.

Along the way, Teresa was encouraged by many people to grow bigger. People suggested she outsource some of her production in order to increase the amount she could make. Twice she tried to set up outsourcing arrangements, first with a more well-known company and then with a smaller operation. She describes both experiments as disastrous. Not only was there the issue of poor quality control, but it also significantly changed her role. Once she set up the outsourcing arrangement her focus necessarily shifted from creation to management. She felt as if all the good energy was sucked right out of the studio and business. Teresa quickly realized that her satisfaction was dependent on actually being engaged with her craft. That was the part she liked best. So despite the time, energy, and money invested, she called off the outsourcing and went back to producing every piece with her own hands.

Still, she was working more than she wanted to. And when she decided to get married she knew kids would follow sometime after. She wanted to have a family and to make space for that without giving up what she loved, so Teresa decided to take a big risk and scale things way back. She switched her business from wholesale to retail. This would allow her to produce less and dramatically reduce her overhead. Because her retail component would be largely made to order, she was really in control of the business's pace. She started by saying no to new wholesale inquiries and then slowly phased out her longer-term wholesale relationships as well. She set up a Web site and reoriented her customers to buying directly from her.

It took the better part of the year for Teresa to implement this new strategy, move to a new city, and dramatically reduce the size of her studio and staff. Soon, however, she was making just as much money as she had been before, despite working less than half the amount of time. And best of all, she was doing work that she loved most. What a win.

Several years later, Teresa continues to embrace the same business strategy. Her new studio sits in the backyard of her house so that, even when she is working, her family is close at hand. Her retail focus has allowed her to control the timing and tempo of her business. It has also enabled her to further develop her craft by creating intricate teaware in addition to her dinnerware sets. Her delicate high-end teapots have not only added to the bottom line but brought acclaim and recognition in their own right.

PART TWO

THE CRITICAL SKILLS:

Mastering Everyday Actions for Business Success

Crafting your business so it meets your long-term needs and goals is paramount to overall satisfaction, but success also depends on your day-to-day reality. Once you've figured out the big-picture stuff—goals, motivations, purpose, and so on—you need to figure out how to take the little steps that will allow you to reach them. After all, your business can only truly work if both the macro and the micro are well attended to and in good order. Thankfully, there's a lot you can do to make that day-to-day enjoyable and productive.

With that in mind, this section is designed to address the things that, in our experience, are most likely to get in the way of success on a daily basis: a too-full plate, not knowing where to draw the line, the expectation of perfection, and isolation.

We will share the critical skills that will help to keep you and your business on track.

- Do less (chapter 5)
- Experiment often (chapter 6)

- Learn to say no (chapter 7)
- Build a community (chapter 8)

We hope the strategies, skills, and examples shared will reinforce what you already know, bolster your existing efforts, and prevent you from learning anything new the hard way!

5

Progress Makes Perfect

Recognize the Value of Doing Less

In business there's a frenetic feeling that if you don't do it right this second, you're going to fall behind. That's just not true. It takes maturity in business to say, "I can come back to that idea."

—JEN MANKINS, OWNER OF BIRD

The Problem: Taking On Too Much at Once

Entrepreneurship is a marathon that often feels like a sprint. Despite knowing that their destination could be years down the road, many entrepreneurs spend each day harried and frantic, racing to catch up or reach the next milestone. Despite our honest intention to move forward, we overcomplicate things and generally make more work for ourselves. Believe us, we know there is a lot to be done. We feel the urgency too. When you're bursting with ideas and salivating over the potential of what could be, it's hard not to get ahead of yourself. But pacing yourself is an important skill to develop. It requires changing your perspective and learning to embrace small steps.

Like all skills, it sounds simple in theory but is hard in practice. It's too easy to convince yourself that everything is a priority and that it all needed to be done yesterday. But trying to do everything at once is a sure way to end up exhausted, overwhelmed, unproductive, and, most important, dissatisfied with your business and experience of entrepreneurship.

However, many of the entrepreneurs we have worked with are not deterred by discomfort alone. They are willing to endure a little frenzy if it means the job will get done. "What's the big deal?" they say. "What do I really have to lose by taking it all on? Isn't that just part of the experience?" Well, we have news for you: the costs of tackling too much at once are very real and they are harmful to you and your business.

This is a short list of things that can happen when you're trying to do too much at once.

- You feel overwhelmed.
- You feel discouraged.
- You are distracted.
- You suck all the fun out of your business.
- You compromise your personal motivations.
- You make bad decisions about the business you are building.
- You burn out.

Let's discuss.

Overwhelmed. Feeling overwhelmed is a terrible thing. But it's easy to do when your to-do list is threatening to swallow you whole or when you're staring your big bad goal in the face. As an entrepreneur you need to realize that your work is never done. There is always another objective or goal looming. But that doesn't mean you need to spend your life running to catch up. So we ask, if you can't pace yourself now, then when?

Discouraged. Let's face it, when the task is always incomplete and the focus is on what is yet to be done, it's hard not to feel discouraged.

Will it ever get done? Will I ever be where I want to be? When can I put my feet up? I have so far to go. It's easy to get stuck in this mind-set and lose sight of what's already been accomplished.

Distracted. This one is important. If you're always too busy rushing to get things done, you will never be able to give proper attention to what's happening *now*. Everything unplanned will seem like an unwelcome distraction, and it's likely that important opportunities will get missed or be turned down.

No fun. Considering the nature of this list so far, it's probably easy to see how taking on too much can suck the fun right out of your business. We've found that our clients who always try to do everything at once are also those who are the least satisfied and having the least amount of fun. Linda De Carlo, a business coach, often reminds us that "stressful journeys don't lead to joyful outcomes." Chances are you became an entrepreneur to attain some level of satisfaction in the first place, so remember, *the fun is in the building*. It can't just be about the destination; otherwise you'll never enjoy yourself.

Compromised. Many of our clients are unhappy with their experience of entrepreneurship simply because the way they are working is undermining the very benefits they were seeking in the first place. And it's no wonder. It's pretty hard to bask in newfound freedom when you don't even have a chance to breathe. The point is to build the business to honor your needs, not sacrifice them for the business.

Bad decisions. When you're under the false impression that your business needed to be built yesterday, you may also be inclined to make decisions that are not in the long-term best interest of you or your business. Your desire for a reprieve from the day-to-day non-sense may eclipse what you really want in the long run and you may be tempted to settle for a less satisfying outcome.

Burned out. Remember . . . it's a marathon. You gain nothing if you're unable to keep going, especially if you expect your business to have any degree of longevity. If you burn out, that's it, game over. Your work, passion, and creativity are gone. You are sad and the promise of your business goes unfulfilled.

The Solution: Do Less

Now that we've established the problem, let's talk about the solution. The antidote to doing too much is doing less and, of course, doing it well. We don't mean you should do less overall; if you want your company to change the world, then great! We want you to do less right now, at this very moment. This is the greatest commitment you can make to the long-term viability of your business.

Doing less at once entails:

1. Prioritizing
2. Taking baby steps
3. Creating accountability
4. Delegating
5. Celebrating progress, not just success

1. Prioritize

Most people complain that there aren't enough hours in the day. But we'd bet that even if you had bonus time you'd be just as busy as you are now. Instead, think about what you really want to accomplish in the time you have. The challenge then becomes defining your priorities. Remembering that time is actually your most valuable commodity, consider what is a worthwhile use of it.

In general terms, there are two to-do lists: *things you need to do* and *things you want to do*. Often prioritizing the things you need to do is not as hard as prioritizing the things you want to do.

In terms of what you need to do, we subscribe to the "to each his own" philosophy. There is no one right way and it can take years to perfect the proper self-management system that works for you. Some people swear by doing the things they hate first, while others always start with what they love. We've always thought one of our In Good Company members got something right when she said to start with what is closest to the money. But whatever your inclination, there are tons of very talented professionals who specialize in helping people get more done and done well. We encourage you to find the guru who sings to you. Let them be your voice of calm.

Let's address the *want-to-do list*. Most entrepreneurs we know are brimming with ideas and eager to get involved with new projects, partnerships, and initiatives. As natural initiators, not only do they have a hard time learning to say no (see chapter 7), but they might also arguably have more opportunities vying for their time. Ultimately your business depends on your deciding which of these things is actually a priority.

In general this is harder than it seems. As entrepreneurs, we are optimists and we fool ourselves into thinking our plate is bigger than others' and that our days are longer too. Convinced that time is our only restriction, we just heap on the work, setting ourselves up for the inevitable explosion. We trick ourselves into thinking the rules don't apply and that if we want it all badly enough we can somehow make it happen. Not only is this false, it's unfair. Like everyone else, we can choose to do it all poorly, or we can do less, but do it well.

In our own experience, whenever we have too much competing for our time and attention we first look at our business goals and our goals for the future.

We ask ourselves:

• What do we want our business to be known for?
• Where do we want to go from here?

These questions help us determine the order in which we'd like to tackle things.

Once we sift out the most important areas of focus, we then look to our resources (broadly defined as our time, capital, and attention) and ask:

• What do we have available to make it happen?

This question helps us know how quickly things need to occur and what, if anything, needs to be done simultaneously. Often this is when our personal motivations come into play. We consider how much of a compromise we are willing to make if need be and weigh our benefits against any potential sacrifices.

For example, we got this book deal in February 2010, when Adelaide was four months pregnant, due in July. We had written a couple of book proposals before but weren't that thrilled about them, primarily because they felt too focused on the nuts and bolts of running a business rather than the strategy of entrepreneurship. However *this* book proposal got us really excited, and it seemed like the right time in our business to focus on a book. We were eager to participate in a larger conversation about entrepreneurship, and since our plans to expand to other cities were on hold, writing a book seemed like a great alternative way to connect with entrepreneurs across the country.

While we knew the manuscript wouldn't be due until the following January, we also knew we wanted to interview a hundred women before we began writing. With Adelaide's short maternity leave now scheduled for midsummer, we realized that the hundred interviews were going to need to be completed before Adelaide's travel restrictions took effect in early June. We were genuinely excited about meeting and interviewing a hundred women, but weren't thrilled about the prospect of doing so in eight weeks or so. This would certainly require a tremendous sacrifice on both our parts. We were already under negotiations for an additional space within our building and knew that we'd likely be opening our new location in the midst of the interviews as well. We considered scaling back our interviewing schedule. Could we do only forty? Did we need a hundred? Could we interview women only in New York?

Did we really need to travel to Boston, Chicago, and Philadelphia? Ultimately we decided that the interviews were important and that for the time being we would sacrifice personal time in order to meet our business and book obligations. We also took some time to quickly take stock of our other responsibilities and immediately eliminated anything that didn't have to be done during that time. Our staff members picked up more of our sales, and additional programming was held to a minimum. We canceled one event that we knew would take a lot of promotional efforts in order to focus on the task at hand.

FEAR FACTOR

Moving things to the back burner takes not only discipline but courage too. When you have a good idea it is easy to be propelled by your fears . . . What if later is too late? What if someone else does it first? What if this is the thing that would make all the difference in getting where I want to go? It's really hard to sit with this uncertainty, but ultimately you need to trust your instincts. Consider what needs attention now and then set yourself up for success by moving other distractions out of the way . . . for the time being. We appreciate the wisdom of Allison Hemming, CEO of The Hired Guns, who reminded us that "there is no expiration date on good ideas." Allison runs a creative talent agency and originally thought of launching her Academy offering more than five years ago. However, she didn't have the space to hold the events or bandwidth to do it justice. She dutifully put the plan aside, which was no small feat for someone who admittedly loves shiny new ideas and has to work hard to keep herself in check. Finally in 2010, after moving her offices into a brand-new gorgeous space, Allison was able to bring her Academy to fruition. Currently staffed by more than fifteen top-notch experts, the Hired Guns Academy offers a full roster of classes on personal brand and career management. So remember, ideas on hold are just that—on hold. You are free to revisit them when you have the time and attention to do them justice.

2. Baby steps

We've all heard the saying that Rome wasn't built in a day, but it's easily forgotten, especially when we are on the outside looking into someone else's business. We romanticize industry giants, forgetting that they too had small beginnings and long journeys. From a distance all we see are strong, clear strides of progress, not baby steps. We aren't witness to the fits and starts, the steps backward, the periods of lethargy, and the misdirection. But they are always there.

The empire of Powell's Books has been forty years in the making. It began with just one small location and introduced what seemed to be a crazy idea at the time: purchasing used books from customers and displaying them together with new books on the shelves. Acclaimed designer and trained optometrist Selima Salaun opened her first Selima Optique retail location in SoHo almost twenty years ago, with no intention of creating her own designs until a customer made a special request. Renowned chef Barbara Lynch was encouraged by a middle school home economics teacher to try her hand at cooking. Fascinated and eager to further develop her culinary talents, Barbara consistently pushed herself out of her comfort zone, first applying for a waitressing job at a fancy restaurant and later raising her hand for jobs that seemed out of her reach.

So while vision is great, progress is often about putting one foot in front of the other and taking baby steps toward your goals. This same philosophy can be used to make a daunting project seem less overwhelming. In our own experience each new project inevitably brings with it minor freakouts and days of feeling stuck. Ultimately it is by breaking up each project into smaller chunks that makes them not just actionable but even possible. For example, when we were tasked with opening our additional space in less than six weeks, the first thing we did was write down every conceivable item that had to be done. There were pages scrawled with notes with no seeming order or direction. At first, the swarm of to-dos looked unwieldy. But a second glance revealed groups of like tasks. Once we recognized that, we were quickly able to divide everything into categories related to construction, setup, and marketing. When looked at separately, each of these projects immediately seemed more doable. We made them even more pint-sized by creating specific project plans that were divided up by week. The major items were prioritized both by chronology (electricity has to go in when the walls are still open) and importance (tenants had to be able to connect their computers, but if they had to go upstairs to receive printed documents for a few weeks that was just fine). Because we could literally see everything that needed to be done, there was never a time when we weren't sure what needed to be done next. Most important, we moved from a place of asking, "How will this ever get done?" to saying, "Here's what we do next."

Although this advice is fairly straightforward, it doesn't mean everyone welcomes it with open arms. So don't feel badly if you're less than eager to actually put it to use. The phrase "write down in one place everything that you need to do" nearly sends Amy into a panic attack. For her, the thought of staring at all her to-do items is scary. But in practice she has found that it is actually quite helpful. Almost always the list shapes up to be not as bad as she feared. And once things are living on paper it is much easier to see a natural order to many of the tasks. Besides, she's learned that if you don't write them down you don't get the satisfaction of crossing them off.

3. Create accountability

Even when your work is prioritized and broken down into tiny steps, it takes diligence and perseverance to make progress. But it's hard to hold your own feet to the fire. Accountability is hands down one of the biggest challenges entrepreneurs face. The good news is that you're not the only one who needs a kick in the pants. The bad news is that lack of accountability is endemic to the experience of entrepreneurship, so consider it worthwhile to find some solutions that work for you. Aside from leveraging the usual self-management principles, such as creating specific goals and deadlines or restricting distractions (ahem . . . the Internet), we have encountered a few accountability strategies that are particularly helpful for those who work independently and that incorporate the regularity and external direction necessary for success.

Find a coach. If accountability is particularly challenging for you, we suggest investing in a coach who can help you strengthen the necessary muscles. Motivating yourself to steadily make progress is one of your biggest responsibilities as an entrepreneur. There will be plenty of other challenges along the way, so this needn't be one of them.

Create a system. Whether you take a good ol' pen-and-paper approach or opt for the Evernote iPhone app, you need something to keep you organized and on task. We really love the example of Gretchen Rubin, who revived a truly old-school system to help monitor her resolutions for her book *The Happiness Project*. She was inspired by Benjamin Franklin to create a daily scoring chart similar to the one he used to track his adherence to particular virtues. By the end of her one-year project, Gretchen's chart was massive, but it served as an important daily reminder of what she strived to accomplish. *The Happiness Project* has inspired thousands of others to revitalize Ben Franklin's system to help keep them accountable too.

Join a group. One of the most common ways to get accountability as an independent is to join a group. There are scores of entrepreneurial groups in every city and loads more online as well. Many of these groups have offerings specifically designed to keep their members moving forward. At In Good Company, we host a dedicated accountability program where a consistent group of people meet to publicly state their goals, get support and ideas, and collectively review their progress. We know several entrepreneurs who have turned to mastermind groups or even weekly networking groups for the same kind of structure and routine. You really can't underestimate the ability of an impending meeting in lighting a fire under your butt. It may take some time to find a group with the right chemistry for you, but in the meantime, sign up somewhere and start getting yourself in gear.

Get a buddy. Two of the entrepreneurs we know, Galia Gichon, founder of Down-to-Earth Finance, and Erica Ecker, owner of The Spacialist, took a different approach. When they were getting started in their businesses eight years ago, they formed a business buddy system. Neither of them had a business partner, yet they still wanted some of the benefits they thought having a partner would provide. So Galia and Erica met weekly for a couple of hours in order to check in, report back, solicit feedback, and make goals for the upcoming week. Over the last eight years they have developed a strong understanding of each other's personality, patterns, and goals. They credit the success of their partnership to the consistency of meetings, a willingness to be extremely honest with each other (both in sharing and feedback), and, of course, the absence of judgment.

4. Delegate

You can't talk about doing less without talking about enlisting help. Delegating is a cardinal rule that all entrepreneurs must learn. Despite being well acquainted with how frequently entrepreneurs grapple with this challenge, we *still* find it to be ironic. Seriously, who has more to do and less to do it with than an entrepreneur? Why is it so amazingly difficult to convince entrepreneurs to relinquish control? Feel free to insert here all the fitting stereotypes: perfectionist, martyr, control freak, untrusting, budget-strapped, etc.

Before you retreat to your own favorite justification, know that we are quite familiar with all the usual excuses about why a particular task should remain on a business owner's task list. Get over it. You need help.

There are lots of good arguments in favor of delegating, but the most important one is this: it costs too much not to use someone else. As we discussed in chapter 3, sticking to what you do best not only keeps you satisfied but will also likely deliver the most value to your company. Taking yourself away from your strengths squanders your talents and puts your business at a disadvantage. So please lose the "I can do it all" mentality and utilize what assistance you can.

Eileen Loeb, owner of BodySmart Personal Training, shared a humorous example of what not to do from her early days in business. Right after Eileen incorporated she was excited and ready to embrace her bootstrapping status. She knew one of the first things she would need was a business card complete with logo. Determined to do it on her own, she bought a computer program and spent hours and hours training herself in basic design skills, ultimately developing what she calls "the world's worst logo." She ended up hiring a designer to give her business a proper identity. However, this experience served up a valuable lesson about delegation and the importance of sticking to your areas of strength.

Grace Bonney, owner of Design Sponge, has three criteria for tasks that should be delegated. She asks herself: Do I enjoy this? Am I good at it? Is it necessary for me to do it? If the answer to any of these questions is no, she makes sure to find someone else to give the job to. Wendy Mullin, owner of Built by Wendy, says that delegation was an important lesson for her to learn along the way. While she started by doing everything herself, over time she learned that not only was she happier when she was focused on what she did best, but she made more money too. By offloading unnecessary tasks and freeing herself up to do what she did best, Wendy was able to focus on generating more value for the company.

5. Celebrate what has been accomplished

A wonderful piece of advice came from Melanie Notkin, CEO of Savvy Auntie. Upon her sharing the news that she had just landed a book deal, her friend texted her: "Keep Going!" What an awesome thing to hear, especially for someone with ambitions the size of Melanie's. It is advice that we too have shared with others and reminded ourselves of. We only add one caveat. *Celebrate*. Then keep going. Then repeat.

We know it's easy to skip the celebration, especially when you're a party of one. But you can't let that deter you. We've worked with many entrepreneurs who despite *years* of hard work have yet to take the opportunity to congratulate themselves or say "job well done."

Believe us when we say it matters and it is deserved. Consider it a demonstration of respect for yourself, the work you've done, and the sacrifices that you've made. So whether you pick a friend or colleague to take out for drinks or choose to do something nice for yourself, make sure to mark the occasion.

Also, it may sound trite, but it's really important to celebrate your progress, not just your big accomplishments. Our own experience has shown that reaching a goal can often be satisfying enough in itself. We typically need a boost when we are in the midst of a big project. It's really the steady, unrelenting progress that carries you the distance, and while others may find it a little odd, that's what we often choose to acknowledge. For example, when we got halfway through our hundred interviews we celebrated with massages. It was the reward/encouragement that we needed to keep going.

Troubleshooting: When You Get in Your Own Way

As you may suspect, we work with a lot of clients who are simply making things more complicated and difficult than they need to be. Bemoaning their own lack of progress or overwhelmed state, they come to us, frustrated and tired, asking what they should do. Generally our answer is: *less*!

There are three classic scenarios that we often encounter: the client who gets ahead of herself by focusing on growth before the business is proven; the client who can't move forward with one business or project because she is spending too much time incubating other ideas; and the client who makes getting set up a full-time job and is endlessly putting other "to-do" items in the way of doing the work.

Sometimes it is very good traits that land entrepreneurs in these situations—a love of learning, an endless pool of good ideas, a vision for where the company could go, a deep sense of pride and attention to detail. But good traits or not, they need to be managed, because they are getting in the way of success and impeding progress.

The Case of Too-Soon Sally

Sally was a former stylist to the stars. She had a great idea to help professionals (like her) and their celebrity clients responsibly and charitably offload unwanted clothes (many of which had never been worn) through an online sale site that allowed a portion of proceeds to be donated to a charity of choice.

As she should have, Sally solicited a lot of advice and feedback on her idea. Her conversations were generating a lot of interest and enthusiasm. In fact, the more she talked to people, the more potential the idea seemed to have. People suggested that interior designers faced a similar challenge with discarded home décor items. Others suggested she get funding or position herself early on for a sale to eBay or another online sales site. She diligently cataloged everyone's advice and folded it into her project plan.

Six months after coming up with the idea, Sally came to meet with us, frustrated about her lack of progress. She had hoped to have had a least ten stylists signed up, merchandise on her site, and some sales by now. However, her site was only partway complete and she was having trouble sustaining the initial interest she had generated with her press contacts. She kept revising her launch timeline and was concerned that she had missed her window of opportunity.

We asked a lot of questions about how she had been spending her time, what her priorities were, and what she imagined the business ideally to look like at six-month intervals for a two-year period. Just a few minutes of talking made it clear that Sally was putting the cart before the horse. Not only had she been spending her time sketching out the initial site and its functionality, but she was also talking with interior designers about expanding into that vertical, as well as folks who had sold their businesses to larger companies. Essentially, she was trying to launch the company and grow the company and even sell the company simultaneously. Her strategy was getting all tangled up and her priorities kept shifting based on what mode (launch/grow/sell) she was in. She would toggle back and forth between being completely focused on the Web site to spreading the word, trying to get more and more subscribers to sign up for updates about the increasingly delayed launch. Her interest in subscriber count was mostly fueled by the assumption that the more subscribers she had, the more valuable her company would be in the case of a sale.

As is usual in our consulting sessions, we also asked Sally about her goals. Why did she want to start this business and what was her desired outcome? Sally told us that ultimately she was bored with being a stylist, and while she didn't want to throw all of her hard work out the window, she wanted a new challenge and also to do something that had more impact in a feel-good kind of way. She wanted to make a difference while also leveraging her reputation, knowledge, and contacts. She was excited about being in a new industry and exploring this new entrepreneurial territory. She also told us that selling her company would be the pinnacle of success for her.

We talked with Sally about the hypothetical pros and cons of selling an idea versus a business. We also talked about growing a business versus a business strategy (see "The Case of Strategy-Only Stephanie" in chapter 2). After some discussion we offered the following insights. It sounded like she was really trying to start a new chapter in her professional career and that selling her idea too early would likely take that opportunity away from her. We also told her that while it was great to solicit advice about best practices for building a company in a way that was attractive for buyers, at this point she should only home in on advice that impacted the start-up stage. For example, it is great to capture subscribers and be mindful about how to grow that number, but not at the expense of solidifying the business. Last, we pointed out the challenges that could come from growing into other verticals before she had solicited feedback on the basic premise.

Our conversation helped her focus on the priorities associated with the start-up stage, namely fleshing out the offering and proving the business model. Together we broke up that work into baby steps that could be tackled more easily and helped Sally examine where she needed help. Sally left much clearer and quite frankly relieved. It is hard enough to pioneer a new concept, or smartly grow a business, or position a company for sale, much less to do all three at once. Within the next six weeks the site was up and running in beta and Sally was getting the very valuable feedback and experience she needed to enhance and strengthen her offering for the future.

The Case of Too-Many Margo

Many entrepreneurs are known for their good ideas. Some are particularly clever and insightful in pointing out potential business opportunities. Margo was one such creative opportunist. In the course of our knowing her, she worked on four different businesses, some product-based, others service-oriented. Despite her genuinely unique ideas, Margo continually expressed dissatisfaction with the progress of her businesses. She always wished the business was farther along than it was. She was excellent at creating the idea and setting up the initial infrastructure, but then she would run out of steam, until of course she was invigorated by the next business idea. All of her businesses were viable, but they weren't performing at the level she desired. Each time she officially closed a business, she felt disappointed and frustrated.

The truth was that Margo had a hard time prioritizing her ideas and subsequent businesses. Instead of directing her energy toward moving a particular business forward, she allowed her creative impulses free rein. She was spread too thin. What was difficult for Margo to see in the midst of her spontaneity was that saying yes to one idea meant that she was also sabotaging and saying no to another.

This is a common challenge for creative entrepreneurs who love putting their ideas out there and making them real. However, there is a time where all entrepreneurs need to learn that just because you have an idea it doesn't mean you need to act on it. This is true in terms of both businesses and projects. Ideas are fun, but execution is what matters. Indulging too many ideas will get in the way of your progress and make it harder to achieve what you want. It is doubtful that several half-baked businesses are reliably and consistently able to deliver desirable benefits.

We know it can be hard to choose among different possibilities, but this is when you should revisit your specific goals and motivations. Taking into account both where you want to go and what is important to you, ask yourself: what ideas should take priority?

The Case of Procrastinating Paula

Another common pattern we see is the entrepreneur who throws endless roadblocks in the way of getting started. Paula was a friend of ours who had this tendency and effectively delayed the start of her interior design business for nearly two years by creating unnecessary things she felt she needed to do before getting launched.

Given her previous professional experience, Paula was perfectly qualified to be in business for herself. When we first met with her, she ran through her business idea with excitement. We told her it sounded great and asked her when she was planning to get started. Paula told us she had to get a few things in order first and hoped to be open for business within a few months. She wanted to get her Web site completed and also complete a marketing training program designed for business owners. It sounded reasonable enough. We periodically saw Paula over the next year, and to our surprise she had yet to make her official launch announcement! She was still working on her Web site and had also found several other training programs in which to enroll. It seemed that Paula was making an entire job out of learning to be an entrepreneur.

Paula was also overly fixated on perfecting her Web site, all to the detriment of actually moving forward and getting to market! It was quite the catch-22. She didn't want to launch her Web site without pictures of her work. However, not having a Web site hampered her ability to connect with a lot of potential clients.

Six months later we got an e-mail from Paula asking if we could meet for a quick lunch so she could pick our brains a bit. We hoped this meant that she had in fact officially launched, but a quick check of her Web domain revealed the same splash page that had been there for nearly a year. At lunch Paula expressed that she was discouraged and disappointed that after almost eighteen months she wasn't farther along. We quickly dispensed two pieces of advice.

First, get out there! There was no need for her to participate in any more training or do any further preparation. It is one thing to use a training to fill a critical skill gap, but it's nonsense to think you would ever be fully prepared for entrepreneurship. There is just no way you can know everything you need to in advance. Part of the experience is adjusting your business to what you learn along the way. And hands down the most valuable feedback you will obtain is from your customers themselves.

Second, stop being a perfectionist! Web sites are a classic place where entrepreneurs' perfectionist tendencies can wreak havoc. We constantly see entrepreneurs agonize over small text changes and particular phrasing. They write and revise many times, often adding more and more unnecessary information on each pass-through. The thing is that Web sites, like many other aspects of your business, are simply part of a conversation that you are having with your customers. That means they will evolve alongside your business and be edited and changed based on what you learn from your experience. Entrepreneurs who wait too long perfecting details are effectively sidelining themselves and missing out on this important conversation. And in Paula's specific case, it was perfectly fine to launch her site with photos of only three client projects. It was unnecessary to wait for all ten projects that she ultimately wanted to have.

BUSINESS SPOTLIGHT

"Out of just listening to our brides and what their needs were, our business evolved."

Becoming an industry leader one step at a time
Claudia Hanlin, owner of Claudia Hanlin's Wedding Library

Like many brides-to-be, Claudia Hanlin found the wedding planning process incredibly taxing. Finding inspiration was easy; it was finding vendors that were reliable, reputable, and well qualified that was overwhelming. This was in 1995 and the best resources available were wedding magazines, which provided little information about specific resources you could use for your big day. Online resources and directories such as TheKnot.com didn't yet exist, but even if they had they wouldn't have necessarily helped to sift worthwhile vendors out of the cluttered marketplace. As a management consultant, trained to focus on effectiveness, Claudia was shocked that there really wasn't a better way for brides to find the services they needed. She yearned for a place where she could go and learn about vendors suitable for her tastes and price range and even thumb through portfolios of their work.

Her wedding came and went and Claudia continued to watch the market. She was sure that something like what she imagined would emerge. Five years later, with no new alternative in sight, she decided to start the business herself. She did tons of research and talked to everyone who was willing to listen. After receiving lots of validation, she took the plunge and found a home for the Wedding Library on the Upper East Side. The goal was to serve as a central repository where New York brides could learn about well-vetted, high-quality vendors for their special day. Claudia knew what a blessing this kind of curated resource could be for brides, but her research had also shown her that it was valuable for the small businesses and artists serving the bridal market as well. By managing a good part of the sale process, the Wedding Library helped these vendors stay focused on what they did best, be that making cakes, taking pictures, or designing stationery.

One of Claudia's first brides was Jennifer Zabinski. Being a creative and entrepreneurial person herself, Jennifer loved what Claudia was doing and immediately offered to join forces and further the mission. Claudia hadn't been looking for a partner, but really enjoyed working with Jennifer and welcomed the infusion of energy and ambition. That was more than eleven years ago. Since then the pair has grown the Wedding Library to offer a full suite of services, establishing it as a clear industry leader not just within the city but across the nation.

Today the influence and prominence of the Wedding Library in the industry is undisputed, but in the beginning Claudia and Jennifer weren't clear about what their specific winning strategy would be. In fact, after they joined forces, Claudia assumed that once they reached critical mass in New York, they would expand to other cities, setting up multiple Wedding Libraries across the country. However, when the time for expansion came they opted instead to grow their footprint within New York rather than head elsewhere. Part of what motivated Claudia to start her business in the first place was the opportunity to be creative. At a certain point it became clear that while replicating a pool of vendors in other cities would certainly take a lot of time, work, and capital, it didn't necessarily provide her the creative outlet she desired. On the other hand, the more they worked with their brides, the more needs they found they could meet within their existing market. And expanding the business to offer these new services certainly provided the opportunity for them to flex their creative muscles. The truth is that by taking consistent small steps toward growth, they have been able to solidify a winning recipe that has not only made the business successful but has also made it work for them.

Their first step was to add an actual retail component. The Wedding Library had become home to many wedding-related products such as stationery, gifts, and bridesmaid dresses. Claudia just found it easier to have the real thing on hand when talking with brides about their options. Within the first year she started wondering if she shouldn't just sell the showcased items as well as educate about them. They started with stationery, and when that was well received they moved on to other items such as bridal accessories, gifts, and bridesmaid dresses. Currently the Wedding Library boasts both the largest wedding stationery department and bridesmaid dress collection in New York City. Most recently, Claudia has decided to enable others outside the New York area to access their goods by creating an e-commerce component on their site.

The second step was adding the actual wedding planning services. After hours of consultation and advisement with Jennifer and Claudia about resources and vendors, the brides routinely asked if the ladies couldn't just manage the planning process themselves. After all, they knew all the details, had all the relationships, and helped to craft the vision. Besides, many of these brides couldn't imagine working with them so closely and not having them there on their big day. So Claudia added a planning component to their menu of services. They currently offer everything from full planning to associates who manage just the day-of details. Shortly after offering the service, the Wedding Library became the largest wedding planning company in the city, planning more than forty nuptials a year.

Later, after saying each year that she would do it, Claudia arranged a Wedding Library–style bridal expo. Typically brides attend traditional bridal expos only to be overwhelmed by thousands of vendors and leave with nothing more than a foot-high stack of brochures and business cards. Instead, Claudia set up an event that was not only well curated but allowed for a real exchange of information between vendor and bride. The event has been such a hit that Claudia has put the wheels in motion to license the concept in other cities and in conjunction with other high-end brands as well.

In the last decade, the Wedding Library has become an undisputed success. Their creative expansion has enabled them to establish their business as an industry leader in several niche markets. Despite their current standing, the ladies say that they still have a lot more they want to accomplish and they see lots of growth options to choose from. Recently Claudia has been styling weddings for various hotel properties, which has really enabled them to put their own stamp on the whole process. In this creative endeavor, Claudia is able to make every decision and bring her own vision to life, quite a different experience from facilitating someone else's ideas. This has opened the door to having more Wedding Library–styled events for properties and individuals.

Also, given her own finely tuned sense of style and built-in marketing channel, they could venture into creating dedicated products as well. And of course, now that Claudia has really perfected the craft and demonstrated how effective the vendor resource/planning/product trifecta can be, she is perfectly poised to expand to other cities if she so chooses.

6

Perfection Is a Trap

Embrace Experimentation

It's really all about dipping your toe into things. I've dipped my toe into a million things. Some worked, some were exceptional, and some I couldn't wait to get out of.
—CHLOÉ JO DAVIS, FOUNDER OF GIRLIE GIRL ARMY

The Problem: Aiming for Perfection

When you embark on the journey to create your own company, you naturally want to make it as good as it can be. You toil over details and obsess over every decision. To a certain extent, this sort of perfectionism is necessary, especially when it comes to getting the big picture just right. But when you apply this mentality to every task and every choice, it can get in the way of your goals. Fooling yourself into thinking there is such a thing as a finished product inevitably just leaves you stalled, subtly tweaking a never-ending project.

Not only does this impair your ability to get things done, but it often causes you to reject much-needed help. Thinking that since you're the business owner, you should know best, you reject useful advice and feedback from people who know better—friends, colleagues, experts, and customers—in an effort to appear like you're in charge. When you do this, you inevitably:

- Become disappointed with the result
- Feel pressured and powerless
- Isolate yourself from the people whose opinions matter most—your customers
- Distance yourself from the lessons learned by your peers
- Underutilize your most important tool: experimentation!

The quest for perfection undermines your chances of success and satisfaction, and most important, it takes the fun out of building the business!

The Solution: Embracing Experimentation

Given the stereotype of entrepreneurs, it may seem ironic that we have to encourage experimentation and urge our clients to just give things a try. What's emphasized and even glorified about entrepreneurship are the stories of risk, luck, chance, and circumstance that make the endeavor seem like a Wild West fit for only the most daring adventure seekers. To be sure, there is a healthy dose of all of those elements in the experience. Most entrepreneurs take significant leaps of faith, and this type of risk requires a strong stomach, thick skin, and good deal of self-confidence, but that doesn't mean most entrepreneurs revel in the unknown.

In fact, more often than not our clients come to us hemming and hawing over an idea, needing both a kick in the pants and permission to "just give it a try." For some clients that is all the push they need. Others are still resistant. They fret about failure. What if it doesn't work? They bemoan the fact that they *just* had things figured out, or at least they thought they did. Do they really want to upset the applecart again? They retreat to false confidence. Maybe things are just peachy the way they are!

We remind them that their business is always going to be a work in progress. Most important, we reiterate that the only way to know what you don't know is through experimentation! Experimenting helps you reveal the unknown, fill in the blanks, and open up unseen possibilities.

Experimentation is a useful and effective way to:

- Discover a different direction for the business
- Test new service or product ideas
- Find untapped revenue opportunities
- Clarify existing business problems
- Revitalize a stagnating offering
- Glean valuable insights and data
- Solicit important feedback

Now, just because you take the leap of faith doesn't mean it will work. Your experiment may be an unprecedented success or it may be a total flop. The goal of an experiment is not necessarily that it work but that you learn something helpful you didn't know before.

Before you get carried away, let's take a moment to recognize the value of careful experimentation. The last thing we want you to do is bet the farm or scrap the whole business. After all, your business is a work in progress, *not* a guinea pig.

Experimentation isn't about being half-baked or haphazard. So if you're cringing at the thought of carelessly tossing ideas into the marketplace, well, you should be. Even when you're trying something new it's still important to be deliberate. Just because the outcome is unpredictable doesn't mean your efforts, questions, and experiments can't be thought out and intentional.

Someone who really understands the value of thoughtful experimentation is Emily Powell, president of Powell's Books, who shared with us the experimentation philosophy she learned growing up in the Powell's culture. She says the staff at Powell's "fires bullets, not cannons." They try "lots of little things, none of which will sink the ship but will tell you if you've hit something." Taking small risks allows you to consistently recalibrate and get feedback without putting too much at risk.

Steps to a Successful Experiment

1. **Start with your questions**. What are you unsure of? Want to know more about? What's been giving you trouble? Maybe you want to better understand a dip in sales. Maybe you'd like to clarify the value that your clients get from your services. Maybe you're curious as to why your customers have chosen you over other alternatives.

2. **Identify your desired outcome.** What is it that you're hoping for? Remember, we're not talking about specific answers here. We're talking about kinds of information. Do you want to know what your customers think of a new product? Do you want to see how viable your business is in a new market? It's important that you don't go into an experiment wedded to one answer or outcome, as you will inevitably miss important data.

3. **Think of ways to find answers**. Perhaps a promotion will tell you if a new offering is interesting or if the price of an existing product needs adjustment. Maybe a pilot client will help you figure out if you want your business to branch out in a new direction. Maybe a survey will tell you what your customers know that you don't. Maybe reconsidering customers' commonly asked questions will reveal overlooked additional revenue potential.

4. **Consider the cost of trying**. What do you have to lose? Literally. What are you risking by doing this experiment? Brand equity? Customer experience? Manpower? Money? And most important, is it worth it?

5. **Consider the cost of not trying**. What do you risk by *not* trying the experiment? Are you in jeopardy of stagnating or launching an unverified offering? Is there any element of first-mover advantage?

6. **Reflect on the experience of your experiment.** Just because it didn't sink the ship doesn't mean it's worth repeating. Consider to what extent you enjoyed the work. Was the business comfortable accommodating that experiment? Did it cause any unforeseen conflicts of interest? Were there any unexpected benefits?

Aside from implementing a good plan, there are several other strategies you can employ to craft a good experiment:

- **Enlist others.** If you're unsure about a particular experiment or direction, see if you can enlist well-informed others, such as an advisory board, to help make decisions and point out things you might not be considering.
- **Be transparent.** If your experiment is going to involve your customers, we encourage you to be transparent. Their trust is critical! Better that they know something is a trial offering than be disappointed by unsatisfactory performance or speculate about curious promotions. Remember, they too want your product or service to be the best it can be.
- **Make it low-risk.** Can you offer a refund or satisfaction guaranteed? Or perhaps use a social media platform to float a question or survey? Make sure your experiment is free to fail; you'll be more open to feedback and a lot less wedded to a particular outcome.
- **Look for validation.** Instead of trying everything you think of, establish experiment litmus tests. Perhaps a certain number of customer requests or answers on a survey can let you know if something is really worth investigating more.
- **Look for inspiration.** Companies you know and admire experiment all the time. Look to the pros for tips and ideas. Think about any time you've purchased a limited-edition flavor or an article of clothing. What about designers who create small collections for other brands? Or that last pop-up shop that you went to? Think about how you

could incorporate some of the same techniques into your experiments.

Our conversations with entrepreneurs have provided countless examples of experiments that worked surprisingly well, as well as those that have crashed and burned, providing important lessons in the process. Some experiments even helped entrepreneurs transform the overall direction of their businesses. We share them in the hope that they give you the courage to try.

A New Start . . .

For many entrepreneurs, it was a random but successful experiment that actually became the seed for their entire business.

For example, Maribel Lieberman already owned a catering company before she started MarieBelle Chocolate. But always having had a passion for chocolate and craving a new creative outlet, she decided in the winter of 2001 to set up a hot chocolate stand in SoHo, taking advantage of the lowered post-9/11 rents. To her surprise and delight, people loved it. She sold $2,000 worth of hot chocolate in the first five hours. Within a few months she built a steady and loyal customer base. She kept extending her sublease, strengthening her presence, and expanding her offerings. Today, MarieBelle Chocolate still occupies the same location with both a retail shop and a café. This small, low-risk experiment paid off in a big way.

Similarly, Michelle Adams, cofounder of *Lonny* magazine, was running her first business, Rubie Green, an eco-friendly textile company, when she and a partner challenged themselves with an experiment. Both magazine veterans, they had witnessed their industry descend into turmoil with the shuttering of magazines like *Domino* and *Blueprint*. Craving their shelter mag fix, they wondered if by using an online format they could shave all the extraordinary costs of publication but still deliver the content. Could they create a beautiful and high-quality magazine that lived only online? At worst, Michelle thought it would be a great interview anecdote should she decide to apply for another print job. They put their noses to the grindstone, produced a 195-page spread, and named it *Lonny*. They were amazed by the response. Readers clamored for more and loved that the online format allowed for direct links to the featured items and resources. Advertisers began to line up, proving that the format could be not only beautiful and functional but also profitable. Within a few issues, *Lonny* had set a new standard within the publishing industry.

A Surprising Success

To some extent, everything you do in your business is an experiment, but some experiments are truly tests of curiosity, taken without any great hope for the outcome. They are interventions you make while saying, "I wonder what would happen if . . ." Surprisingly, these happy accidents can end up having a significantly positive impact on the business.

For Andrea Miller, CEO of Tango Media, one runaway success immediately comes to mind. Once she moved her print publication to its new online home, Andrea was thinking up various ways to leverage the digital platform to generate conversation and community. After first trying an online forum, which didn't work well, she landed on success with the "Ask Your Tango" feature. This section allows users to submit questions that can be answered by others within the community, which helped to generate the conversational aspect they were looking for. Users were eager to submit their relationship questions and get advice from others. And as a bonus, advertisers love it too!

It was actually an employee who brought Amy Voloshin, owner of textile design studio Printfresh, a winning idea. Printfresh primarily sells textile design patterns to a variety of clients ranging from Michael Kors to Billabong to J.Crew, primarily in women's and children's wear. A couple of years ago a salesperson who had worked her way up in the ranks asked Amy if she'd consider producing graphic T-shirts. Amy took some time to debate it; after all, it really wasn't what they were known for. After some reflection, she decided to give it a try, and now these T-shirts make up about half of Print-fresh's total business.

A Different Direction . . .

The results of an experiment are sometimes so profound that they serve as the start of something new. We've worked and spoken with a lot of entrepreneurs whose experiments went beyond success and ended up transforming the future direction of the business.

Jen Hill, graphic designer and owner of JHill Design, loves to travel and learn about new places. One year she decided to create a desk calendar as a gift for her clients. Eager to create an opportunity to marry all her interests, Jen made the calendar about places she had never been. Each month would correspond to a different city. After researching the location, she would create a custom design that represented the city's special features. Her clients went nuts for it, and more important, Jen loved creating it. It was fun doing the research, and the pattern-making was a joy. It all got her to wondering whether other people might be interested in it too. Until this point, her business was entirely made up of custom design work for independent clients. This would certainly be a whole other kind of business. Since the calendar-buying time had come and gone, she made the designs into stand-alone prints and produced a new calendar for sale the following fall. The overall impact of these experiments has been astounding. Today, the *Places I Have Never Been* print series and calendars make up 70 percent of Jen's revenue, with the remaining 30 percent coming from ongoing custom design clients. The series is hands down what Jen is best known for and certainly what she enjoys doing most. This shift in her business has not only enabled her to pick and choose her design clients, taking on only the most interesting and creative products, but has also given her the freedom to travel extensively to all the places she has never been.

In 2003 an experiment proved to be a defining moment for

Cyndee Sugra and her company Studio 7 Media. For its first year and a half, Studio 7 was known as a Web design company. However, Cyndee wanted to push the envelope. She really wanted her business to be known for developing innovative products and charting new territory. She experimented with their ability to branch out by accepting a software development project. It was this experiment that forever changed the company's direction and reputation. Cyndee says this project was a crazy learning experience. Her staff was worked to the bone, Cyndee herself ended up in the hospital from exhaustion, and by her standards today she certainly would have proclaimed the final product to be a failure. But they got the job done well and in doing so created a brand-new software product/technology. Her experience, as exhausting as it was, only whetted her appetite for more challenging work and similarly difficult projects. This would mark the beginning of Studio 7's transition from a Web development company to a software development company and the start of its reputation as a company that develops excellent products.

FAILURE ONLY COUNTS IF YOU TRY?

Sometimes when we are really afraid of failing, we tell ourselves that the failure doesn't count if the trying isn't real. This ridiculous psychological twist leads us to further undermine our own efforts, all but ensuring failure. We see this self-sabotaging behavior especially in an entrepreneur's early days when fledgling business owners are quick to explain that they are not a "real" entrepreneur or say they are "sort of" in business for themselves. These ambivalent business owners dangle in entrepreneurial purgatory, waiting until it is safe enough to confess that they are doing something bold! Even if you're not 100 percent committed to your new venture or a particular direction, you gain nothing by undermining your own efforts to try.

After two years of being in business, Angie Davis was finally able to recognize that she is not "just a maker but a maker who is in business." "I used to be really uncomfortable even calling my business a business, but that's really not the case anymore," she said. "I think part of that was to 'keep it casual' and not commit to this being a real thing because if it's real, it can fail."

So own your actions, open yourself to learning, and be willing to fail if necessary!

An Informative Failure

Of course, not every experiment goes well. Some experiments fizzle, others go down in flames, but all yield valuable lessons. Here's a look at how some not-so-hot experiments actually provided some important business insights.

Creating stationery seemed like a natural business extension for Joy Cho, founder of Oh Joy!, who was originally trained as a graphic designer. About two years into her business, Joy decided to try it. She designed and manufactured her own line and was thrilled at the response. She received some terrific press and was picked up in several reputable stores. Unfortunately, the quick momentum also caused a significant shift in the business, which wasn't necessarily a welcome one. Joy realized that a product-based business required a whole different set of business activities, such as production, shipping, and wholesaling. Designing was by far the smallest part of the process, and these other activities required an extraordinary amount of time. What's more, the stationery line also encroached on her design work for clients and running other more fruitful parts of the business. After two years of producing the line on her own, Joy knew that in order to make the stationery efforts worthwhile, she would need to produce on a much larger level or change the way the production was handled. Knowing that more production volume would just pull her further away from the work she loved most, Joy decided that licensing was a better direction for her to go in. With licensing arrangements, she can focus her energy on designing and leave the manufacturing and sales to someone else! She has created card designs for Wedding Paper Divas and Tiny Prints as well as product designs for a whole host of companies including

Anthropologie, Urban Outfitters, Hygge & West, and Chronicle Books.

Jennie Nevin started Green Spaces as a place where sustainably minded green businesses and social enterprises could support each other and work together. At some point it dawned on her that, space being the premium it is, there might be an opportunity for a pop-up retail market alongside the workspace. Green Spaces could leverage the same square feet to feature and sell various members' green products in addition to providing office space. Given that an interest in green goods and a green lifestyle is a common dominator for those at Green Spaces, it seemed like a perfect marketing opportunity. In reality, Jennie discovered that there just wasn't enough money to justify the extraordinary amount of work it took. So before long they abandoned the effort in order to focus on alternative expansion strategies, such as additional programming and another location in Colorado.

We also have deliberately tried things that have failed spectacularly. One failure in particular was our Ning network. Most of our members are probably asking themselves, "What Ning network?"—which is not surprising since after investing much time and effort the dang thing wasn't even launched. Here's what happened.

We have struggled for years over determining the right balance of online versus in-person activity, the best way to connect our members virtually, and the appropriate type and amount of social media presence. We know there is a huge market for online communities, but we also know the business model is tricky and online communities can be quite expensive, gobbling up inordinate amounts of both time and money. We are also always very aware that part of our unique value proposition is our community focus on connecting people the old-fashioned way . . . in person. This fact has made the right online implementation a bit elusive. Further, we individually suffer from being a social media amateur (Adelaide) and a social-media phobe (Amy). Needless to say, we are far from being the tech-savvy talent behind most good sites.

After at least eighteen months of puzzling and researching and abandoning and reinvigorating the question, we decided to leverage an existing technology instead of building something proprietary. We had heard terrific things about the Ning platform and were also big fans of the founder and the business model. We determined we could run an extended and very low-cost test by setting up an online community through Ning. This experiment would allow us to play around with functionality and features, gauge interest and usage, and determine the overall benefit to our business. We decided to invest the time and energy to get it set up and then let it run for four months before sitting down to evaluate it.

Good plan, huh? Well . . . not so much.

We did invest (a lot of) time and energy to develop it and set it up, and then we stalled. Why? Well, we weren't excited about it. We knew it was going to take a tremendous amount of energy to get the community to log into another place and use it. And more than anything, since neither of us regularly used any online communities besides Facebook, we found it really hard to get involved in a technology that we weren't accustomed to using ourselves.

Needless to say, when we look back on the experiment, we are thrilled that we chose to start with Ning first, rather than invest any funds in creating something new. Our uncertainty about creating a more robust online community also solidified our interest in our in-person programming, which we immediately beefed up.

Troubleshooting:
When You Get in Your Own Way

We know more than a few entrepreneurs who have run into trouble because they held their cards too close to their chests and were overly committed to their "perfect" solution or idea. In many cases the businesses could have been saved if the owners had used experimentation as a way to gather valuable information and feedback. So you don't end up in the same situation, here are two cautionary tales, each of which addresses a particular perfection struggle.

Overly Committed to a Mediocre Offering?
Don't Throw Good Time After Bad

Nothing feels worse than backtracking. Undoing work is frustrating and discouraging. But it's not as bad as pursuing a path that's sure to fail. Unfortunately, even when the writing's on the wall, it's tempting to think that if we can just push through a little bit more, then just maybe it will turn out the way we want. We close our eyes and ears and pretend that what we're experiencing is just naysaying instead of valuable insight and feedback. The more we bury our heads, the harder it is for us to be objective about the future and willing to do what needs to be done.

The Case of Headstrong Haley

Haley had an idea for a different kind of brush that made styling hair easier and more comfortable. She believed that both professional stylists and regular women like her would appreciate the design and functionality of her improved brush. Because her creation was a product with special features, she immediately connected with a lawyer and began the patent process, which is both time-consuming and expensive. While she was waiting for the patent to be official, she set up a manufacturing relationship, sourced the materials, and began perfecting the design. All the while she was telling her friends and colleagues about this great brush with unique features. We met Haley during this time, and though we kept hearing about this amazing brush we never were told what the extraordinary features were, nor did we see a picture or prototype. We were happy for Haley, but it was hard to be excited about a product that we knew nothing about.

A few months later, Haley asked us to have a conversation with her about marketing her product. Her first batch of brushes had come in and she was eager to get them sold. It seemed like a straightforward problem and we were happy to brainstorm ways to connect with both individual customers and professional stylists. A few minutes into the meeting, however, it was clear that Haley had a bigger problem on her hands. She hadn't gotten much validation on the product's design. All this time she had been talking about features that very few people had weighed in on. We knew that the issue at hand was much bigger than marketing.

We asked Haley to take a few steps back with us and start from the beginning. What were the unique features and how did she know that the marketplace cared about them? According to Haley the handle was more comfortable and the brush itself was more aesthetically pleasing, plus it was made of eco-friendly materials. Haley explained that she came up with the idea based on her own experience and frustrations but that she really hadn't sought too many other people's opinions. At first she had worried about people stealing her ideas. Now that her patent was almost official, she worried about knockoffs.

Unfortunately, it was clear that other potential customers might not feel the brush was compelling enough. When Haley, now with product in hand, showed people the brush, they all had a positive reaction but for the most part didn't make a purchase. Haley worried that maybe her price was too high since she had positioned the brush as a premium product. We asked her to clarify for us what problems her design solved. Compared with other brushes, Haley believed that hers was more comfortable, attractive, and environmentally friendly. We suggested that while the brush was certainly a nice product, maybe it wasn't really a solution that people were looking for. We asked Haley if she would consider holding some focus groups so people could weigh in on both the brush that she had designed and what they found to be problematic about their current products. It seemed important that the brush really speak to existing pains, especially since Haley had counted on professional training schools and salons to be the primary sales channels. In our minds, if the brush was going to be a standout product in these places then the technical merits and benefits had better be sound *and* solve problems that professionals experience.

Haley was disappointed and resistant. She had already designed the brush; she just wanted to know how to sell it! Through our conversation we explained that if you wanted people to pay a lot more for special features they had to be features people really felt made a difference. Haley could certainly sell the brush she had as a nice alternative to existing products, but in order to do that the price had to be comparable. While we did share the marketing suggestions we had, we also encouraged Haley to be open to learning and reapproaching the problem as an experiment, which is what we wished she would have done in the first place. If she held focus groups to get feedback on her existing version, they might validate the product or they might point out some areas for improvement. In either case she'd be armed with more information.

We also cautioned Haley about letting her investment to date dictate the fate of her company. It was true that she had already submitted the patents and developed one batch of the product, but if the product wasn't viable there was no business to be had. Better to be open to feedback and tweaking than to be wedded to something that wasn't going to work.

Confusing Encouragement with Need?
Get a Broader Base of Feedback

For the most part when people are thinking of doing something new they are given positive encouragement by those around them. Of course there are always naysayers, but by and large people respond with "That's great" or "How interesting." But it's important to remember that just because people are intrigued by what you are doing doesn't mean they are going to line up and be customers themselves. We often witness some disappointment from early entrepreneurs related to this false expectation. Our clients will say things like, "Everyone said what a great idea this was and how many people they knew who needed it, yet none of them have signed up!" Get used to it, we reply!

There are two things at play here. First, you can't rely on those you know to be your customer base. Second and more important, sometimes what people say they want is different from what they actually want or will do. They are not trying to be misleading or deceitful. It's just that when things are in the idea phase, people aren't really asking themselves the same questions that they will when considering a purchase. Sentiments such as "It'd be great if you were a massage therapist" become "I really don't want this person who I know professionally to be massaging me." Theory is very different from practice.

The Case of Take-You-at-Your-Word Tiffany

Tiffany, a former client, was a yoga instructor with a background in social work. She had very close relationships with her clients and often offered them advice alongside their yoga routine. One of her longtime clients was turning forty and had had a particularly difficult year. As a gift, Tiffany got a T-shirt printed with one of the inspirational phrases she was always saying. The client was touched by the gesture and remarked that the T-shirt was a great way for her to keep Tiffany's words of wisdom close at hand in between sessions. Tiffany wondered if more people would want T-shirts like this. In an instant, a future business flashed in front of her eyes, one that was product-based and didn't rely on the same hourly billing model that her yoga practice did. She excitedly sent an e-mail to her clients asking for their feedback. With each positive reply, Tiffany inched closer to taking action. By the end of the week, she had contacted a graphic designer and a printer who could make the shirts. Within several weeks she had a first run of one hundred T-shirts in her apartment.

She excitedly sent out another e-mail to her clients announcing the news and sending them a link to purchase. Then she waited, and waited, and waited. A few weeks later, no one had bought a shirt. Frustrated, Tiffany widened her circle. She sent e-mails to her larger contact base and posted links to the shirts on Facebook. She also signed up for a small craft market for the following weekend. Although she sold only five shirts at the market, it proved to be an incredibly valuable exercise for her. Face-to-face with customers who weren't her yoga clients, she was inundated with feedback. They did like the T-shirts and the design. But some didn't understand the sayings; others wondered why the quote was attributed to her on the shirt. They told Tiffany that if they didn't know who she was, they weren't comfortable wearing her name on their back.

At first she was disappointed and felt she had failed. Maybe she should just give away the shirts as a gift to her clients and call it a day. She wished she had gotten feedback from people she didn't know in the first place. She felt foolish for having thought her clients would each buy multiple shirts themselves. She was pretty sure she wouldn't do that if she was in their shoes!

After thinking about it for a couple of weeks, though, Tiffany decided to take the feedback seriously. She decided not to be overly invested in her initial idea but to be open to a little failure and experimentation. First, she eliminated the saying that caused the greatest confusion and redesigned the shirts without her name. They never ended up being a hot item among her clients, but Tiffany did continue selling shirts on the side in a few local boutiques and online. Eventually she found it hard to nurture the business and give it the time it needed while still managing her thriving practice. When push came to shove she decided the T-shirt business wasn't what she wanted to be known for. However, she was able to leverage what she had built by selling her existing designs and accounts to someone who made yoga accessories. What the experience really provided Tiffany was a lesson in the importance of soliciting the right feedback early on and not just looking for a confirmation of what you want to hear. She also learned that you can't tie your whole experience to the actions of those you know. The most valuable opinions often come from outside your family or friends.

BUSINESS SPOTLIGHT

"Like every other great idea, we fell into it. It turned out to be the missing link in our business model to actually be both sustainable and scalable."

A pioneer uses experimentation to work out the kinks in her big idea
Rebecca Kousky, Nest

Rebecca always knew her professional life was going to be about helping people. However, when she graduated from her social work program she had a fair amount of trepidation about her industry-to-be. As important as social work is, it isn't a creative profession, and the job itself can often be repetitive, as the workers shuffle through a new pile of cases each day. After some serious thinking and reflection, she decided the only way she would feel truly fulfilled was if she started something of her own.

Once Rebecca made up her mind, coming up with the focus and mission of the actual business was easy. She had always been passionate about design, women, and economic development abroad. She had also been reading a lot about Mohammad Yunus and microlending. While she was in love with the concept of cyclical, self-sustaining lending as a way to help people establish themselves as entrepreneurs and bring them out of poverty, she also saw some room for improvement. From her perspective, the only downside of microlending was the high interest rate attached to the loan. Yes, the interest rate was what sustained the lending organization and accounted for the risky nature of the loan. Nevertheless, it instilled a lot of fear in the very people it was intended to help.

Inspired to remove this fear from the equation, Rebecca pioneered a new process she termed microbartering. Instead of tacking on interest and asking the recipients to repay their loans in cash, the new microbartering arrangement allowed the women to repay their loans in product, which Nest would then help to market and sell to Western consumers. Not only did this eliminate the interest rate, but it gave Nest a way to make money to fund more loans and be self-sustaining.

As an added bonus, if Nest placed orders that were bigger than what was required to repay the loan, the loan recipients would have ongoing access to Western markets and added income. Excited, Rebecca spent the next several months going through her cell phone contacts, calling everyone she knew and seeing what advice they had or how they could help. She gathered momentum quickly, and before long, social work was already a distant memory.

However, as with every new idea (and business for that matter), there are bound to be some hiccups. And one of the liabilities in creating a new way to do things is running into new, unforeseen, and unanticipated challenges. Ever the innovator, however, Rebecca spent the first three years in business harnessing the power of experimentation to find creative solutions to the difficulties she encountered.

Soon after launching, Rebecca started to receive products from her loan recipients as repayment. She was surprised to learn, though, that many of the goods, while beautiful and well made, were difficult to sell in the U.S. marketplace, which had totally different quality control and retailing standards. Even more surprising was just how difficult it was to explain the reality of a large retail environment, the concept of merchandising, and the standard procedures that stores used, such as SKUs. When Rebecca realized how pervasive this need for education was, she quickly created and deployed a training program for each of her loan recipients that focused on business and financial skills, covering topics from product development to exporting to greening your business. The training encompassed essentially everything one needs in order to start an art- or craft-based business. As a result, the Nest loan recipients were empowered with a tremendous amount of knowledge and Nest was provided with products that sell well in lots of markets.

Aside from helping get the products to the right market, Rebecca didn't realize how laborious and difficult it would be to find the right sales channels within the United States. Originally she thought Nest would be a wholesaler and she looked for appropriate boutiques to feature the Nest goods. This proved to be more difficult than she thought. Aside from standard wholesale challenges such as managing store owners, waiting for payments, and worrying about how the product was being featured, Rebecca was concerned about the margins on the goods and adding another layer of sale between the women and the marketplace. So she quickly decided to shift gears and become a retailer instead.

Of course Rebecca knew this decision would shift the focus and responsibility of the business substantially. In order to create retail opportunities, she planned to host lots of trunk shows featuring the artisans' products as well as set up an e-commerce site. She knew she needed dedicated supporters and ambassadors across the country to set up a robust sales network. Plenty of people were inspired by the mission and had written her with offers to volunteer and get involved. On a whim, Rebecca decided to start local advisory boards in a few cities across the nation. Her hope was that she could get volunteers to help set up and sponsor events as well as spread the word to their contacts and friends. She started in New York and Washington, D.C., both cities where a lot of people had expressed interest. Today Nest has a total of twelve city boards across the country, involving more than two hundred women. These boards not only serve as cheerleaders for Nest, but they fund-raise and host trunk shows as well. Each event not only functions as a retail sales channel but drives grassroots awareness and support for the organization as a whole.

Once Rebecca got the bones of the business established and working well, she turned her eye to the future. With so much need and interest, she wanted to be able to fund as many people as possible. But it was clear to her that her current model couldn't support that. Nest's ability to give loans was fundamentally limited by its ability to sell product. She knew she'd have to find another way to reach more people, as she didn't want to commit the majority of her organization's time, now or in the future, to retailing. Luckily, a serendipitous meeting with Lauren Bush, founder of FEED Projects, provided the seed for a great solution. FEED Projects is an organization that designs and sells products whose sale funds donations to antihunger efforts worldwide. After talking with Rebecca, Lauren had an idea. What if they leveraged the artisan communities that Rebecca was tapped into to create some dedicated products that would help to fund hunger initiatives in the women's own countries? By establishing a sourcing arrangement Nest would be able to provide sustainable and potentially long-term income opportunities while of course cultivating and preserving the women's artistic traditions. And by partnering with organizations like FEED, it would benefit from having an automatic sales and distribution channel built in. Nest would be responsible only for the sourcing and production, not the retail component. What a win-win! Rebecca decided to experiment with an initial order, fulfilling fifty thousand specifically designed FEED bags. It was a huge success! Quickly Rebecca set up other product partners and established seven other sourcing collaboratives around the world. This additional service has diversified and solidified Nest as an organization, making it possible to engage more women with more certainty. As Rebecca said, "It turned out to be the missing link in our business model to actually be both sustainable and scalable."

7

Enough Is Enough

Learn to Say No

When you can say no, that's when you know you're in business.

—PATRICIA HELDING, PRESIDENT OF
FAT WITCH BAKING COMPANY

The Problem: Unable to Draw the Line

Saying no may be one of the hardest things for entrepreneurs to learn. But setting limits is essential, not only for your sanity but also for your satisfaction and the health of your business.

Don't get us wrong, we believe in being generous. After all, we're entrepreneurs and giving is just a part of our ethos. Our own scrappy roots and pleas for help are still fresh in our minds and we feel a sense of duty to pay it forward on behalf of all those who helped us. We have also learned that, in general, the more you put out there, the more you get back. But still, there needs to be a limit.

Sometimes our good intentions—like a desire to be helpful—get in the way of saying no. Other times we are simply scared to turn away any potential business, no matter how unsatisfactory it may be. A holdover from our start-up days tricks us into thinking that any business is better than no business. But we soon end up overburdened and overcompromised in situations that are complicated and unfruitful. When we say yes for the wrong reasons, we waste our time, give away valuable information, and leave money on the table. And the kicker is that most of the time we already know that saying yes is a bad idea, but we do it anyway.

Have you ever:

- Accepted a client who you don't like or with whom you've already had a bad experience?
- Agreed to a meeting that you know will yield little value?
- Answered too many of a potential competitor's questions?
- Accommodated a request to speak at an event that will have little return?
- Added another major project to your already full plate because it seemed like something you should do?

Every time we say yes when we should say no we become determined not to make the same mistake again. We swear off everything but the essentials, roll up our sleeves, and refocus on work. But then the requests return. Flattered, guilty, or obligated, we relent again. All the while proclaiming, "Why?" The fact is, you really can't avoid these situations. There will always be time-sucking favors, pushy clients, intriguing but distracting opportunities, and networking coffees galore. But just because you're asked doesn't mean you have to accept. After all, as chief it is your job to marshal your resources, determining what is truly worth your time. It is your job to understand the costs of not being able to say no.

Remember, each coffee, favor, or phone call takes time away from the other things you want to be doing. And that time really adds up. Each difficult or underpaying client prevents you from taking on better work that is rewarding and adds value to your business. Each divergent opportunity detracts valuable resources from the projects that will really move your business forward.

By saying no you are able to say yes to the things that really deserve your time and attention. By saying no you are able to be available for the right opportunities when they come along. By saying no you are able to preserve the clients and parts of your business you enjoy the most. Saying no isn't just something you should do; it's something you should enjoy and be comfortable doing!

Sometimes that is easier said than done, however. One of the biggest reasons we have a hard time saying no is that we don't know the right way to go about it. No one wants to appear rude, ungenerous, or arrogant. Are we really such hot shots that we can't take five minutes to (fill in the blank)? While every situation is different, remembering these three universal techniques can make for a more successful and comfortable no.

1. **Know your soft spots.** We each have our own weaknesses. Some can't turn down clients, while others are forever fulfilling tiny personal favors. Identify in advance where you usually cave and pay extra attention to your boundaries in those scenarios.

2. **Set limits ahead of time.** It's much easier to adhere to an existing rule than to respond to each particular and nuanced request. Establish business-savvy guidelines in advance so that decisions feel less personal.

3. **Offer alternatives on your terms.** Remember, it's not always an all-or-nothing situation. Sometimes it's about saying no to what's being asked and offering an alternative that is acceptable to you. Reframe requests in terms that honor your needs too, but be prepared to let the situation go if your proposed alternative doesn't fly.

The Solution: Learning to Say No

We used to think the art of saying no was a skill that, once learned, could be universally applied to many different business situations. It turns out that's not the case. For whatever reason, some people have no problem saying no to a client but can't turn down a networking coffee. Whereas others would never give up a strategic opportunity but are able to decline charitable requests with ease. The way we see it, you need to be comfortable saying four kinds of no: no to clients, no to opportunities, no to favors, and no to goodwill.

Say No to Clients

There was probably a time when you couldn't imagine how turning down clients would be a significant business challenge. Starved for revenue and eager to build a testimonial bank, you were probably all but giving away your services. (Or maybe you were.) But now the shoe is on the other foot. You're established and have a track record. Your concern is not necessarily survival but getting to the next level. However, even now when people approach you and propose a less than ideal arrangement, it's still hard to say no. You know, deep down, that the client or situation will be difficult, but something feels funny about turning away business. It's a good problem to have, but it's a problem nonetheless.

Funny as it may feel, turning away a potential client can often be the right thing to do, particularly if the client:

- Wants something different from what you offer and is requesting irritating changes to the product or service
- Wants something you *can* deliver but isn't what you want your business to be known for
- Promises to refer you to others in exchange for free or reduced services for them
- Proposes a confusing or unbeneficial barter arrangement so they can get free service from you
- Can't afford you and wants you to reduce your fee but not your deliverables

Learning to say no and asserting limits in these situations is practically an entrepreneurial rite of passage. As such, we have dedicated a lot of programming at In Good Company to handling situations like this. Lots of terrific best practices have come out of these discussions, but unfortunately so have a lot of horror stories. As the saying goes, hindsight is 20/20. And when these nightmares are recounted, we often have to fight the urge to ask, "How the hell did you get into this mess?!" But we all must remember that bad situations often start with a small request that snowballs into something preposterous. Chances are that if you have a hard time saying no up front, you won't be that keen on doing it once a client engagement is under way. So it's the small and early questions you need to pay attention to.

The good news is that there are lots of tools at your disposal when it comes to saying no to client requests. Here are a few we want you to master:

- Trust your instincts
- Give away less for free
- Give what they pay for
- Say no, but what if?
- Say no, and here's why

1. Trust your instincts

Hands down the most valuable data you have at your disposal is your instincts. Like most people, we have said yes against our better internal judgment, only to regret it later. But when we think about our own horror stories and the times we should have said no, one situation in particular comes to mind. We ultimately did say no to this request, but what is astounding to us is just how much time and energy it took for us to do it. We should have known from the start that the proposal wasn't worth entertaining, yet we did.

In the summer of 2008 we were contacted by a woman who was starting a Web site for women professionals. This particular woman was a quite well-known TV personality, and she and her partner contacted us because they were looking for temporary office space in the city. We were flattered that they were considering In Good Company and were excited to meet them.

Our meeting was strange. It started with lots of questions about our actual business (the first red flag). They wanted to know how it ran, what the rent and square footage were, and how we were funded, among other things. We tentatively shared what we were comfortable sharing and tried to move the conversation back to the topic at hand—their need for office space. They then proposed that we form a relationship with their to-be company. Um, yeah, we thought, the kind of relationship where you rent space from us!? Apparently they had something else in mind. They offered that in exchange for space (second red flag) we could have a "relationship" with their company and "perhaps" some presence on their new site. We were very confused. Their site wasn't even developed and they couldn't be more specific about the kind of relationship they were proposing.

They also told us they didn't have the money to rent space for the remainder of the summer (third red flag). Taking space with us would have cost them between $300 and $800, given our prices at the time and the length of time they were interested in. We aren't saying that $800 is something to sneeze at, but this woman clearly had funds at her disposal. We continued to ask as many polite questions as we could to get more information, but it didn't get any more specific than that. Twice the woman said she didn't want to "give away the farm" (fourth red flag) but she'd be open to considering different solutions.

We should have been able to say no on the spot and point out how lopsided and quite frankly stupid their proposal was. Instead, after they left, we questioned ourselves. Confused, we actually consulted one of our advisers (subsequently wasting her time too) and walked her through the situation. Had we misunderstood something? Was there a terrific opportunity buried in this vague proposal that we weren't seeing? She encouraged us to get clear about what we would be interested in exchanging and offer that. So we did. It was generous but did require payment for space because in our experience straight barters are tricky. We also pushed them to define what their side of the bargain would entail and offered several specific options that would be satisfactory. We sent the e-mail and hoped they would say they weren't interested (fifth red flag). Our adviser had also wisely told us that if they declined our offer we should tell them to kiss off. Sadly, we never got the opportunity. Why? Because they never even bothered to reply to our e-mail. The nerve!

We ended up wasting several hours of our own time, as well as the time of our adviser, dealing with this nonsense. Of course, there was no major damage caused, which there most certainly would have been had we just said yes. But we learned a valuable lesson about being able to say no, even to someone famous. We should have listened to our gut and said no on the spot. Or if we wanted to avoid making our meeting more awkward we certainly could have followed up with a clear no instead of bothering to make an offer we hoped they'd refuse. We should have remembered that most of the time when something doesn't seem to add up, it's because it doesn't.

2. Give away less for free

With most clients there is a lot of wooing that goes on. You might talk, then answer some questions, then talk some more, then answer more questions. The longer the process, the more and more time you spend and the more and more you give away without any guarantee it will be worth your while. In the best-case scenario the overly curious and cautious prospect commits to becoming a client and you work together happily ever after. In the worst-case scenario you end up giving, promising, or compromising too much before the work has even begun, lending a new definition to bending over backwards. You effectively throw good time after bad, working to secure a client you're not even sure you want.

While every business is different, it is important to have guidelines in place to protect against these situations. It's far easier to prevent them than to turn them around once they are heading in the wrong direction.

Still, it can be nice to give potential clients a flavor of what it's like to work with you. Not only that, but it is nice for you to have an opportunity to test-drive potential clients and make sure you want their business. It is for these reasons that many business own-ers build in some sort of consultation process, either for free or for fee. The key to consultation success is to stick to your own rules. If you limit the time to thirty minutes, then spend only thirty min-utes. If you plan only to discuss the way you work instead of tack-ling a real challenge, then don't take the bait when the client asks what kind of solution you might suggest. If the client presents a long and involved question, you must reply with a standard line: "I'm sure we could discuss that more if we choose to work together." It's hard to do when you also want to win the client, but it sets the right precedent for the future.

In other instances it's a matter of thoughtfully deciding what your policies are and sticking to them. For example, we don't let any-one "try out" the space before signing up. We know other coworking spaces do this quite routinely, but we feel it compromises our busi-ness goals. We are, above all else, a community, and we believe it is disruptive to have a bunch of unconnected folks auditioning the facilities and their potential coworkers. At other spaces, we have seen prospective members trying out the space and spending hours literally talking to the other coworkers, getting their opinions and mentally sizing them up (can I see myself working next to this per-son?). We don't want our members to feel compelled to do our sales for us. We can also imagine getting pretty annoyed if someone we didn't know continually interrupted our work to ask about a service we were using. We know we may lose some people with this policy, but to us it seems that a visit and a space tour and a conversation with us should give you all you need to know when determining if In Good Company is the right solution for you.

3. Give what they pay for

No matter how thoughtfully you have priced your goods and ser-vices, there will always be clients who will ask you for a discount or a custom option. There are all sorts of philosophies about asking for things (as a buyer) and changing the terms of the deal (as a seller). Some people think it never hurts to ask for what you want, while others firmly believe it makes them appear cheap and disrespectful. Some entrepreneurs swear by a friends-and-family rate. Some are forever reinventing their offering to suit the needs of the particular client. Others issue a flat-out *no* to all special requests.

We don't believe there is one right answer. In our experience, customization and discounts are trickier in some businesses than in others. In some industries discounts are standard, while others frown on them. Some proprietors thrive on custom work, while others find special requests insulting. We think it is important for you to identify your own beliefs and then establish business guidelines that reinforce those practices.

However, it's *always* a bad idea to automatically say yes to what the client asks for. We guarantee you will end up with the short end of the stick, and often the principles that are important to you as a business owner will be undermined.

Instead, we are big advocates of making sure clients get what they pay for. If they want to pay less, then make sure to scale your offering so they receive less too. If they want a more time-consuming product, then make sure they cover the expense of the added work. Again, this principle is much simpler in theory than in practice.

Maybe you've had the experience of putting together a terrific proposal for a client that you're really excited about. After submitting it, they tell you they would love to work with you too. Yay! But there's a catch—their budget won't cover the full amount that you've outlined. While it's tempting to begin negotiating with them on the price, DON'T! Instead of thinking about whether you can come down a little bit, ask them what they can live without. Even if you need to make some recommendations about pieces they can do in-house, it is important that you adjust your deliverables to meet their budget. This way you are getting to do the work with the client you want without compromising on your fees. The value stays the same and you're still being paid what you're worth. The same rule applies if the customer asks you to go above and beyond to accommodate their situation. If they want more and you want to accept the job, put the cost back on them.

Ceramist Teresa Chang has encountered many such scenarios. She is routinely asked if she will do a custom glaze on her dinnerware sets for clients. Historically she had always said no without explaining why. Dissatisfied with where that left the conversation, she decided instead to say yes, but for a fee. She would explain that coming up with a glaze was both very time-consuming and very arduous and that if a client wanted to cover the cost of what was involved, she would be happy to work with them on it. She found that once they heard the number involved, they'd change their minds and instead choose from one of the very lovely colors she already offers. Using this approach Teresa found that she was not only able to have a more positive conversation, but also that her clients came to respect her established work even more.

4. Say no, but what if?

Sometimes you have to say no even when you don't want to— maybe because you don't have the time or the resources. In these cases you should pat yourself on the back for respecting your limits even when you'd like to do otherwise. When you find yourself in this situation, though, it's important to take a moment and consider if there are any feasible alternatives. Sometimes the prospect of saying no is made easier when it is followed by a "but what if?"

Selia Yang, bridal wear designer and entrepreneur, shared with us our favorite "no, but what if?" example. As someone who has always been self-funded, Selia has had to juggle her boundaries and limitations while creatively finding a way to make an opportunity work. She has artfully stuck to her guns while also finding a way to create some possibility or opportunity, even if it is different or on a smaller scale than first imagined. After many years of being a made-to-order retail shop, Selia added a wholesale component to her business. There was tons of interest, more in fact than she could initially finance.

Early on in her first season, Selia was approached by a store that wanted to purchase seven of her dresses. The terms they proposed were net 60, meaning that Selia wouldn't get paid for up to sixty days after the delivery of the dresses. Being that many of her dresses are exquisitely adorned and expensive to produce, this was a huge financial burden for her. The store indicated that they couldn't shorten the terms and meet their own financial obligations. After some thinking, Selia declined the order but then proposed that they consider buying two dresses at a time. It would take longer for them to build their collection but neither business would be overstretched and in the meantime their relationship could build. It was a risk and it took some courage to tell the store that they couldn't have what they wanted. However, the store agreed and hopefully will carry her line for years to come!

This example has served as a good reminder of taking the time to consider how to reposition a client request in terms that are mutually beneficial. It won't always work, but it's a way to respect your boundaries while also looking for common ground.

5. Say no, and here's why

Sometimes there isn't a feasible or comfortable alternative. Sometimes the answer is just simply no. And that's okay too. In these circumstances it's important to be crystal clear on your rationale, whether or not you decide to share it with your client. Being clear on *why* you are saying no makes it easier to stick to your decision and also reminds you of what you are choosing *instead*.

We have heard lots of stories from entrepreneurs who have had to turn down clients altogether. Each situation offers a unique glimpse into their choices. We are able to see the real impact of adhering to their principles.

For example, Courtney Davis and Lauren Paradise, cofounders of Kelly & Olive, love to help people design their living space to reflect their personal style. Their affordable and fun services allow even the budget-strapped to have access to great interior design advice. The pair spends much of their time getting to know their clients' preferences and lifestyles in order to improve their homes. As designers, they often have been asked to do some real estate staging work in order to get a home ready to go on the market. Although in the early days they did accept a few of these clients,

Courtney and Lauren quickly decided they didn't want to offer this service any longer. They dislike the work, and even though they can do it, it goes against their business purpose. The reason they love their job is precisely because they get to find creative ways to reflect someone's personality and individuality through the design of their home. Staging, on the other hand, is all about stripping away unique elements and making a space look as generic as possible. So now, when asked, the ladies decline the work. They would rather have more time for work they love.

Say No to Opportunities

Turning down an opportunity can be agonizing. As entrepreneurs we are accustomed to taking risks, leaping into the unknown, and hoping for the best. We know better than anyone that you just never know what is possible. We are also well acquainted with the costs of taking on too much. We customarily walk the very fine line between making sure we aren't haunted by "the one that got away" and spreading ourselves too thin. And sometimes, given the thousands of things going on at once, it's hard to separate ourselves from our day-to-day reality enough to objectively assess a given opportunity. Instead of questioning the individual merits of the opportunity, we readily evaluate our capacity to do more. We ask, "Do I have the bandwidth? Will I regret it? What's the worst that could happen?"

Instead of challenging yourself to do more, we encourage you to analyze the worthiness of the opportunity in question. Ask yourself a few questions to determine if it is worth your valuable time and resources before you sacrifice anything to accommodate it.

1. Is it a priority?
A few years ago, Andrea Miller of YourTango.com, was in earnest talks with Sirius Satellite Radio to create a branded radio show—think *Sex and the City* meets *Car Talk*. Everyone was really excited about it, but ultimately Andrea's plate was too full at the time. She knew that adding the show was going to detract from the other

projects they had going on. Though it was tough, they forced themselves to be focused and judicious about their energy. They determined that at that point in time the show was not a priority. So, as difficult as it was, they put the show on hold, with the option to revisit.

2. Does it get you where you want to go?

There aren't many people who can claim to have said no to Google. A few years ago Lotta Anderson, founder of Lotta Jansdotter, did just that. As an expert pattern-maker with a large grassroots following, Lotta was surprised when Google approached her to design a custom iGoogle page. It was a really intriguing opportunity that boasted huge marketing potential. But Lotta was hesitant. Her brand was all about being small and handmade. She was embraced by the DIY and craft markets and was known for high quality and sharp design. Google didn't match with that image. It seemed too big, too mainstream. She was worried about what the collaboration would say about her brand. Lotta had worked very hard to position her brand and products as higher-end and exclusive. What if this made her look like she had sold out to the man? After a good deal of hemming and hawing and tons of advice, she said no. Lotta knew the opportunity wouldn't reinforce the image she was working toward.

Interestingly, Lotta's goals have changed since then and she says that if she were offered the same opportunity today, she'd probably take it. Now that the "crafting" movement has exploded and is so well regarded by the mass market, Lotta has been able to position herself not just as a maker of beautiful patterns but as a DIY connoisseur. Lotta Jansdotter the brand has matured and taken on a bigger role in educating and influencing those who love handcrafted goods and unique design. Now with the new iteration of the business she wants to reach the mass market and she can do so without compromising her brand integrity. The same opportunity today would move her closer to her goals but might have sabotaged her ambitions back then. By listening to her instincts and saying no when it was appropriate, Lotta has been able to grow her company organically and with integrity.

3. Does it require too much of a compromise?

Joy Cho, founder of Oh Joy!, is a blogger, graphic designer, and overall lifestyle expert. Her creative eye and sense of style has seduced thousands of people into following her and seeking her advice. The Oh Joy! brand has grown into a multiplatform business encompassing a blog, full-service graphic and product design studio, pattern licensing, writing, and consulting. Joy appears regularly in the media, sharing her tips on fashionable living. She has been offered several opportunities to collaborate with or be featured within the scrapbooking market. Each time, she has turned them down, despite the impressive marketing potential they present. The truth is, the scrapbook market is not really congruent with her brand and it feels disingenuous to create scrapbooking products while not being a scrapbook enthusiast herself. Each time the opportunity has been presented, Joy has determined that even a large number of new eyeballs really is not worth compromising the essence of her brand.

Say No to Favors

It feels good to give back, especially after receiving a lot of help along the way yourself. However, at some point it is important to realize that if you helped everyone on their terms you'd have no time left for yourself or your business. Now, of course, we aren't talking about learning to say no to those idiots who call up and brazenly ask for your business plan. It's easy to say no to them. We're talking about the people you'd like to help if time weren't an issue: the aspiring entrepreneurs, the fans, and the friends of friends.

Here are a few suggestions that will help you stave off time-sucking favors while maintaining good business karma.

1. Put it on your terms

Setting limits for people who want something for free is about putting the work and hassle on them. If they want the help they should be willing to exert some effort (and gratitude) to make it happen. Nothing is more frustrating than going out of your way to help someone who is taking that help for granted. We've all agreed to a networking coffee or call, only to have the other person not show or cancel at the last minute. The extent to which you inconvenienced yourself in the first place makes this situation exponentially frustrating. The key to helping is figuring out a way to do it that is easy for you.

Michelle Madhok receives a lot of requests for advice. As CEO of SheFinds.com, a successful online shopping blog with a large following, she clearly has a lot of information and experience that others would like to learn about. Instead of wasting time scheduling various phone calls or coffees, Michelle instituted "office hours." Every once in a while she sets aside a couple of hours to meet with aspiring entrepreneurs and people who want to learn more about her business and industry. During those hours she makes herself available to meet new people, answer questions, and give advice. When she receives a request to meet or talk, she tells the inquirer about the next upcoming office hours and invites her to come. If someone doesn't show, Michelle uses that time to get some miscellaneous desk work done. Her office hours ensure that the time and location are convenient for her, and by putting these meetings all together, she cuts down on the time it takes to set up and attend individual meetings.

2. Make it public

Grace Bonney of Design Sponge is literally inundated by questions from admirers and fans about her business, design ideas, and resources. In her first several years, Grace really liked the idea of replying to every e-mail she received, but in time there was literally no way she could keep up with the requests. A primary part of her role is maintaining a public conversation with her community, both through her blog and her social media platforms. This job is so big that she really can't afford to dedicate too much time to one reader. Brilliantly, she leveraged the Formspring.me platform as a way to manage these common questions and answers. Formspring.me allows anyone to ask questions of a user, anonymously if they'd like. The format encourages the questions to be short, and the answers are posted publicly so others with the same question can find them. This solution keeps Grace easily accessible to her community and it makes her information and resources available to all. Grace also shares these posts through her social media platforms, which allows others to follow along with the conversation, thereby strengthening the Design Sponge community even more.

3. Refer to other resources

Because we have always been generous with our time and information, we tend to get a lot of e-mails asking for favors, and it is our policy to reply to each e-mail we receive. In the old days we were much quicker to extend our time and knowledge, but once we began building the In Good Company community and the requests for help and advice quickly grew, we knew we needed a better system. So we did two things. First, we decided that In Good Company members obviously received priority. Second, we sorted all other favor requests into two groups: those with questions related to our expertise, and those with questions about things we knew about but weren't experts on. It actually surprised us how many people were sent to us asking questions about topics that weren't our core competency but instead were lessons we had learned along the way through experience or research. Perhaps it was our reputation for being resourceful and generous that netted these requests, but in any case it became clear that servicing them didn't directly advance our business goals and really wasn't a good use of our time. They didn't help build the reputation we wanted, nor were they likely to generate clients or members. So we got in the habit of determining what kind of information someone needed and quickly directing her to resources that we ourselves found valuable.

Instead of spending the time rehashing what we have learned, we will direct a seeker right to the source. We regularly refer people to various workshops and programs, Web sites, and services. Some are free, some not, but all provide excellent answers or experiences. As a bonus, this timesaving strategy has unintentionally helped to strengthen several of our referral relationships.

NO TO FAMILY AND FRIENDS

Doesn't it seem ironic that just as you hit send on the e-mail sharing the news of your company launch, the personal requests start pouring in? You probably have never had less time on your hands, but something about not regularly disappearing into a big building for defined hours every day screams "I'm available" to everyone you know. Whether it's a casual cup of coffee, a quick look at someone's résumé, or a trip to pick up Granny at the airport, those who love you are excited and ready to cash in on your newfound flexibility. Not so fast! Remember, you worked very hard to earn that flexibility. Don't give it up so easily.

If you find that these personal requests are particularly hard for you to avoid or decline, try to fulfill them only outside of work hours. This way they won't eat up valuable work time or replace your critical business to-dos. But more important, we're willing to bet that when it means giving up your personal time, you'll learn to say no much quicker!

Say No to Goodwill

It never feels good to say no to charity. And if time and money weren't an issue, we are sure you'd say yes every time you were asked. But the truth is that there are only so many times you can donate free merchandise, products, or services without undermining the stability of your own business. The key is having a limit and choosing opportunities that count—either in terms of meaning to you or strategic return for the business.

Space is a hot commodity in New York City, which is of course part of the reason we started In Good Company. Once we were open for business, we were flooded with requests for free space by tons of nonprofits and small businesses. We couldn't possibly say yes to them all, and while we wanted to help, we were a fledging business ourselves! So we took a few steps to set some limits. First, we chose to focus on organizations that were close to our own mission—professional development of women and girls. Second, we limited the number of times a month we'd lend out the conference room and the number of times a year we'd lend out the whole space. Third, we designated December as the one time a year that we would entertain a different kind of charitable project. One year we ran a clothing drive, another year a toy drive, and a third a food drive. Each year during this time we also donate money to entrepreneurial women in developing nations through Kiva. These parameters give us enough latitude to entertain a variety of requests and collaborate with a good number of interesting and worthwhile organizations. This also allows us to contribute in ways that don't overwhelm the business and that make sense given our own purpose.

Several of the entrepreneurs we spoke with had set similar limits in order to combat the onslaught of requests they received. Selecting dedicated partners or particular areas of interest made it easier for these entrepreneurs to decline other charitable requests. Noha Waibsnaider, founder of Peeled Snacks, has carefully selected her charitable partners, making sure the partnerships were not only long-term but substantive as well. For example, they partner with American Farmlands Trust, which works to help farmers and ranchers protect their land. This is obviously a priority for Peeled Snacks as well, which sources many of its ingredients from these very farms. Ellen Diamant, owner of Skip Hop, has selected four charity partners that are all congruent with the company's focus and have high charitable impact. For example, the company donates excess product to Baby Buggy, a charity that collects new and used baby items for parents in need, and collaborates with a pediatric AIDS organization. Patricia Helding, president of Fat Witch, also limits her charitable donations (a generous ten thousand brownies a year) to organizations with a focus on children and education.

NO TO ENTREPRENEURIAL EXPECTATIONS

Most entrepreneurs feel tremendous pressure to be technologically engaged. Social media platforms such as Facebook and Twitter are considered critical marketing tools for almost every business. Most entrepreneurs sweat inactivity, fearing lost visibility, sales, and (God forbid) followers. The challenge is that these platforms can be both time-consuming and a bit intrusive. And social media are, quite frankly, not how many entrepreneurs want to be spending their time. This is certainly true for Paige Arnof-Fenn, CEO of Mavens & Moguls. She is very pointed about abstaining from social media herself. The irony is that she is a marketing expert, which makes her absence seem like a bit of a contradiction. Paige sees it differently. She knows the platforms well and advises her clients on their use all the time. But she also knows that her great advice isn't contingent upon her "leaving a paper trail" to her own life.

For Paige, this is an important boundary. It helps her to preserve her work/life balance and privacy as well. She serves as a great reminder that sometimes it's important to say no to industry and business expectations too.

A No That You Later Regret

At some point you're bound to regret saying no to something. But don't lose the opportunity for a lesson learned. Here are a few things to consider to help you avoid repeating your mistakes and beating yourself up unnecessarily.

- **Were you in a good place to say yes?** Or were you overcommitted or unhealthily stressed? Maybe if you had been juggling less you might have been in a position to take advantage of this opportunity. Take responsibility for your daily state so there is room for good opportunities when they come your way.

- **Could you have known?** Should you have been able to recognize this opportunity for what it was, or is this a case of hindsight being 20/20? If so, don't beat yourself up about it. Instead, think about how you might inform yourself differently about future opportunities so you can see them more clearly.
- **Can it be rekindled?** It may be worthwhile to consider how you can create a similar opportunity now that you recognize the potential. If not, brainstorm ways that you might be better able to take advantage of an opportunity like that in the future.

Linda Lightman, owner of Linda's Stuff, shared an example of an opportunity that she passed on and still regrets. Linda gets all of the clothes that she sells on consignment from individuals. The benefit, of course, is that she doesn't have to lay out cash for inventory, except for the merchandise shipping costs, which she covers. A couple of years ago, eBay put her in touch with a liquidator, a company that accepts unsold merchandise from larger chain stores. Linda had the opportunity to purchase literally a ton of merchandise directly from the liquidator. However, it would obviously have been a tremendous outlay of cash and very different from what the business was accustomed to. In addition, Linda wasn't able to inspect the merchandise prior to purchase. All the clothes were stored in giant bins and she would have to take the liquidator's word about the contents and the condition of the clothes. Linda decided that the risk was too high. Aside from the financial hazard, it was difficult to determine whether the clothes were congruent with the brands she was known for selling. Now Linda says she wishes she had taken the chance. The worst-case scenario would have meant a big financial hit, but it wouldn't have been disastrous. Instead of working with her, the liquidator partnered with a competitor of Linda's. Linda would now entertain similar opportunities more optimistically.

Troubleshooting:
When You Get in Your Own Way

As you can imagine, businesses can get all tangled up when people have a hard time saying no. Other people's wants, needs, and priorities end up dictating the business and just about everything that you want gets compromised on. In extreme cases this can even lead to threatening the viability of the entire business.

The Case of Anything-Goes Agatha

Agatha was a huge self-improvement junkie. She invested a lot of time and energy in strengthening her self-awareness and well-being. A couple of years ago she went to a personal development training that was really terrific. She got to know the owners of the program and found they were licensing the program to practitioners all over the country. Agatha told them she would be very interested in purchasing the license for her market. The fee was fairly steep, and there were certainly some additional start-up costs involved, but she would have a lot of latitude in terms of marketing and positioning the training. Plus there were lots of ancillary products she could sell, and she could even create some of her own. Ultimately she was very optimistic for the revenue potential of this opportunity.

In order to make it work financially, Agatha sought out a few investors. Believing it was wise to select investors who had relevant skill sets that she didn't, she looked for someone who had a lot of experience doing trainings and another who had experience selling products directly to the consumer. While she was asking for referrals and suggestions to appropriate investors, two other people indicated that they too wanted to invest in this great opportunity. Great, Agatha thought! The more the merrier! Not so. It turned out that these investors came with strings. Both wanted to play a role in the business, but neither really had the right experience or skill set. But, flattered that they wanted to get involved and eager for funds, Agatha said yes and added them to the team.

One of these investors had a sister who was a professional trainer, and they strongly encouraged Agatha to reach out to her about this opportunity. Agatha did. It turns out that the sister was interested and willing to invest, but wanted to offer this training as a part of her own brand. Agatha felt stuck. She felt uncomfortable saying no because her current investor really wanted to bring his sister aboard. She did seem to have the right skill set, but Agatha feared that adding another brand to the mix was going to be bad for the business. Her investors reminded her that she could have more of nothing or less of something. She yielded.

At this point there were already a lot of cooks in the kitchen, so Agatha was hesitant to bring on yet another person. However, they still needed someone to manage the creation, marketing, and sales of the products. After a group meeting someone suggested that Agatha take this role if she really didn't want to bring anyone else on. Again she yielded.

So just a few months later the license was purchased and Agatha and her three partners were in business. Not surprisingly, Agatha wasn't very excited about the new venture anymore. Her vision had been hijacked, they had to navigate another brand, and she was in a role that was completely unsuitable for her.

We probably don't need to tell you that it didn't end well. The company puttered along for two years before imploding, and the experience was miserable. There were so many competing priorities and agendas on the table that the company didn't have a chance of establishing or executing a coherent strategy. Agatha's inability to say no meant she had compromised on everything that was important to her and ultimately sacrificed the opportunity she was so excited about. The good news was that by the time she wised up and left the organization she had learned a lot of lessons about setting boundaries and saying no. She was hopeful that the next time around she would be much more protective of her own needs and wants, because that is, after all, the only way the business could truly work for her.

BUSINESS SPOTLIGHT

"One of the hardest things is trying to figure out how to best capitalize on what I've already created instead of saying, 'That's done. What's next?'"

An entrepreneur learns that sometimes growth isn't about more, it's about better
Jen Mankins, owner of Bird

With a rodeo horse rider for a mom and a race car builder for a dad, it's not surprising that Jen Mankins would have an adventurous spirit. And although she earned her stripes at bigger fashion companies, such as Steven Alan and Barneys, Jen was never afraid to go out on her own. Nor was she afraid to grow.

In fact, in 2003, instead of opening her own store, Jen decided to buy Bird, an established cutting-edge boutique in Brooklyn, so that she could hit the ground running. She had a big vision for what fashion-forward boutiques could really do in Brooklyn and was eager to put the plan into motion, and she didn't want to spend the time building a new customer base and fussing with a logo. Instead of laying the foundation, she preferred to take something that was already working well and make it much, much bigger! Jen wanted to leverage Bird's excellent reputation and great relationships with vendors and customers in order to grow the business.

Being a Brooklynite herself, Jen knew that multiple smaller, neighborhood-based stores would be more successful than one larger emporium. So after she took ownership of Bird, she set to work on an aggressive expansion plan, opening three new stores in four years (moving the one in Park Slope and adding another in Cobble Hill and one in Williamsburg) and increasing her staff from two to twenty people. During that time each location experienced tremendous sales growth. A buyer and fashion lover at heart, Jen was (in addition to scouting, designing, and opening stores) having a great time cultivating unique fashion-forward collections from over three hundred brands each season. It was an enormous job but one that she really loved and was very good at doing.

Then the recession hit. Customers stopped buying and sales weakened. Gone were the days when anything could be bought and everything could be sold. Jen put her remaining expansion plans on hold and took the time to acquaint herself with what she calls the other side of the business. In order to make do, she had to "face the things I didn't like to do," including operations and the financials. Not only did she watch expenses and cash flow, but she had to make major reductions in inventory and really analyze the performance of the items they carried. Although it was painful, Jen forced herself to edit the store's collection so that only well-selling items remained.

It turns out that this period, what Jen has described as introspection mode, has had a lasting impact on both her and Bird. And she says that they are both better for it. Surprisingly, Jen's prudence led to a growth in profits despite overall sales being down. And most important, it taught her how to rein it in, sit still with what she had, and say no to herself! She continues to have a new idea every five seconds, but she's removed the pressure to act on them all. She's realized that everything doesn't have to happen today and it's okay to put ideas on hold. Taking on less didn't mean she was going to fall behind. Instead it allowed her to make sure she was doing things to the highest level. Her efforts have been recognized too. In addition to being awarded Top Women's Boutique by *New York* magazine, Bird also won Top Visionary Boutique in the United States by *Lucky* magazine.

As Jen looks to the future, she is committed to the idea that entrepreneurship is about finding out how your business can best work with what you want at the time. This may come in the form of additional stores or it may be through an expansion into menswear, which they did in 2008, or through creating their own line of clothes, which they experimented with in 2007.

When Jen thinks about additional locations and further expansion, she sees it primarily as a way to facilitate the lifestyle she wants. She has toyed with opening a store in Manhattan, which has experienced a drain of independent boutiques, but has also thought about future iterations of her business that might coincide with changes in her life. Perhaps she could have a store in Sweden, where she hopes to live someday. Or maybe she would like to have a Beach Bird that would allow her to spend her summers at the beach. Or when the time comes for kids, maybe revitalizing Baby Bird would be fun (the original Bird store had a Baby Bird outpost when Jen bought it). But in the meantime Jen is focused on making her existing stores the absolute best they can be and is consciously filtering through her great ideas to see which is the next good one to implement.

8

Don't Go It Alone

Leverage the Power of Community

One group is never enough.
—EMILY POWELL, PRESIDENT OF POWELL'S BOOKS

The Problem: It's Lonely at the Top

Working for yourself often means spending a lot of time working by yourself. Most entrepreneurs are surprised to learn how isolated they feel once they are running their own show, even when they're surrounded by employees and customers.

But there is something to be said about shared experiences. Sure, you can bond with your staff and clients, but it's different. You're still always on, tending to the culture and navigating the relationship. You can't really let your hair down. You can't complain freely about that client. You can't admit you're concerned about cash flow or freaking out about a difficult decision. But it's important to do these things. You just need to find the right forum to do so. You need the comfort of knowing that this wacky ride of entrepreneurship is just as wacky for other people too. You need time with your people.

We would be underestimating the importance of peers, though, to think that isolation only means you feel lonely or have an absence of moral support. Actually, the toll of isolation can be quite significant. When you are isolated you are more likely to:

- Reinvent the wheel, wasting both time and money
- Be less informed about what is going on in your industry
- Fail to spot general business trends
- Suffer from your own blind spots
- Miss out on valuable feedback and brainstorming
- Falsely perceive more people as competitors
- Lack necessary emotional support and encouragement
- Have access to a smaller network of people
- Be overlooked for key opportunities

The Solution: Find Your People

Strength comes in numbers; numbers of colleagues, that is. Hands down, one of the best ways to enhance your business is by forming relationships with your peers. The more people you know, the more collective wisdom, experience, resources, and information you can access—plain and simple. However, we know that with a mile-long to-do list, it is easy to consider time spent with peers as optional, or even a luxury. But trust us when we say that friends are every entrepreneur's secret weapon.

If you're an extrovert, like Amy, you're probably saying to yourself, "Obviously, the more the merrier!" And if you're an introvert, like Adelaide, you may be wincing and looking for excuses to avoid this chapter altogether. But we say to extroverts and introverts alike, read on! Whether or not making lots of professional relationships comes easily to you, we want you to take advantage of *all* the benefits that a strong community will bring.

While it certainly takes a lot of work to establish a large entrepreneurial network, the bigger challenge is making sure that you're properly using it to its full potential. Too often, entrepreneurs, who are connected to terrific colleagues, still stew on problems alone, neglecting to ask for advice when they need it. On the whole, we tend to underutilize our peers, figuring they are only valuable for an occasional introduction or brainstorming lunch. What a waste! If you engage them, your peers and community can have a huge impact on the quality of your business and experience. We want to ensure that you are making your community a priority, both by making the most of the community that you have and filling in the gaps where need be.

The Top Ten Benefits a Community of Peers Can Provide

1. Reality check

Sometimes you just need a good reality check—a healthy dose of sanity from someone who has been in a similar situation. Someone to whom you can say, "Is it just me or _____." You can fill in the blank: Is this client being unreasonable? Have you also seen a drop in sales? Does the craze of the moment seem stupid?

Sometimes peers can help demystify the process, showing you it isn't rocket science after all. Or perhaps their own experience will help demonstrate that, contrary to how it can sometimes feel, no one else has it easy. Since time really is money, a quick e-mail or phone call is worth it to avoid spending hours mulling over something in your own head.

2. Information

With all the information out there, how come it is so difficult to find what you need? Sometimes a seemingly straightforward question can result in hours of research and data-gathering. Even the question about how best to legally register a business can be a needle-in-the-haystack kind of experience. We've yet to meet a business owner who doesn't share this complaint. Wouldn't it be great if there was a shortcut? A way to get tried-and-true information from someone who has been there, done that? Good news: there is! A strong community is a great way to find valuable information without wasting your precious time.

Melanie Notkin, founder of Savvy Auntie, commented on how different are the standards of behavior between corporate America and the entrepreneurial community with regard to sharing information. She believes that "in corporate America there is very little karma. You get the information and you keep it because that information is power. That information may get you the corner office. And in the entrepreneurial community we're all there to help each other because we've been there."

We see this firsthand all the time. When we bring a group of business owners together it is incredible how much knowledge and information is buzzing in the room. We often have Give & Get resource sessions where participants ask for resources they need and share resources they currently utilize. Whether it's an online business tool, prize vendor, cautionary tale, social media secret, or a great accountant, each suggestion makes at least one person's life a lot easier.

When we were in the planning stages for In Good Company, we contacted Joy Parisi and Lila Cecil of Paragraph, a writer's space in New York City just a few blocks from where we are located now. They had already been in business for three years, and we admired what they had created and hoped they would be willing to share some of their experience and knowledge with us. Thankfully, they were.

For example, they graciously shared their version of their rules and regulations so we didn't have to start from scratch. In addition, Joy offered lots of operations advice about running a workspace. There were dozens of things in there that we hadn't yet thought of and undoubtedly would have had to learn the hard way. The best piece of advice from Joy was to accept only credit cards. Honestly, we hadn't spent a great deal of time thinking about collecting payment, seeing as how we didn't have customers yet. And although we wanted to accept credit cards, we didn't have a merchant account set up. We had figured we could accept checks to start. Once we heard what Joy had to say, though, we were made very aware of the problems that a check-only situation could bring: nonpayment, bounced checks, a huge receivables balance, time spent chasing down members to pay their bills, as well as the yucky feeling that accompanies the chase. We set up our merchant account the next day, undoubtedly saving ourselves lots of aggravation and expense. We have continued to share information with Joy and Lila over the years, swapping ideas about operations, infrastructure, and expansion. It has been an invaluable relationship.

TRADE SHOW TREASURE

Every single designer we know seems to have learned at least half of their industry secrets from peers they meet at trade shows. Honestly, given the value they seem to get, you'd think that having buyers place orders was only a secondary benefit. Ellen Diamant, owner of Skip Hop, reminisced about an early group of peers in the baby product market, many of whom she initially met at trade shows. She said the group functioned as a support system for its members, who openly shared industry information with each other, such as what manufacturers to avoid, what customers didn't pay, and how to find out if your designs were being ripped off. In the early days they even set up a Yahoo! message group called "Training Wheels" to help facilitate their exchanges. Pauline Nakios, owner of Lilla P, echoed that sentiment. She said that her trade show peers saved her countless hours of time and effort, particularly by sharing best practices for dealing with vendors and buyers.

3. Feedback

The right feedback can prevent you from making a disastrous mistake, can bring some of your blind spots to your attention, and can even help validate something you were hoping to be true. However, if you *really* want to know what's up, you need to give your colleagues permission to give their *honest* opinion. We can all be guilty of asking people what they think without really meaning it. Instead of their honest opinion, we'd prefer to just hear a confirmation of our own thoughts. Make sure your colleague knows this isn't one of those cases. Say something like, "I really want to make this product the absolute best it can be, and given your experience in this market,

I'd love your feedback. Please feel free to be honest." Yes, it can be uncomfortable to open yourself up and potentially hear negative things, but it's worth it if it improves your product in the end.

One of the most exciting programs that we facilitate at In Good Company is GROW it!—a four-week class designed around giving and receiving honest feedback. Each participant has an opportunity to present a business challenge and solicit the group's perspective and ideas. The presenter inevitably walks away with a bevy of ideas and suggestions that they hadn't thought of, as well as valuable feedback on their basic business assumptions. We are always so impressed by the content of the participants' feedback. And participants have transformed and reshaped their entire businesses based on what they learn. However, what is most remarkable about the experience is the way in which feedback is delivered. All of the participants are so generous, genuine, and helpful. They want nothing more than to further their peers' businesses and help them achieve their goals. They elegantly articulate even the most difficult messages and skillfully give suggestions that keep the presenter's goals and needs in mind. It is incredible to witness how supportive the entrepreneurs are of one another and how effectively they can repurpose their own lessons and knowledge for someone else's gain. Each class reinforces our belief about the importance of feedback and reminds us how much you can benefit if you're brave enough to ask people to share their honest opinions.

However, just because everybody has an opinion doesn't mean you want to hear them all. While feedback is obviously a key to your success, we caution you to be thoughtful when asking for it by being both specific and selective.

If you are not specific about the kind of feedback you are requesting, all is fair game and you may hear things about your business that you do not want to hear! That is not to say that it is not valuable, but it may not be constructive or welcome in the moment. By not being specific, you might also be opening the door to ongoing unsolicited feedback. When you ask someone for her opinion, make sure to tell her what and why.

Further, it is important to be selective in who you ask for feedback. We all have a lens through which we see the world, and despite our desire to be objective, we are colored by our own experience. So make sure that those you ask have experience and perspective you truly appreciate. This doesn't mean that you like what they say, but at least you know they know what they are talking about.

However, despite your best efforts to solicit helpful opinions, you're still bound to get some feedback that is not only unhelpful but discouraging too. Remember to take everything with a grain of salt! Shazi Visram, founder and CEO of HappyBaby, still has notes from a conversation she had with a colleague and entrepreneurship expert in the early days of her business. This colleague told her that she thought her business had no chance of success and was an absolute sure way to bankruptcy! She proceeded to say that even if they did create something worthwhile it would immediately be gobbled up by a competitor. Luckily Shazi took the feedback in stride and used it to further fuel her fire. Nearly eight years later, with product in more than five thousand stores, she's glad that she knew to trust herself and not put too much stock in what others, expert or not, had to say.

4. Brain trust

Sometimes you need more than just feedback. You need full brainpower. Whether you're dealing with a problem, question, or new frontier, some things require, as our friend Karen Rancourt says, noodling. Who better to turn to than a fellow enterprising, initiative-taking, roll-up-your-sleeves-and-get-it-done entrepreneur?

While it can certainly be good to get input from someone on your team, there are times when you need a perspective that is both objective and totally honest. Employees may not be totally comfortable sharing their unvarnished perspective, and they may not be privy to all information (for good reason) that would help them give informed ideas. In these cases you may need to look outside of your own sandbox.

Several entrepreneurs we spoke with referenced a regular "brain trust" of people they relied on to help think through business questions and challenges. For example, Ellen Galinsky, president of the Families and Work Institute, pointed out that her prized brain trust, which includes her daughter, Laura Galinsky, senior vice president of Echoing Green, helps her think through challenges, point out things she might not be seeing, and listen for historical areas of weakness that may be playing a role. With no stake in the outcome, her trusted confidantes are free to contribute their unedited thoughts about how best to proceed. Ellen believes that this practice has ultimately made her a better leader of her organization.

Another way we see entrepreneurs use brain trusts is by enlisting the collective brainpower of their peers to help solve a troubling challenge or advance a common cause. This is an interesting way to build community and improve your industry at the same time. Two examples from our own community stick out.

One group, the We Own It Summit, was created as a consortium of businesses and influencers to help break down barriers for women in high-growth entrepreneurship. The group, which includes a cross section of entrepreneurs, investors, and academic, government, media, nonprofit, and industry organizations, meets once a year to discuss, learn, and further the conversation. Each year goals are set out for the next. This event is by invitation only and is powered by an informal network of colleagues. The attendees not only get to make a meaningful contribution to the dialogue around entrepreneurship and business growth, but also connect with peers who share a similar focus.

Another such initiative is the Young Entrepreneur Council, an advocacy group whose mission is to teach young people how to build successful businesses and fight youth underemployment and unemployment. The council is made up of various entrepreneurs and thought leaders who are eager to share their own business experience, expertise, and insights with young aspiring entrepreneurs. Created by Scott Gerber, author of *Never Get a Real Job*, the council helps him achieve his mission of encouraging Gen-Yers to embrace entrepreneurship as a viable career alternative.

5. Collaboration

Sure, you may love being the one in charge, but sometimes it's fun to work together. And the impact of business collaboration really cannot be underestimated. There are so many examples of great brands working together to make something infinitely cooler. Think about when you go to a hotel and the brand of toiletries they carry just happens to be one you love. The hotel then goes way up in coolness points. Or think about when other designers, like Dwell or Splendid, create a line for Target. It is truly a case of 1 + 1 = 3.

One of our favorite examples of collaboration is the adorable uniforms donned by the staff at BabyCakes, a vegan bakery based in New York. Vegan cupcake Erin McKenna knew that the style of her shop was a critical part of the business's overall success. That included the staff uniforms. Erin has collaborated with local design talent (Built by Wendy, Earnest Sewn, and In God We Trust) on three different uniform collections. Not only do these custom duds perfectly suit the BabyCakes vibe, but they strengthen Erin's ties to the indie scene in New York.

We have loved our own collaboration with Raandesk Gallery. Jessica Porter, founder of Raandesk, approached us with an offer to curate the space in exchange for allowing IGC's walls to serve as a gallery for her artists. How could we say no?! Our start-up art budget was seriously meager, yet we knew that the aesthetics of the space were really important to our offering. So now every eight weeks or so IGC gets a new exhibition and vibe. It's fun for us. The changing shows bring new inspiration, conversation, and beauty to the space. Jessica gets a place to hang her artists' work as well as a space to host buyers and events.

6. A show of force

Sometimes you need backup. Whether it's people coming to a book signing, your latest event, or maybe even a simple retweet, you need action! Of course, you can rely on your customers, but you'll find that many of your biggest cheerleaders are your colleagues too.

We have counted on our community and colleagues time and time again. Recently their support was critical in helping us to combat a tricky business situation. Last fall we had a copycat emerge in the form of In Good Company Ireland. Some (lazy) lady in the Emerald Isle went ahead and set up a Web site and Facebook page for a seemingly identical business. She even felt compelled to use our tagline (work.meet.learn) and exact Web copy. We were understandably annoyed. Having no contact information, we blogged about our experience and started a social media campaign about the importance of professional etiquette. To our delight, we received an outpouring of support from our colleagues. Many weighed in on copycat experiences of their own and shared some valuable strategies. Our plight was even picked up by a *New York Times* blogger, who was kind enough to solicit support and feedback on our behalf. In the end our efforts did persuade our copycat to make some changes. She replaced our exact copy with a shoddily written version that fell just shy of plagiarism and got our tagline changed in most places to a suspiciously similar one (connect.work.grow). It was a frustrating situation overall, but the support we received from our colleagues really was a silver lining. It was a great reminder of the power of being connected to so many fantastic businesses.

On the other end of the spectrum, your peers can also help you create a movement or catalyze change. Doing something interesting on your own is great, but it's even better when several like-minded businesses take notice of each other and act in concert. When Wendy Mullin, owner of Built by Wendy, got her start in the early 1990s, buyers didn't really know what to make of her stuff. They liked it, but her indie, hipster-esque vibe didn't really fit into the few traditional fashion categories that existed at the time. It wasn't until there were a few other bourgeoning indie designers on the scene that people were able to define the look. By banding her work together with what other designers were doing, Wendy was able to be part of a movement and get even more people to take notice.

7. Business!

Most businesses rely heavily on word-of-mouth referrals as a source of new business. So chances are that your success, in part, hinges on people knowing about you so they can spread the word. A larger, more engaged network undoubtedly leads to more referrals, which lead to more business.

Here's the catch: in order to leverage word of mouth to the fullest, your colleagues need to know, in plain English, first what you offer, and second, the problem you solve. For example, we provide opportunities for women entrepreneurs to learn and work together by offering a community, classes, and workspace just for them. We help them feel less isolated physically, intellectually, and emotionally.

Again, this may sound like stating the obvious, but think about how many times you are still clueless after people tell you what it is they do. And think about when you are actually in a position to refer something to someone else. Do they say, "I need a good accountant"? Sometimes. But sometimes they don't know what they are looking for and they just state the problem they are having. "I have no idea what I can expense or how to organize my shoebox of receipts." Or, "I'm not sure if I can really afford to hire another person or if I should just use a contractor." Or, "I don't know if I should register as an LLC." So it's important that your colleagues understand the problem your business solves as well.

8. Differentiation

Our experience with clients has shown that different industries regard their competitors quite differently. In some industries competitors are held at arm's length, while others abide by the "keep your enemies closer" philosophy. Unless a competitor has proven itself to be particularly nasty or unethical (rarely the case for us), we tend to see them as just another kind of colleague. And we actually have found our relationships with them to be quite beneficial, primarily because the more you know about another business the better you are able to see distinctions between you.

A more nuanced understanding of how you differ from similar

businesses in your industry not only helps to enhance your own value proposition but also gives you a place to refer business that you don't want. We often redirect customers to other places when we feel that it might be a better fit. For example, we steer people toward Green Spaces when it seems that they will benefit from a network of sustainably-minded businesses.

Michelle Adams, founder of *Lonny* and Rubie Green, also reminded us that competitors can be allies if your business goals are aligned. In college, Michelle was particularly struck by a professor who challenged his students to think about what impact their future products might have on the market and earth. He made them think about how they could advocate for sustainability in whatever they were going to do. In part due to his influence, Michelle became very dedicated to creating eco-friendly products. During the launch of her fabric company, Rubie Green, she reached out to a strong competitor who was more established than she was. To her surprise, the competitor was far more generous than she had ever imagined. Why? Because the goal was to help revolutionize a toxic industry, not stamp out others trying to advance a sustainable product.

9. Self-esteem

A lot of the time, collegial relationships aren't about what you can get but what you can give. After all, it is a two-way street. Aside from making us feel good, helping others also reminds us that despite how we sometimes feel, we actually know what we are talking about! Sharing our lessons with peers gives us the opportunity to remember what we have learned and reflect back on how far we have come. This boost of confidence can be a welcome respite from the current batch of questions circling our minds.

Participants of our GROW it! class consistently report that in addition to getting great ideas about their own challenges, they were surprised by how much they were able to share and how good it felt to do so. They enter the class because they need help themselves and are looking for assistance solving a problem that they are experiencing. However, after spending four weeks working hard to give others good ideas, they end the class not only with suggestions for their own challenge but also proud of and confident in their ability to help others.

10. Skills

In addition to confidence, helping someone else work through a problem actually improves your own skills and knowledge in that area. Like circuit training, this insight will help you strengthen your business muscles for a variety of situations, leaving you better prepared overall for the challenges ahead.

GROW it! participants also often remark that by helping other business owners with their challenges they end up getting answers to problems they weren't even aware of. They are able to capitalize on transferable lessons, saving them for future use. For example, nearly every time someone presents a marketing challenge the other five classmates walk away with several concrete new ideas for their own businesses. They often find it is easier to think of solutions for someone else, and it's only later that they wonder, "Why don't I do that for my business?!"

Types of Friends to Have

Now that you're sold on all the super-duper benefits of friends, let's address the different types of colleagues that you should have:

Groups

Okay, so this isn't really a type of colleague, but professional associations and groups can be a great way to get a lot of bang for your buck. They provide a regular opportunity to meet new people who have some commonality with you and serve as a source of information about industry trends, business opportunities, and referrals.

And remember, diversity is key. As Emily Powell, president and owner of Powell's Books, reminds us, "One group is never enough." Emily told us about the many groups she participates in, each providing a unique benefit and different set of colleagues. Not only is Emily well connected to other independent booksellers, but she also belongs to groups for family-owned businesses and started a group for women CEOs. Aside from these groups, Emily makes an effort to be in touch with other retailers in her area as well as other businesses that have strong e-commerce components, like Powell's. Her collective experience with these peers has helped her get advice and ideas about how to handle various aspects of the business. Despite being in a unique situation herself, running the leading independent bookseller in the country and having inherited the business from her father, Emily has made sure she's not alone!

Following Emily's example, think about the range of groups you can join. You may benefit from joining a group based on your type of business, like a group for nutritionists; stage of business, like businesses with annual revenues over $1 million; target client, like businesses that target pregnant women; or business interests, like businesses with significant media components.

Since the beginning, Claire Chambers, founder of Journelle, has relied on peers to help her along her entrepreneurial journey. Before launching, she says she was lucky enough to work at a fantastic consulting firm that went to great lengths to support and cultivate their people. While employed there, she had the freedom to start an entrepreneurial peer group with seven other employees who were also nurturing various business ideas. They met biweekly to go over their evolving business plans, brainstorm, get feedback, and exchange contacts. These folks were critical in helping to shape her concept and give her encouragement to keep moving forward. Despite being interested in divergent industries, Claire said they were all able to relate because "the struggle was the same."

OUTGROWING GROUPS

Remember, as your business matures and evolves, your needs will change too. It is very likely that groups that worked for you in the past won't pack the same punch as they used to. Don't take this as a sign that you have outgrown networks or groups altogether; instead find a new one that is properly positioned to help you move forward. We have met lots of entrepreneurs who become more isolated over time because they don't replace the groups they have outgrown. It is not a good thing if you were more connected as a young entrepreneur than you are now. Make new friends!

Buddies

Buddies are the people you can ask anything of and say anything to. They are business contemporaries who are more or less figuring it out at the same time you are. There is no false pretense. There are no ramifications if you admit your fears. Lessons are readily shared. Not much is held back. You need lots of these folks. Some you will see every once in a while, but others may end up playing a very significant role in your experience.

As someone who teaches creative and independent workers how to best manage their careers and represent themselves, Allison Hemming, founder of The Hired Guns, is well versed in the importance of leveraging your relationships. "Sometimes it's just a matter of being able to take a break from your issue and asking the opinions of the people that are going through it with you. Human touch is important in this process. If you try to work in a vacuum you will definitely make unnecessary mistakes."

During our interviews we met two such buddies who even decided to team up and share an office space. When graphic designer Jessica Sutton, owner of JSGD, started getting more freelance graphic design business than her full-time job left time for, she knew she needed to reevaluate her employment situation. She loved Fresh, the beauty company she worked for, but she ultimately wanted to work for herself. Her boss at the time was very understanding and suggested that Jessica first reduce her schedule at Fresh as a way to comfortably transition to independence. Jessica also got in touch with Jen Hill, another graphic designer and Fresh alumna who had been on her own for several years at that point. Jen had lots of sage advice for Jessica and the two formed a close relationship. After being in touch for a few months, Jen and Jessica decided their experience would be more fun if they actually shared an office. Their professional friendship has continued to strengthen, and today in addition to sharing advice and an office they also share staff.

If you have a brick-and-mortar shop, it is wise to make pals with your surrounding neighborhood businesses. You will have many areas of commonality that will be helpful to confer about over time. Alice Cheng, owner of A.Cheng, has found friendship in Hannah Macdonald and SaSaDi Odunsi, owners of Bump Brooklyn, which is located only a few blocks away. Not only can they compare notes on neighborhood changes but they have also helped normalize the landscape of sales during seasonal changes and throughout the recession as well. Similarly, Erin Waxman and Megan Brewster, owners of Art Star, team up with local boutiques to host trunk shows and special events on the same days in an effort to drive more traffic and awareness to all the stores involved.

Strategic partners

We define strategic partners as other organizations that have the same client pool as you. Your shared target market gives ample opportunity for collaboration, and you can learn a tremendous amount by observing their strategies and tactics. You will often be impacted by the same market trends and can have congruent goals. We are lucky to have loads of strategic partners, as there are a lot of organizations that also target women entrepreneurs. We have collaborated with many of them to teach classes, host a joint event, and share information with our respective audiences.

A great example of partnership is of Amanda Hofman, founder of Urban Girl Squad, and Silfath Pinto, founder of Stylosophy. Amanda produces networking events in New York City for women in their twenties and thirties and is always looking for exciting and innovative events that her membership will enjoy. Silfath is a stylist who works with women to find their style in a fun and nonjudgmental manner. The Urban Girl Squad membership is Silfath's target market and she welcomes the opportunity to get in front of this audience. Her repeat events have enabled her to build up her reputation and name recognition within the community as well. For these ladies, working together is both mutually beneficial and fun.

Another example is between Shazi Visram, founder and CEO of HappyBaby, a premium organic baby food company, and Dr. Bob Sears, one the country's best-known pediatricians. Dr. Sears serves as a medical adviser to HappyBaby and gives input on all of the products they make. Each HappyBaby product prominently displays Dr. Sears's stamp of approval. Shazi and Dr. Sears also cowrote a book that serves as a parent's organic guide to their baby's first twenty-four months. This partnership is clearly mutually beneficial and helps bring brand awareness and notoriety to both HappyBaby and Dr. Sears.

Mentors

In addition to those folks who are stumbling along the entrepreneurial path beside you, you need support and help also from those who are just ahead of you. Good mentors and advisers are critical to your business's success. Some businesses choose to formalize their advisery relationships, creating either a panel or a cohesive group, while others choose to call on people in their network more informally as the need arises.

Andrea Miller, founder of Tango Media says her panel of advisers has been truly invaluable. Andrea worked hard to secure support from many well-known executives and entrepreneurs who had relevant professional experience. One of these advisers, Geraldine Laybourne, who founded and ran Oxygen Media, has been quite generous with her time, feedback, and connections. From time to time Andrea accompanies Geri on her morning walks in Central Park. We understand from several of our interviewees and colleagues that this is a mentoring practice that Geraldine is known for. (It is also a terrific example of helping people on your own terms. See chapter 7.) During the early morning jaunt, Andrea is able to share her challenges, and Geri is able to pepper her with questions and things to think about.

Virtual friends

Social media platforms have become a very valuable source of community and connection. We know that many entrepreneurs hold Facebook and Twitter at arm's length, regarding them as the *last* thing they have time for. Because these platforms are often positioned as a marketing vehicle, our clients sometimes get frustrated when their efforts don't yield direct business. In our experience, these tools have been much more valuable in serving as connectors, which is what they were originally intended to do. We love engaging with people we wouldn't otherwise know and participating in a conversation with a community of people.

For some, including Angie Davis, owner of Byrd & Belle, which designs modern felt MacBook and iPad sleeves, social media tools have been a great way to connect with a unique community. Since Angie conducts business exclusively online, she relies on other online business owners for feedback, advice, and best practices. Through social media, Angie is able to connect to a broad network from around the world to compare notes and get advice.

Troubleshooting:
When You Get in Your Own Way

We have worked with many entrepreneurs who are suffering the effects of isolation. By not building a robust community they have cut off access to opportunities, such as new business leads, and valuable information, such as industry trends and best practices. Their businesses become islands and they feel stranded without a lifeline.

Far and away the two most problematic issues that stem from the lack of community are becoming obsolete and attracting work you don't like.

Becoming Obsolete? Leverage Peers to Get Up to Speed

From time to time we work with business owners who really had it going on at one point but whose present-day business is a bit lackluster. What seemed like a temporary dip in sales has became a long-term downward slide. Sometimes this happens because as entrepreneurs become more established they also become complacent in the business practices that helped bring them their initial success. This is particularly the case when it comes to community and colleagues. By pulling back from their peers and exclusively focusing on their business, they end up metaphorically sticking their head in the sand. Over time this can be quite dangerous for your business.

The Case of Obsolete Olivia

Olivia owned a small recruiting company that focused on placing creative professionals in New York City's media industry. She was great with people and had a knack for knowing who was the right person for the job. She had a reputation for her professionalism among both clients and candidates. Her business did well. Over time, though, something changed. And about eleven years into her business, Olivia came to us for a consultation.

She said she was concerned about the viability of her business and presented two specific challenges. First, she felt that most of her candidates had evaporated and she was finding it difficult to connect with new ones. Second, she had recently lost several good job opportunities because negotiations took too long. She was frustrated because she used to be many of her clients' go-to person. It was clear that that was no longer the case. She wondered whether she should hire more people to work on business development but felt hesitant because of her previous experiences. A few years prior, Olivia had employed up to four people, but she struggled to keep any of them for more than twelve months. They kept leaving for positions at other firms. Frustrated about the wasted time, money, and energy the staff had taken, she returned to running the business herself.

After listening for a while we asked Olivia about how her company's changes matched what was happening industry-wide. How did other people stay connected with candidates? Were client negotiations become more difficult for everyone? Was it customary for employees to jump around a lot, or were they particularly unhappy with their arrangement with her? Perhaps she was dramatically underpaying them? She looked at us blankly and said she wasn't sure. When we asked who in her industry she consulted with to share best practices and resources, she told us she felt it wasn't appropriate to ask competitors how their business was doing. Olivia made it clear that she had few industry peers. We began to wonder whether this wasn't the source of the problem, at least in part.

In an effort to gather more information we dug a little deeper on both of the challenges she had presented. We asked Olivia to tell us why she felt she was losing connection with so many of her candidates. Was this always a problem? How had she done it in the past? Olivia told us she used a paper-based system that she had developed years ago. She said she had known for some time that she would inevitably have to move over to a more technologically advanced system at some point, but she held out for a long time because she hated the thought of not being able to "see" all her information at once. When storage got unmanageable (which it had after ten years), Olivia investigated online databases. Twice she tried migrating to an online solution, but ultimately abandoned both efforts. She felt frustrated that she had wasted lots of time and money trying to find a solution that would make her business more efficient. If anything, she thought the whole process was slowing her down. Worse still, the time wasted on these projects only compounded her fear that she was losing business by not being able to search candidates she had met in the past in a timely fashion.

When it came to the negotiations, Olivia said her clients had begun to push back on the traditional standard rates, which were 30 percent of the candidate's first year's salary with a guarantee that the candidate would stay at the job for at least thirty days. Recently she felt as though every client was angling for a 20 percent fee with a ninety-day guarantee. Several times she had spent weeks negotiating with her client, and by the time they came to an agreement the job had already been filled.

We empathized with Olivia's frustrations and concerns. However, more than anything we were sad, as these situations seemed unnecessary. At one point in Olivia's business past she had been well connected and well informed, but it was clear that that was no longer the case. Both of Olivia's problems could have been solved or at least dramatically improved by getting input and suggestions from her peers! Surely she wasn't the only one who needed a good online database. And certainly she would have had more information about the changing standard of pay if she was more in the loop. By being out of touch with her colleagues, Olivia had become an industry dinosaur.

While we were happy to be a resource to initially help her navigate her tricky situation, we felt that having peers to bounce ideas off of, exchange information with, and boost her morale was what she needed in the long run. It was a community that would best help her get up to speed and solve these significant business challenges.

We shared our thoughts and rationale with Olivia and encouraged her to find comfortable ways to connect with those in her industry as well as other small business owners. Over the next six months, she experimented with different groups to find the right mix of communities. In addition to a couple of groups, she established a more regular relationship with two other recruiters who worked with different kinds of clients than hers. Through her relationships and the information and support they yielded she was able to bring her business up to date and stabilize her revenue stream.

Only Have Work You Don't Like?
Use Peers to Hone Your Sweet Spot

When you're in start-up mode you're desperate for validation and eager to practice your new skills. All you want is a client—any client. So what if they are not exactly who you were looking for, right?

While taking on a few off-track clients in the beginning won't make or break your business, you want to be careful about seeing all clients as equal. Sometimes people fall into the trap of accepting *all* clients. This challenge is particularly problematic when you are isolated, because not only do you not have a place to refer business you don't want, but you're also cut off from feedback that may help you understand why you are attracting off-target clients in the first place.

The Case of Any-Client Annie

After being laid off at the height of the recession two years ago, Annie started a small coaching practice. She had always dreamed of having her own business, so she welcomed this new opportunity to go out on her own. Despite her background as a marketer, Annie had found the most rewarding part of her previous jobs to be managing other people. She was a natural facilitator. Also, during her corporate tenure she had had the opportunity to work with a coach twice and really enjoyed the experience. She knew that being a coach was something she would love to pursue. She wanted to focus on helping people to live more authentic lives, specifically by working with them to identify and pursue careers that would reflect their goals.

After enrolling in a training course and spending hours on research, Annie asked a Web-savvy friend to help her set up a Web site. Excited to get started, Annie sent an e-mail to everyone she knew announcing her career change and the launch of her new business. She encouraged people to refer clients who were seeking a change and emphasized her corporate experience and credentials. Things got off to a pretty slow start and she was disappointed that she hadn't received more referrals. Whenever she saw people at social events, they were very encouraging of her work and often remarked how they knew lots of people who needed to find work that was more fulfilling for them. Hopeful, she would follow up via e-mail, but inevitably she wouldn't get a response.

Annie did have a few clients she enjoyed working with, but she noticed that the majority of her clients resisted her transformative approach and preferred her to help them stay accountable to their specific goals or help with their career-search nuts and bolts, like résumé reviews. While she could help people make steady progress, she was frustrated, because she preferred to work with people who wanted to make big changes! Alas, she was reluctant to turn away any business, so she continued taking these clients, who in turn referred friends with similar issues.

Annie felt discouraged and suspected she was doing something wrong. Concerned it might be a marketing problem, she worked on her branding. She invested time and money into redesigning her Web site, logo, and marketing materials. The response was underwhelming.

After a while, Annie's eye started wandering to other kinds of services and businesses. She wondered if holistic health counseling might be a better fit. Surely those clients would be eager to make lasting and meaningful changes in their lives. Annie came to us asking our advice. Should she start over? Was there an easy way to switch?

After hearing Annie's story, we asked her who she regularly turned to for advice. She said her boyfriend was a good listener but knew little about issues related to building a business. She also said that her former colleagues had been helpful with the marketing and Web site aspects of the business. So we asked her how she got business advice. Did she belong to any groups or professional affiliations? Annie said she didn't really participate in groups targeting business owners because she had been primarily concerned with getting clients. The networking she did was mostly within her old industry in the hope that she would connect with people unhappy with their corporate experience.

It was clear to Annie that she was running a business without any entrepreneurial colleagues or connections to other small businesses. Wow, was she making it difficult for herself!

We talked with Annie about the value of connecting with different types of communities. We explained that these peer relationships would help improve and build her business in the long run. We also talked about the cost of operating without any feedback or access to lessons learned. Before Annie threw in the towel on this business and changed direction, we suggested she try a few things. First, we suggested she join a network or group specifically for coaches. Among other things, it would help her to see how her offering compared with others and perhaps help her to more clearly articulate her points of differentiation. Second, we suggested that she select a few coaching colleagues who had different areas of focus and form a closer relationship with them. In addition to swapping best practices, they could cross-refer clients who were more appropriate for another practice. Third, we suggested that she join a group that had a diverse pool of entrepreneurs. They would be able to give feedback on business practices and might help Annie think outside of her industry box, especially about good places to connect with potential clients. Plus, networking with businesses that also serviced her target market was a great way to get more referrals.

Six months later Annie had a completely different business experience. She had received some critical feedback about the language she was using to describe her services and had made changes to her Web site and verbal pitch. She had several referral sources and had begun getting many more of the kinds of client that she liked. She also had places to send clients that she didn't want to work with. More recently, she started offering joint programs with colleagues who also worked with the kinds of clients she did. Not only was it fun, but it was a great way to meet new potential clients. Most important, Annie felt well supported, well resourced, and reinvigorated. She quickly abandoned the idea of changing her business focus and embraced her original business, which was now working for her.

POSTSCRIPT

Brava! We know it's not easy to take time away from what's likely a very long list of things to do, but by reading this book you have chosen to invest in your own success and satisfaction.

Before closing we want to leave you with some final thoughts.

We know things can get hectic. Entrepreneurship is not easy and it's far from straightforward, but it's much simpler when you keep the following in mind:

- The fun is in the building
- Honor your own definition of success
- It's not about big, it's about big enough
- The "right" choice is the one that works for you
- Entrepreneurship is an opportunity

With these principles close at hand it is easier to stay on track and build a business that works for you.

One more thing. We want to remind you about the cardinal rule of entrepreneurship: pay it forward!

We are still amazed by how generous the women that we interviewed were with both their time and advice. But in truth, we must admit that while we are very grateful, we are not at all surprised. After all, nearly every entrepreneur we spoke to said that hands down what had been most helpful to them in their journey was other women entrepreneurs. It was the women who came before them who helped to pave the way for their success. Whether it was industry secrets, key introductions, words of wisdom, or best practices, they learned the lessons of entrepreneurship from those who were gracious enough to share the truth about their experiences. In turn, the women we interviewed felt a clear duty to reciprocate the favor, passing on their own experiences to you—our readers.

This gift—their gift—also comes with a responsibility. As you're working on your own business, think not only about how others can benefit from what you have learned, but also how you can share the value and importance of making your business work for you.

In doing so, you will help shape the next generation of women entrepreneurs. We are confident that your example will help them see new ways to build their own business, and that your success will help them to create a business that is big enough to meet their needs.

IN GOOD COMPANY:
ADVICE FROM ENTREPRENEURS
INCLUDED IN
THE BIG ENOUGH COMPANY

Alexandra Mayzler
Founder and director, Thinking Caps Tutoring, a tutoring company located in Manhattan.
"It is important to consider networking outside of your immediate professional circle. It is helpful to meet people of different careers and different perspectives, as they can always shed light on the way an entrepreneur does and thinks about business."

Alice Cheng
Owner, A.Cheng, a clothing boutique located in Park Slope, Brooklyn.
"When you're doing well, you can't take it for granted. Constantly reevaluate what you're doing and what you have. This also means you should apply for a loan when you don't need it. Have a little line of credit at a good rate when you need it. Because when you do need it, they're not going to give it to you."

Allison Hemming
Top gun and founder, The Hired Guns, a talent agency located in Manhattan.
"Make sure to have your business checkbook separate from your personal checkbook as soon as you can. Otherwise it is too easy to forget to pay yourself; it's too easy to forget that your time has value."

Amanda Hofman
Founder and CEO, Urban Girl Squad, a social group for women in their twenties and thirties, located in Manhattan.
"Don't underestimate how different different markets can be."

Amy Voloshin
Studio director, Printfresh Studios, a textile designs and vintage archive located in Philadelphia.
"Have a standard noncompete with your employees. It allows you to be much more open and transparent about the business."

Andrea Miller
CEO, Tango Media, a digital media company dedicated to love and relationships, located in Manhattan.
"One thing I always do if I'm at an event is to try to introduce myself to the keynote speaker or panelist or whoever is there, especially back in the early days when Tango was just an idea. Most of the time the relationship doesn't necessarily go anywhere, but you just never know, and enough of the times it does. It's worth it to me to take the time and make those connections.

Andreea Ayers
Founder, Tees for Change, an inspirational apparel company dedicated to spreading positivity, making a difference, and giving back, located in Manhattan.
"Focus on selling the benefits of your product instead of the features."

Angie Davis
Owner/designer, Byrd & Belle, a company specializing in handmade sleeves and cases, located in Minneapolis.
"There is a lot of negativity in the world and sometimes somebody is going to have a bad day and say something about you, and you just have to let it go and know in the large scheme of things that those

little hiccups aren't really going to affect you and so try not to take them personally, because it's not really about you. Don't worry about what other people think makes you successful, just do your thing."

Ann Mehl
Certified coach helping clients facilitate life change and forward momentum through one-on-one sessions, located in Manhattan.
"Learning to love your weakness as much as you revel in your strength requires courage. But the potential rewards far outweigh the risk."

Barbara Lynch
Founder/chef, Barbara Lynch Gruppo, a collection of entities offering unique and memorable culinary experiences, located in Boston.
"Lead by example."

Carol Mills
Partner, Malia Mills, a beauty company focused on swimwear, ready-to-wear, and accessories, headquartered in Manhattan with retail locations in New York and California.
"Keep your business fresh."

Caroline Green
Chief marketing officer, IvanExpert Consulting, a company that provides superior Mac, iPhone, iPad, and iPod support for small businesses and home users, located in Manhattan.
"Sometimes you should just try it and go for it."

Chloé Jo Davis
Founder, Girlie Girl Army, a Glamazon Guide to Green Living, located in Manhattan.
"I think there is power in numbers. If you can, pair with someone who's really got a lot of strengths that you don't have."

Claire Chambers

Founder and CEO, Journelle, a new breed of lingerie store, located in Manhattan and Miami.

"Don't take experts too seriously."

Claudia Hanlin

Founder of Claudia Hanlin's Wedding Library, an innovative research boutique created especially for the bride-to-be, located in Manhattan.

"Always be open to learning. If you think you have learned everything, you are doing your business a disservice."

Claudia Romana

Designer/owner, Claudia Romana Enterprises, a fashion line created with the needs of the golfing woman in mind, located in Manhattan.

"It's not just the goal that is important, but how you get there. On every step, you need to ask, 'Is this the right thing to do? Is this the fair thing to do? Am I hurting anybody doing this?' Really try to keep your integrity. Because if you lose that, you lose everything."

Courtney Davis

Cofounder and designer, Kelly & Olive, a company specializing in a fresh, personal approach to interior design, located in Chicago.

"You don't have to give your firstborn to a client. Even in the beginning you need to realize, 'This is what I do, this is what I am, and this is what I cost. I value what I do and this is an appropriate compensation for my services.' "

Cyndee Sugra

Owner/CEO, Studio 7 Media, LLC, a sophisticated technology, design, and marketing firm that blends engineering expertise with creative passion to create breakthrough brands and business solutions, located in Los Angeles.

"You need to remember why you're doing it to get you through, because it's not all rainbows."

Darcey Howard

Owner, LifeStyled Ltd., a company that combines the marketing concept of creating a brand with a natural talent for substance and style, located in Seattle and Manhattan.

"Read *Inc.* magazine. I thought it was for someone with a bigger company than me but found that there are tons of great tips, info, and nuts and bolts to learn from."

Darla Cohen

Owner, Fork in the Road, a personal chef focused on delivering healthy meals, located in Austin, Texas.

"Think about what your *big* goals are. It's really easy to get caught up in the do-more, make-more mentality without stepping back and thinking about what it is that you're actually accomplishing and what it means for your life. Ambition is great! But resist the urge of doing more for the sake of saying you did so. You may want to say, 'Hey, look at this big thing I built.' But the question is whether that big thing makes you happy."

Eden Abrahams

Founder, Clear Path Executive Coaching, an executive coaching firm located in Manhattan.

"Set realistic goals. The initial stages of building a business can be tough going, and there will be days when you feel like you are moving sideways, or even backwards. Establishing clear, specific and action-oriented goals (such as the number of networking meetings you will have per week) versus vague status-related goals (such as getting a lot of early media buzz) helps put you in control and will give you a sense of forward momentum as you accomplish them."

Eileen Loeb

Owner, BodySmart Personal Training, a wellness company that designs and delivers high-quality fitness programs to small companies and discerning individuals, located in Manhattan.

"There is room for lots of different people under the entrepreneurial tent."

Ellen Diamant

Owner and chief creative officer, Skip Hop, a company focused on creating unique, innovative, and highly functional products that make parenting easier, better, and more fun, located in Manhattan.
"It is always good to get a second opinion on legal issues."

Ellen Galinsky

President, the Families and Work Institute, a nonprofit, nonpartisan research organization that studies the changing workforce, family, and community, located in Manhattan.
"Don't stop because you're afraid. Fear means go."

Emily Powell

President and owner, Powell's Books, one of the world's great bookstores, with seven locations and an online business, located in Portland, Oregon.
"Remember to lighten up and not take yourself so seriously."

Emily Wolper

Founder and president, E. Wolper Inc., an admissions consulting firm located in Morristown, New Jersey.
"Do not give up pieces of the business that you enjoy."

Erica Ecker

Owner, The Spacialist, a professional organizer company, located in Manhattan.
"My number one piece of advice is progress not perfection. I would call myself a recovering perfectionist and it has kept me totally stuck at times. But I've learned to just keep moving. Doesn't matter if you make mistakes, doesn't matter if you don't love your logo 99 percent. If you love it 92 percent, perfect, keep going, keep going, keep going."

Erin McKenna

Founder and president, BabyCakes NYC, an all-natural, organic bakery with locations in Manhattan, Los Angeles, and Downtown Disney.
"Don't be a perfectionist. Learn to trust others."

Erin Waxman

Co-owner, Art Star, a gallery and boutique showcasing work and products by emerging artists, located in Northern Liberties, Philadelphia.
"Take advantage of free tools for small businesses."

Fauzia Burke

Founder and president, FSB Associates, a company that promote books online exclusively, located in New Jersey.
"Hiring is about fit. Ask yourself, do you want to work with this person every day?"

Frances Lappé

Principal, Small Planet Institute, an organization dedicated to changing failing ideas in order to turn our planet toward life, with offices in New York and Boston.
"If we have somebody with us, we feel that we can just keep going and the challenges seem so much less daunting. So to have good friends that you cultivate and stay with you for a lifetime, that's really what it's all about."

Gail Epstein

President and creative director, Hanky Panky, a lingerie and sleepwear company, located in Manhattan.
"There's no such thing as an overnight success."

Galia Gichon

Founder and owner, Down-to-Earth Finance, an independent resource dedicated to clients—especially women—about investing and financial control, located in Manhattan.

"Just do it. If you really want to start a business, just start it. Start it on the weekend, start it at night, stop talking about it, and just get out there."

Genevieve Thiers
Founder, Sittercity, an online source for childcare, pet care, senior care, housesitting, housekeeping, and tutoring, located in Chicago.
"When it comes to investors, the more you have created, the more you will keep."

Grace Bonney
Owner, writer, and editor, Design Sponge, a daily Web site dedicated to home and product design, located in Brooklyn.
"Don't forget the reason you started."

Jackie Gusic
Principal, Inhabit Architecture & Design, located in Philadelphia.
"Find an opportunity to say no to. Being able to say no is really refreshing, and I think it helps you grow as a person and as a business to know that you have that option."

Janet Hanson
Founder and CEO, 85 Broads, a global network of twenty-five thousand trailblazing women who are inspired, empowered, and connected, located in Greenwich, Connecticut, with chapters in eighty-two countries around the world.
"It's easy to lose sight of the core mission if you have people underwriting the process."

Jen Boulden
Cofounder, Ideal Bite, a Web site offering bite-sized tips for eco-living. She is an environmentalist, entrepreneur, author, public speaker, and a fierce animal lover, located in Los Angeles.
"If you don't love your idea so much it hurts, don't even bother."

Jen Hill

Owner and designer, JHill Design, a graphic design company, located in Boston.

"When you're working with clients and customers, try to set boundaries with them. If customers or clients think that you work on Saturdays at eight in the morning and you start your relationship like that, then that's how they're going view it for the rest of the time. So it's really important to let everyone know exactly how the relationship is going to stand and stick to that."

Jen Mankins

Owner, Bird, a fashion boutique, located in Brooklyn.

"There should only be one boss."

Jennie Nevin

Founder, Green Spaces, a coworking space for green entrepreneurs, with locations in Manhattan and Denver.

"The hardest part is knowing if you have a product that could sell and that people are willing to buy. Once you know that, then the rest is details."

Jennifer Thomas

Founding director, director of Civic Innovation Labs, 2003–2010, currently program director at the John S. and James L. Knight Foundation, located in Ohio.

"I would say that the most critical piece of starting a business or having an idea or a product or a service is understanding demand and understanding your market. Who wants it? Who is going to use it? And why do they need it?"

Jennifer Walzer

Founder and CEO, Backup My Info!, a company that provides businesses with fully managed online data backup services, located in Manhattan.

"You have to be passionate about what you do."

Jessamyn Waldman
Founder and executive director, Hot Bread Kitchen, a nonprofit social enterprise that creates better lives for low-income women and their families, located in Brooklyn and Manhattan.
"Be patient—innovation is tough!"

Jessica Dunne
Founder and owner, Ellie D Perfume, a luxury perfume company, located in Chicago.
"Do your research! Figure out what it takes to bring it to fruition before diving in."

Jessica Porter
Owner, Raandesk Gallery, a premier resource for art collectors and art enthusiasts to purchase works by emerging artist talent from all over the world, located in Manhattan.
"Never hesitate or ignore an opportunity to meet someone new, ever, even when you aren't 'in the mood.' Go to that networking event you are too tired to go to, chat up the person next to you in line for the bathroom, it doesn't matter, just connect with as many people as you can."

Jessica Sutton
Owner, Jessica Sutton Graphic Design, a design firm focusing on company branding, marketing, and Web design, located in Boston.
"Go with your gut on everything. No matter how many pro/con lists you make, and no matter how heavily you weigh a decision, whatever your gut or heart is telling you to do, it's always going to be the best for your business."

Jessica Jackley
Cofounder, Kiva, a social enterprise organization that empowers individuals to lend to an entrepreneur across the globe. Cofounder of Profounder, an online crowdfunding platform that provides tools for

entrepreneurs to raise their investment capital from their communities. Jessica is located in San Francisco.

"Involve those around you. Harvest their ideas and energy to move you forward."

Jill Diamond

Founder, president, and CEO, Lanartco, Inc., an executive coaching and training firm, located in Manhattan.

"The customer isn't always right: when starting a business, clients can be intimidating as we try to scramble for our first dollars. As we build confidence, it becomes clear that the customer's attitudes and needs may not always suit the values you hold for your business. Get a jump-start on this understanding and look for customers who match your business ethics."

Jodi Glickman

President, Great on the Job, a company focused on providing a road map for effective communication in the workplace, located in Chicago.

"Find role models."

Jodi Morgen Katz

Owner, JMK Creative, a beauty creative agency specializing in developing retail marketing, packaging, advertising, and e-marketing for beauty brands, located in Manhattan.

"Don't pressure yourself to be there now."

Joy Cho

Founder and designer, Oh Joy!, a studio dedicated to home accessories and textile design, located in Philadelphia.

"Work hard to study your craft, whatever it is."

Joy Parisi and Lila Cecil

Owners, Paragraph, a workspace for writers, located in Manhattan.

"Start a business you truly believe in—not just something you believe will make money or get you something else you want, but one that you feel in your bones serves a need, or feeds a great cause. In all decisions big and small, follow your instinct. You can ask for advice, but you'll have to be able to withstand those who tell you not to, you can't, or it's a bad idea. Ultimately, you know what's best for your business, and you know if your business will succeed. Nobody else can tell you that, or tell you how to do that. Trust yourself."

Joyce Szuflita

Founder and president, NYC School Help, a company that helps Brooklyn families with school search, public and private, nursery school through high school, located in Brooklyn.
"It is important to connect to a variety of communities."

Jude Stearns

Owner, Judy Jetson Salon, a hair salon, located in Cambridge, Massachusetts.
"Listen to everything—the good and the bad."

Judi Rosenthal

President and founder, Bloom, a community for female financial advisers to learn how to cultivate their business with creativity, develop their own personal brand, and create marketing efficiencies, located in Manhattan.
"The best way to get people to refer you is to treat them better and better and better. Better than anyone else that they know or have ever known."

Julia Archer

Owner, @WorkDesign, a retail and online boutique specializing in workspace furnishings, products, and supplies for the home, located in Chicago.
"The reality is that not everyone is going to 'get' what you do or what you have to offer."

Julia Pimsleur
Founder and CEO, Little Pim, a company that creates foreign-language videos/DVDs for toddlers, located in Manhattan.
"Have people around who can help you think bigger, dream bigger, and make the business the best it can be."

Justine Lackey
President, Good Cents Bookkeeping Inc., a firm that provides a variety of bookkeeping and management services, located in Briarcliff Manor, New York.
"You have to have an incredible amount of motivation and discipline."

Lauren Paradise
Cofounder and designer, Kelly & Olive, a company specializing in a fresh, personal approach to interior design, located in Chicago.
"Don't waste your time being intimidated. Dive in."

Lida Orzeck
CEO, Hanky Panky, a lingerie and sleepwear company, located in Manhattan.
"Open your own mail."

Linda Lightman
Owner, Linda's Stuff, an eBay clothing seller, located in Philadelphia.
"Do your homework."

Lotta Anderson
Founder and designer, Lotta Jansdotter, a design studio specializing in home and lifestyle accessories, located in Brooklyn.
"Don't get overwhelmed by the big picture."

Lunden De'Leon
Founder and CEO, Dirrty Records, an independent punk record label, located in Marion, South Carolina.

"Learn all the aspects of your business; don't leave it up to others who you hire to know more than you do."

Malia Mills
Founding partner and designer, Malia Mills, a beauty company focused on swimwear, ready-to-wear, and accessories, headquartered in Manhattan, with retail locations in New York and California.
"Don't compromise on your values, even if it means saying no to opportunities like press."

Maribel Lieberman
CEO, MarieBelle Chocolate, a retail and online chocolatier, with two locations in Manhattan.
"Hard times teach you more. They force you to become more disciplined and more reflective."

Marie Scalogna-Watkinson
Owner, Spa Chicks on the Go, a full-service spa event marketing company that delivers customized spa and beauty experiences for private, corporate, and media clients, located in Manhattan.
"Own your expertise!"

Marissa Lippert
Founder, Nourish, a nutrition counseling company, located in Manhattan.
"You have to be confident in your idea. A positive vibe will help it grow."

Megan Brewster
Co-owner, Art Star, a gallery and boutique showcasing work and products by emerging artists, located in Northern Liberties, Philadelphia.
"Constantly remind your customers that you exist."

Melanie Notkin
Founder, lifestyle expert, and author, Savvy Auntie, a community for aunts and all women who love kids, located in Manhattan.

"If you want to be happy, entrepreneurship may be the right path for you. But you have to understand that there is a tremendous amount of work and dedication and devotion. That you're not going to be able to take weekends off. You're not going to be able to go to every wedding that you're invited to that's not near where you live. You're not going to be able to afford to go out for dinner or buy the clothes that you want or the shoes that you want or the hair that you want. But it's the most amazing journey you can take to find yourself."

Michelle Adams

Founder and editor of Lonny, *a bimonthly online magazine that focuses on lifestyle and home décor. Michelle is also the founder of Rubie Green, which specializes in fabrics that represent vitality, energy, comfort, and style, all while maintaining respect for the environment by using only 100 percent organic cotton, located in Manhattan.*

"You always hear that it takes companies so long to take off; it can happen overnight, it can happen in a couple years. So keep plugging away and don't let anything stop you, because if you have a genuinely good idea and you're passionate about it, it will take off at some point."

Michelle Kedem

Founding partner, On-Ramps, a full-service search firm that helps organizations recruit the best talent available for full-time, part-time, and project-based work arrangements, located in Manhattan.

"If you have partners, make sure to assign decision-making. Understand authority around decisions—when they can be made alone and when they need to be unanimous."

Michelle Madhok

Founder and CEO, SheFinds (White Cat Media Inc.), distributor of online publications SheFinds.com, MomFinds.com, and BrideFinds .com that help busy women everywhere shop the Web for the latest beauty and style finds, located in Manhattan.

"Do something every day that will move yourself a little bit forward, even if it's not a big step."

Noha Waibsnaider
Founder and CEO, Peeled Snacks, a company specializing in snacks made with organic and all-natural ingredients with no sugar or oil added, located in Brooklyn.
"Create an advisery board."

Paige Arnof-Fenn
Founder and CEO, Mavens & Moguls, a network of seasoned marketing professionals with experience at the highest levels in small, medium, and large companies, located in Boston.
"Don't get caught up in other people's definition of success. Life is too short. Don't get caught up living somebody else's dream. Live your own dream."

Pat Helding
President, Fat Witch Baking Company, a retail and online business dedicated to brownies, located in Manhattan.
"My measure of an entrepreneur is whether they are wearing sensible shoes. Even if you're not physically on the move you're mentally on the move."

Pati Drumm Grady
Founder and president, Cooperstown Cookie Company, a bakery that celebrates the love of baseball and cookies with delightful and delicious baseball-themed gifts, located in Cooperstown, New York.
"Remember that you are only as good as your word!"

Pauline Nakios
Founder and designer, Lilla P, a fashion collection that is perfectly tailored for a casual lifestyle, located in Manhattan.
"Always demand to be treated like a client. Don't give over control just because you're a novice."

Rebecca Kousky

Founder and executive director, Nest, a nonprofit organization that empowers female artists and artisans around the world, located in St. Louis.

"You should have some sense of where you are going, but it's really important to have a clear picture of your daily to-do list in order to make progress. It can be really overwhelming to just be visionary. You have to find a way to balance the two: the big picture and the daily details."

Robin Wilson

Chairman and CEO, Robin Wilson Home, a national eco-friendly design firm focused on creating a healthy lifestyle for residential and commercial clients, located in Manhattan.

"Say no three times to every yes."

Samantha Edwards

Founder and creative director, Gif+d, a creative collective that specializes in branding, art direction, and graphic design, located in Manhattan.

"Never burn a bridge! Even if you've pissed a client off to the fullest, never burn the bridge. You want people to be singing your praises."

Sara Holoubek

Founder and CEO, Luminary Labs, a boutique consultancy focused on strategy and innovation, located in Manhattan.

"Think about the difference between price and value."

Sara Horowitz

Founder and executive director, Freelancers Union, a national membership organization for independent workers, located in Brooklyn.

"You need to surround yourself by people who always tell you what your blind spot is."

Sarah Endline

Founder and CEO, Sweetriot, a human, globally responsible, irreverent, and built-for-a-new generation chocolate company, located in Manhattan.

"It is all about problem-solving. The day you become stuck in the mud and focused on the problem instead of the solution is a day that nothing moves forward."

Sarah Grayson
Founding partner, On-Ramps, a full-service search firm that helps organizations recruit the best talent available for full-time, part-time, and project-based work arrangements, located in Manhattan.
"Have an off-site meeting once a year to celebrate accomplishments of goals met and set goals for the coming year."

Selia Yang
Founder and designer, Selia Yang, a fashion company dedicated to evening and bridal couture, located in Manhattan.
"It is important to always give yourself a break when things don't go as expected. I would much rather be a failure making an attempt than not striving at all, never knowing what I could have been. You should be proud of yourself just for that."

Selima Salaun
Founder and designer, Selima Optique, a trend-setting designer and professional optician and optometrist with eight boutiques in New York and Paris.
"Don't be ashamed to admit when things go wrong, because you have an opportunity to own the failure and do something about it."

Shazi Visram
Founder and CEO, HappyBaby, makers of baby and toddler food as healthy and delicious as homemade, with the essential nutrients needed for optimal growth and development, located in Manhattan.
"Even bad advice can have a positive impact because it can drive you to do better."

Shobha Tummala
Founder and CEO, Shobha, a spa for natural and effective hair removal services and products, with three locations in Manhattan.

"Assume that it will succeed instead of always fearing that it may not."

Sunny Bates
CEO, Sunny Bates Associates, a recruiting firm specializing in online media, located in Manhattan.
"Everything always takes longer than you think."

Suzanne Muchin
Founder and lead strategist, ROI Ventures LLC, a strategy firm that works at the intersection of social impact and market opportunity, located in Chicago.
"Have a partner. I just don't think you should go it alone. It could be a thought partner or a business partner, but you need a real partner."

Tara Hunt
Cofounder and CEO, Buyosphere, a tool to help you take control of your shopping history: organize it, share it, and track how you influence others, located in Montreal.
"I have days where I think, 'What the hell am I doing?' and I feel like I'm not making any ways forward. But then if I hold out just a little longer there are little victories that come along and show me I'm going in the right direction. So watch for those."

Teresa Chang
Owner, Teresa Chang Ceramics, a studio offering high-end, hand-thrown porcelain dinnerware and teaware, located in Philadelphia.
"As an artist, try not to think of what people want to buy. Try not to look around and see what's selling, because when people do that their work is absolutely soulless."

Trisha Anderson
Owner and president, Frontier Soups, producer of creatively crafted, wholesome, and nutritious soups, stews, chili, and chowders, located in Waukegan, Illinois.

"As an entrepreneur you have to figure out a way to get what you want. You're not accomplished if all you're doing is working all day long. There has got to be more. Success is about being able to take advantage of the benefits of the job."

Trish Karter
Cofounder, Dancing Deer Baking Company, an all-natural gourmet brownie, cake, and cookie gifts company, located in Boston.
"Just being there, just pushing forward, and not shrinking back is big."

Wendy Mullin
Owner and Designer, Built by Wendy, a fashion boutique dedicated to classic, clean American style with contemporary flair, located in Manhattan.
"If you want something done ask the busiest person you know."

ACKNOWLEDGMENTS

BOTH OF US WANT TO THANK:

All the members of In Good Company past and present. You bring meaning and life to our business. We have learned a lot from you. We are grateful to be part of your journey and thankful that you are a part of ours.

All the interviewees who participated in this book. We admire what you have created and are amazed by your wisdom and spirit of generosity.

A few people who have made a really big impact on our journey:

Karen, we can't miss an opportunity to thank you

Marci for putting us on the map and becoming a loyal friend and colleague

Marissa for being our first client, twice.

Emily, Galia, and Erica for getting on board when IGC was just a seedling of an idea. Your feedback and contributions continue to make IGC all it is today.

Elie, Karen, Gary, Heather, Jordan, Cari, and Dan for taking a chance and believing that women entrepreneurs are worthy of investment.

Donna, the ever gracious hostess of IGC, for helping make hundreds of people's every day better, especially ours!

Victoria for your ability to juggle an endless number of projects while also keeping our heads screwed on and feet moving in the right direction.

Alexandra for your encouragement and confidence and ultimately the kick in the pants that made this book happen. You are a wonderful example of what things look like when people find the perfect role for themselves.

A big thank-you to the entire team at Portfolio. We can't imagine being in better company. We have felt welcome and supported from day one. We especially appreciate Adrienne's initial interest and advocacy; Brooke's willingness to carry the torch and skill in helping us to navigate this experience—not to mention her sharp eye and clear wording; and Adrian's insight and willingness to think big (enough)! Also, a huge thanks to Amanda for her enthusiasm and expertise. We know there is a large team of people behind each of you and we are grateful for their work as well.

And a special thanks to Rebecca, who was always willing to lend her eyes and brain and gave great feedback. We appreciate your support.

ADELAIDE WANTS TO THANK:

My support team: Mom, Jim, Cort, Adam, Jennifer, Wayne, Josh, Andrea, Michael, Celia, Prudence, Dana, Jenny, Anne, and Christina. Everything is easier with your love, enthusiasm, and encouragement.

Amy. You make everything we do better and more fun. Thanks for bringing spice and heart to what we do. I've learned so much from you, but most important you've taught me to better practice what we preach. Thank you for showing me the strength in asking for help, the relief in saying no, and the fun in the unknown.

Most important, Tim. You know more than anyone that an entrepreneur's job is never done. Thank you for honoring my work and believing in me. I'm grateful for your partnership, unwavering support, and clear commitment. Your calm and confidence are inspiring. And despite no desire on your part to be an entrepreneur, I learn a lot of business lessons from you. I'm honored to be your wife and can't wait for what's in store. Next step? 3/15/12.

And, of course, Ella. You've changed my world. Thanks for making us a family.

AMY WANTS TO THANK:

Thank you to my Grandpa George, who helped form my earliest impressions of entrepreneurship and continues to run his own business.

Thank you to my grandmothers, Naomi and Bess. (Grandma Bess became an entrepreneur in her nineties, proving it's never too late!)

Thank you to the first entrepreneur I ever knew (and adored), Bonnie Levin, who owned Hearts Desire and made the indelible impression about the possibility of running my own business one day.

Thank you to Barbara, Yossi, and Talia, who love, accept, and get a kick out of who I am.

Thank you to my best girlfriends, Naomi, Jenny, Jennifer, Rebecca, Laurie, and Aliza. You have taken friendship to a new level, especially this past year. Thank you for really being there when I needed you.

Thank you to my parents, Carol and Chuck, who gave me wings, taught me to fly, and instilled the confidence that I could achieve whatever I set my sights on.

Thank you to my sister Caryn Aviv, who loves and supports me unconditionally.

Thank you to Adelaide, first my friend and confidante, second my business partner. Your tenacity is something to marvel at, especially when it comes to dealing with me. Thank you for your stick-to-it-iveness, your patience, your kind ear, sound advice, and support, and for being the *best* business partner in the world.

Thank you to Laura Paul, who has helped raise our girls and to whom I give full credit for teaching my children good manners.

pure joy, delight, laughter, and love and it is pretty clear that you are already taking the world by storm.

And the biggest thank-you to my husband, Ronen. None of this would be any fun at all if I could not share it all with you. Thanks for loving me and for sharing you with me.

ABOUT IN GOOD COMPANY

For many years we ran a consulting practice focused on women business owners. What we found over and over was that many of our clients were isolated. They reinvented the wheel too often and missed out on the opportunity for collaboration. So we decided to change our business to meet these needs. In 2007 we created In Good Company, a community, business learning center, and workspace where women can come to learn the business of building their businesses. In addition to professional work and meeting space, IGC offers dozens of learning opportunities, classes, and workshops each month. Over the years, thousands of women have connected through IGC to become more confident and successful as entrepreneurs.

In addition to running In Good Company Workplaces, we continue to consult with entrepreneurs around the country on building businesses that work for them. We also work with people interested in setting up shared workspaces and learning centers.

We'd love to hear from you and learn about your business! To get in touch with us visit www.ingoodcompany.com.

INDEX